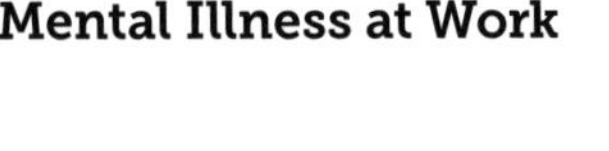

Mental Illness at Work

A Manager's Guide to Identifying, Managing and Preventing Psychological Problems in the Workplace

Mental Illness at Work

Mary-Clare Race
University College London, UK

Adrian Furnham
University College London, UK

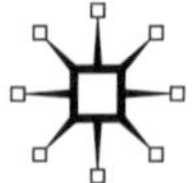

Some sections of this book have been based on previous publications of Professor Adrian Furnham.

First published 2014 by
PALGRAVE MACMILLAN

Palgrave Macmillan in the UK is an imprint of Macmillan Publishers Limited, registered in England, company number 785998, of Houndmills, Basingstoke, Hampshire RG21 6XS.

Palgrave Macmillan in the US is a division of St Martin's Press LLC, 175 Fifth Avenue, New York, NY 10010.

Palgrave Macmillan is the global academic imprint of the above companies and has companies and representatives throughout the world.

Palgrave® and Macmillan® are registered trademarks in the United States, the United Kingdom, Europe and other countries.

ISBN 978–1–137–27204–1

This book is printed on paper suitable for recycling and made from fully managed and sustained forest sources. Logging, pulping and manufacturing processes are expected to conform to the environmental regulations of the country of origin.

A catalogue record for this book is available from the British Library.

A catalog record for this book is available from the Library of Congress.

Typeset by MPS Limited, Chennai, India.

For Alison: whose emotional stability I value above gold, diamonds and rubies,

and

For Alan: who drives me mad and keeps me sane in equal proportions

Contents

List of Figures and Tables

Figures

Tables

Preface

Our interest in two related topics led us to the decision to write this book. The first was on mental health literacy, which concerns the extent to which laypeople are able to recognize mental illnesses in people that they meet in daily life. Whilst we know that people are pretty good at spotting depression and may have a good idea of how to help a depressed person, they are much less able to recognize schizophrenia or other conditions. They seem particularly poor at recognizing the personality disorders which can give the person with the disorder and all those working with them considerable distress.

The work on mental health literacy is growing fast. We know more about what problems people at work fail to acknowledge or misdiagnose. This can, and does, lead to many very significant problems. The idea of this book is to improve the mental health literacy of people at work: not to turn them into amateur psychiatrists, but rather to know what different behaviour means and the sort of help and intervention that can be offered.

The second topic is the dark side of behaviour at work. A surprisingly large number of people at work 'fail and derail'. Estimates put this to be around 50 per cent for senior managers. In plain terms this means that half of all people appointed to senior management conditions will either plateau below the level they were expected to reach, will cause poor moral and business results or, worse, widespread collapse, and in extreme cases will get sacked or end up in prison. The paradox here is that so many of these derailed leaders were once thought of as having high potential and being talented. The obsessive-compulsive can seem well suited to quality control and internal audits; the narcissist may thrive (initially) in marketing and sales; and the paranoid may perform well in the security industry. Articulate and confident psychopaths can do very well in poorly regulated sectors. The newspapers are full of stories of 'bailed out, booted and busted' executives who cost their company millions.

A partial explanation of this is the extent to which people with certain sub-clinical personality disorders like narcissism and anti-social personality disorder can thrive in business. Thanks to the brilliant insights of Robert Hogan and others, we have begun to understand how the personality disorders can lead to people being promoted to senior positions, only to cause mayhem all around them.

But what impact do personality disorders have in a broader business context? And how does this fit in with the wider mental health agenda? How do we tell if a colleague is suffering from a serious mental illness or if they are just suffering from the winter blues? How can we distinguish between those with personality disorders and those 'normal' difficult individuals we all come up against at work? It is a complex landscape and one which we hope this book will make more straightforward and easier to navigate.

We have been assisted in this book by many people, including, but not limited to, the following: Rebecca Milner, Steen Tjarks, Luke Treglown, Philippa Robinson, Elwyn Thomas and Robert Care.

chapter 1

Introduction

Would you recognize if a colleague at work was having a serious mental breakdown? You may be able to see signs of stress or depression, but can you detect schizophrenia or alcoholism? Are any of the top people in your organization psychopaths? And does anyone have full-blown obsessive-compulsive disorder? What should you do if you recognize symptoms of a major mental health problem? Is this essentially an HR issue?

Do some workplaces make you psychologically as well as physically sick? Are there pathological organizations which almost require you to be disturbed in order to work in them: the paranoid or psychopathic organization? Do certain workplaces cause mental illness? And are people with a particular propensity towards certain disorders attracted to certain jobs and organizations?

This book is about mental illness in the context of the modern workplace. It deconstructs the mythology and misconceptions surrounding mental illness and offers a useful taxonomy for understanding how the impact of mental illness in the workplace can be managed, mitigated and prevented. One aim is to help people recognize a range of psychological problems for what they are and offer appropriate help and advice before the problems become too serious.

People are frequently physically ill at work. Over the course of a working life, people are likely to experience a wide range of physical illnesses such as the common cold, broken limbs resulting from accidents and chronic conditions like hypertension. Many are also likely to experience a range of 'psychological issues' and sometimes these may result in mental illness. Whilst physical health and mental health are closely related, it is much more difficult to identify and deal with mental health problems in the workplace. One of the biggest challenges is the stigma that is still associated with mental health problems. People suffering from mental illness are among the most stigmatized and marginalized in society, and although a lot has been done in recent years to address this, there is still a long way to go before mental illness is regarded in the same light as physical illness. The stigma of mental illness is consequently one of the biggest barriers that people with mental illness face as the social distance and exclusion that they often experience as a result of other people's prejudices can make it very difficult for them to integrate successfully with other people and maintain a normal life. Another negative side-effect can be that people suffering from mental illness are reluctant to accept professional help until a late stage because of the fear of being labelled if people find out they are receiving treatment.

One of the biggest challenges is the stigma that is still associated with mental health problems

In the workplace this often means that employees will withhold information from their line manager, HR professionals or other decision makers because of the perceived impact on their career progression. As a result, the very people who are in a position to help them manage and cope with their illness at work are often the last to know.

Depictions of mental illness in the media do not help, with a typically negative focus on the link between mental illness and violence, failure and unpredictable behaviour. The formation of these stereotypes is normal and to be expected in situations where we are basing our assumptions on often very limited personal contact with sufferers of mental illness. For example, a 2002 study of over 200 students in Malaysia highlighted the impact of stereotypes about mentally ill people, with the results showing that students with knowledge of, and contact with, mentally ill patients were less likely to have negative attitudes than students who had no prior exposure (Mas and Hatim, 2002). But what if we told you that most of us have more exposure to people with mental health than we think? Current estimates suggest that one in four people will experience some form of mental illness in any given year and yet awareness of, and attitudes towards, mental health would suggest otherwise. Proper education to dispel these myths and exposure to people with mental disorders is therefore an important step in overcoming these stereotypes, and later in this book we will explore this further.

1.1 Defining mental health

Mental health is a broad and complex topic and we will not seek to provide education on every disorder listed in DSM-V (the most recent psychiatric manual), but rather will focus on those conditions which can have the greatest impact on the business world.

To a large extent, psychologists have thought about mental health as an absence of mental illness. Most psychologists accept that we are bio-psycho-social animals. Our health and welfare is not determined exclusively by our biology, our psychology or our social lives and networks, but by *all* of these. Abnormal and clinical psychologists are most concerned with mental health. However, the comparatively new discipline of health psychology is more interested in mental health and how it affects physical health (Seligman, Walker and Rosenhan, 2001).

When a professional attempts to make an assessment of a person's mental health, he or she tends to look at very specific features. Nevid, Rathus and Greene (1997) have listed 11 of these:

- Appearance: appropriate and clean.
- Behavioural characteristics: verbal and non-verbal.
- Orientation: knowledge of correct places, space and time.
- Memory: for recent and long-term past, people and events.
- Use of senses: concentration and awareness.
- Perceptual processes: sensing reality from unreality.
- Mood and affect: having an appropriate emotional tone.
- Intelligence: vocabulary knowledge.
- Thought processes: logic and coherence.
- Insight: self-awareness and psychological awareness of others.
- Judgement: rationality and decision making.

It still seems rare for psychological textbooks to deal with mental health and wellness as not being anything more than an absence of signs of mental illness. On the other hand, there are lists of characteristics that epitomize mental health (Seligman, Walker and Rosenhan, 2001). These include the following: emotional stability and awareness; being able to initiate and sustain satisfying long-term relationships; being able to face, resolve and learn from day-to-day work, and personal and financial problems; being sufficiently self-confident and assertive; being socially aware, empathic and socio-centric; being able to enjoy solitude; having a sense of playfulness and fun; and showing signs of merriment, joy and laughter from time to time when appropriate.

Mental illnesses can be caused by environmental, cognitive, genetic or neurological factors. Clinicians are concerned with the assessment, diagnosis and management of psychological problems. They are both scientists and practitioners who often specialize in the treatment of various disorders like anxiety disorders (anxiety, panic, phobias, post-traumatic stress disorder (PTSD)), mood disorders (depression, bipolar), substance disorders (alcohol, stimulants, hallucinogens, etc.) or complex problems like schizophrenia.

Happiness is another widely discussed state that is essentially about mental wellness. However, it has been known for 50 years that happiness is not the opposite of unhappiness – the two feelings are unrelated (Bradburn, 1969). What this taught researchers was that absence of illness and unhappiness was not the key to understanding happiness, but that we need to know those factors that lead to stable happiness in an individual.

The relatively recent advent of studies on happiness, has led to a science of well-being (Huppert, Baylis and Keverne, 2005). All the early researchers in this field pointed out that psychologists had long neglected well-being, while preferring to look at its opposites: anxiety, despair and depression.

All the early writers in this area struggled with a definition. Eysenck (1990) noted telltale signs, both verbal and non-verbal. Argyle (2001) noted that different researchers had identified different components of happiness like life satisfaction, positive affect, self-acceptance, positive relations with others, autonomy and environmental mastery. Happiness also constitutes joy, satisfaction and other related positive emotions. Myers (1992) noted the stable and unstable characteristics of happy people, who tend to be creative, energetic, decisive, flexible and sociable. They also tend to be more forgiving, loving, trusting and responsible. They tolerate frustration better and are more willing to help those in need. In short, they feel good so do good. Diener (2000) has defined subjective well-being as how people cognitively and emotionally evaluate their lives. It has an evaluative (good-bad) as well as a hedonic (pleasant-unpleasant) dimension.

1.2 The incidence of mental illness

The understanding and awareness of mental illness in society has improved dramatically in the last 15–20 years and at the same time there appears to have been an upward trend in its prevalence rate (Deverill and King, 2009), with the most commonly quoted statistic estimating that *one in four people* in the UK will experience a mental health problem in any given year (http://mind.org.uk). It is not clear if the rate of mental illness has truly increased or if the increase in understanding of the topic has led to more accurate diagnosis and therefore a greater frequency of reporting symptoms.

Regardless, this increased prevalence of mental illness is quite alarming and particularly given the evidence that approximately three-quarters of adults with a common mental health problem are not in receipt of medication or counselling, including two-thirds of those who have been assessed as having sufficient a level of symptoms to warrant treatment (Deverill and King, 2009). The rate appears to be higher among women and in people in the 45–54 age bracket, and the prevalence rates are mirrored among working-age adults, with approximately one in six workers experiencing depression, anxiety or stress-related problems at any one time. This rate can increase to one in five when drug or alcohol dependence are included (Sainsbury Centre, 2007) and later in this book we dedicate a chapter to understanding the implications of drug and alcohol dependency.

1.3 Why we should care: the costs of mental illness to business

We have all experienced the negative impacts when a colleague is off sick: increased workload for the rest of the team, disruption to the operations of the business, a drop in sales revenue, etc. Mental illness falls into this category and is a silent epidemic impacting the business world at an alarming rate. In the UK, for example, it is estimated that around 80 million days are lost every year due to mental illnesses, costing employers £1–2 billion each year, and in the USA, according to recent collaborative research by Harvard University Medical School and the World Economic Forum (Bloom *et al.*, 2011), it is estimated that untreated mental illnesses costs the country at least $105 billion in lost productivity annually. The very nature of mental illness also means that absences from work are rarely characterized by the odd day here and there; instead, sufferers are likely to experience prolonged periods when they are not able to work, and when they do return to work, they can take some time to get back to their previous level of performance.

Estimates for national spending in the USA on depression alone are $30–40 billion, with an estimated 200 million days being lost from work each year. Similarly, in the UK, depression is estimated to cost approximately £2 billion a year and, on top of absenteeism, can have a profound impact on reduced productivity, staff turnover, poor timekeeping and work-related accidents. In a study of US workers, Kessler *et al*. (2006) estimate that a single depressive disorder is typically associated with an average of over five weeks of lost productivity per person. Compared to other mental illnesses, depression would appear to be the most costly of all health problems to employers (Wang *et al*., 2003), although there is a vast amount of evidence to suggest that all mood disorders are associated with significant costs, including absence from work and reduced functioning whilst at work. In addition, it is quite probable that a diagnosis of depression is often used as an umbrella term for some other mood disorders.

Reduced functioning can take many forms, including poor cognitive performance, problem behaviour directed towards other colleagues, lack of attention to the core tasks of the job, poor interpersonal skills when dealing with clients and a greater need for frequent breaks and time off. In a recent study in the Netherlands, De Graaf *et al*. (2012) carried out extensive research to compare the effects of mental disorders on work performance. They found that drug abuse, bipolar disorder, major depression, digestive disorders and panic disorder were associated with the highest number of days of lost work (once co-morbidity had been taken out of the equation). At a wider population level, they found that depression, chronic back pain, respiratory disorders, drug abuse and digestive disorders contributed the most to lost productivity and days off work.

Other research suggests that those with a psychiatric disorder (in comparison to the rest of the population) do not always have more days off work, but will certainly have a greater number of days during which they are either unproductive or unable to function at their full capacity (Boyle *et al*., 1996; Kessler and Frank, 1997). So, in other words, those with mental illness may be just as likely to show up for work as the rest of us, but they will need extra help in performing at the required level. This highlights the need for increasing the awareness of how to manage, mitigate and prevent mental health problems in the workplace. In order to get the most from workers who experience mental health problems, it is critical that managers and co-workers understand the nuances and respond appropriately.

1.4 The impact of the global financial crisis on mental illness

The report of the World Health Organization (WHO) in 1996 suggested that depression would emerge as the leading cause of disability by the year 2020 and the indicators seem to be that we are on trend for this to be true. One of the main catalysts contributing to this trend in the last decade has been the global financial crisis, with indicators that the economic crash of 2007 and the subsequent fallout has increased the prevalence of mental illness. The prolonged economic downturn has led to an increase in job insecurity, work stress and the helplessness associated with unemployment and redundancy. The mental health charity *Mind* found that one in ten workers in the UK visited their GP for support with mental health issues as a result of recession-related work pressure and in 2011 the BBC reported figures indicating that prescriptions for anti-depressant drugs such as Prozac rose by more than 40 per cent between 2006 and 2010.

Economic recessions have numerous social and psychological consequences. Many people lose their jobs or are compelled to work part-time. Young people are often hit hard and struggle to find work. A sense of a lethargy and despair pervades many communities, industries and organizations. In some countries people take to the streets in protest, while in others they seem quietly resigned to their fate. There have been numerous studies of the psychological distress that unemployment brings (Bjarnsasson and Sigurdardotter, 2003), with the most extreme cases resulting in suicide.

Redundancies in particular usually lead to two problems: first, affective or emotional consequences; and, second, cognitive consequences which impact an individual's thought processes. Some of those 'laid off' from work genuinely experience all the symptoms of PTSD, experiencing anxiety and depression. Some cannot stop thinking about it (sensitizers), while others cannot bear to face reality (repressors), becoming withdrawn and soon falling into the vicious cycle of decline. Depression leads to withdrawal and low self-esteem, which lead to fewer attempts to find a new job or adjust, which in turn leads to a greater level of depression. Some see threats as opportunities, while others see them as disasters.

Figure 1.1 below represents a typical, negative vicious spiral. People feel uncertain and anxious about their jobs. This distraction can lead to poorer performance as well as illness. This often leads to worse results for an individual, a group and a whole organization. This, in turn, threatens the individual's work status which caused the problem in the first place.

The most extreme impact of the recession is evidenced in the increasing rate of suicide amongst adults of working age in the hardest-hit countries. In 2011 the British medical journal *The Lancet* reported the results of a study from 10 European Union countries which indicated an increase in suicide rates in hard-hit economies like Greece (up 17 per cent on figures before the recession) and Ireland (up 13 per cent). Research suggests that men may be more susceptible than women to suicide; a 2012 study published in the *British Medical Journal*

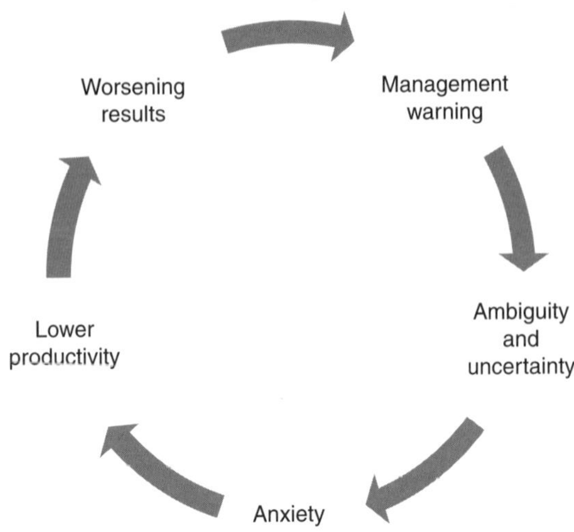

FIGURE 1.1 **The vicious cycle of job uncertainty**

reported that each ten per cent increase in the number of unemployed men between 2008 and 2010 was significantly associated with a 1.4 per cent increase in male suicides. Men may be more vulnerable to the adverse effect that unemployment and job insecurity can bring, particularly in households where they hold the traditional 'breadwinner' role.

The nature of mental illness is such that symptoms can take many months to appear and so even though the signs of financial recovery are there to be seen, the impact on human well-being is likely to be felt for many years to come. Indeed, at the time that *The Lancet* study was published in 2011, Bloomberg warned that increased suicides would be 'just the tip of the iceberg', alerting researchers to the likelihood of a mental health crisis and the spiralling incidence of depression across the world.

This worrying trend highlights the need to invest in better systems to support people back into the workplace who may have lost their job as a result of the recession, to ensure that those in work who may be feeling vulnerable have the adequate support systems in place and to educate managers and the general workforce so that they are more able to spot the warning signs of mental illness.

1.5 A brief history of mental illness

Attempts to understand and categorize mental illness can be traced back to ancient times where many cultures viewed mental illness as a form of punishment from the Gods. People were commonly assumed to have been possessed by demons and treatment included exorcism, physical punishment and treatment with balms and ointments.

There was no clear distinction between physical and mental illness until the time of the early pioneers, including Hippocrates, who began to question this assumption. Hippocrates was one of the first people to start treating mentally ill people with techniques not rooted in religion or superstition and focused instead on making changes to the environment and administering specialist substances. Throughout the Middle Ages, the preoccupation with a religious connection persisted and priests and other figures of authority still thought of mental illness in terms of the person needing to be cleansed of evil spirits. Treatments during this era were of a harsh and brutal nature.

These negative attitudes persisted into the eighteenth century in the Western world, following which a more enlightened and scientific approach began to emerge. In 1752 the first 'lunatic' asylum was opened in the USA at the Pennsylvania Hospital based on a model of care established at the famous Bethlehem Hospital in London (commonly known as Bedlam), where there are records as far back as 1403 of mentally ill patients being admitted. Treatment in these institutions was not much better than that doled out by priests in the Middle Ages and patients were often beaten, chained to walls and put in straitjackets for days at a time. Another cruel aspect of such institutions was that local people were often permitted to visit the asylum, pay an admission fee and subsequently observe patients and poke fun at them.

Things began to change in the mid-1800s and activists such as Dorothea Dix lobbied for better treatment and living conditions for the mentally ill. Dix wielded considerable influence over state legislature and was eventually successful in persuading the US government to fund the building of 32 state psychiatric hospitals. During this time, new ideas about treating mental illness were also introduced and physicians became convinced that the act of physical confinement itself would go a long way towards treating the illness. Thus, the institutional inpatient care model, in which many patients lived in hospitals and were treated by professional staff, became accepted as the most effective way to care for the mentally ill. Asylums subsequently began to spring up in many countries in the Western world.

By the mid-1950s, particularly in the USA, there was a push for deinstitutionalization as growing evidence had begun to show that this model was not working. Understanding of mental illness had progressed considerably and the focus at this time was on understanding and treating the psychosocial causes of mental illness. As a result, outpatient treatment began in many

countries, accelerated by the development of a variety of anti-psychotic drugs. This international move towards a more community-centric model of care was based on the belief that people with mental illness would have a higher quality of life if they were treated in their own communities.

1.6 Modern treatment and cures for mental illness

Psychiatry has gone in and out of fashion. One of the most famous anti-psychiatry studies was done in the early 1970s. Eight 'normal' mentally healthy researchers tried to gain admission, through diagnosis, to a number of American mental hospitals. The only symptom they reported was hearing voices. Seven were diagnosed as schizophrenic and were admitted. Once in the hospital, they behaved normally and were ignored when they politely asked for information. They later reported that their diagnostic label of schizophrenia meant they had low status and power in the mental hospital.

They then decided to 'come clean' and admit they had no symptoms and felt fine. But it took nearly three weeks before they were discharged, often with the diagnosis of 'schizophrenia in remission'. So, normal, healthy people could easily be diagnosable as abnormal. But could the reverse happen? The same researchers told psychiatric hospital staff that fake or pseudo-patients pretending to be schizophrenics might try to gain access to their hospital. They then found that 19 genuine patients were suspected as bring frauds by two or more members of staff, including a psychiatrist. The conclusion was that it is not possible to distinguish the sane from the insane in mental hospitals. Though this famous study has received considerable criticism on ethical and experimental grounds, it added great impetus to the anti-psychiatry movement.

There were three main origins of the anti-psychiatry movement. The *first* started in the early 1950s and was a result of the war between *Freudian-inspired psychoanalytic* psychiatrists and the new *biological physical* psychiatrists. The former favoured protracted, dynamic, talking cures, but were losing power and were being challenged by the latter, who saw this approach not only as costly and ineffective but also profoundly unscientific. The biological psychologist treatments were surgical and pharmacological, and they had some important early successes.

The *second* attack on psychiatry began in the 1960s with famous figures like David Cooper, R.D. Laing and Thomas Szasz becoming highly vocal in different countries about the use of psychiatry to control those deviating from societal norms. Thus, people who were seen to be sexually, politically or morally deviant or different were subjected to psychiatric processing and control. The famous book *The Myth of Mental Illness* (Szasz, 1961) explains this position well.

The *third* force were American and European sociologists, notably Erving Goffman and Michel Foucault, who saw the devious power of psychiatry and its effects on labelling and stigmatizing and hospitalizing people. The high point of this movement occurred at the time of the 1960s counter-cultural, challenging zeitgeist. Popular films (*One Flew over the Cuckoo's Nest*) and radical magazines appeared that challenged the biological psychiatrists, state services and practices.

The anti-psychiatry movement was always a loose coalition between social action groups who tended to focus on very specific problems like schizophrenia or sexual disorders. They talked of *authenticity* and *liberation*, of *empowerment* and *personal management* rather than pharmaceutical intervention. Many began to attack the pharmaceutical industry and, particularly, established psychiatric institutions like the great Victorian mental hospitals.

The movements did share some fundamental beliefs and concerns. The *first* was that families, institutions and the state are as much a cause of illness as a person's biological functioning or genetic make-up. *Second*, they opposed the medical model of illness and treatment. They believed those who were living by different codes of conduct were erroneously and dangerously labelled delusional. *Third*, they believed that certain religious and ethnic groups were oppressed because they were in some sense abnormal. They were pathologized and therefore were made to believe they needed treatment.

The movements got and still get very concerned with the power of diagnostic labels. They see such labels as giving a bogus impression of accuracy and immutability. They have succeeded to a large extent such that 'schizophrenics' are now regularly described as 'people with schizophrenia' and 'AIDS victims' as 'people with AIDS'. Diagnostic labels and manuals are rejected because people either meet none of the criteria or they meet multiple criteria and there is little agreement between experts.

The movements against psychiatry also focused their opposition on very specific therapies, particularly drugs. This was especially the case with drugs designed to treat primarily childhood problems (like attention deficit hyperactivity disorder (ADHD)) and depression. They were attacked because of their cost and side-effects, but also because patients were not told the truth

about them. Anti-psychiatry movement activists have focused on all aspects of pharmaceutical company behaviour, arguing that they fake their data and massively overcharge for their drugs. This in turn has led the industry to be carefully monitored and policed by legislation.

Other targets have been electroconvulsive therapy (ECT) as well as very specific procedures like brain surgery (prefrontal lobotomies). Despite some evidence of success, critics argue they are 'forced upon' naïve patients and cause massive permanent side-effects.

Although there are still a number of large inpatient psychiatric hospitals, particularly in Central and Eastern Europe, the deinstitutionalization movement has been fairly widespread and has changed the nature and perception of modern care. What was once the common has become the uncommon, with lobotomies being almost totally eradicated and the media branding psychiatry as a pseudo-science, not empirical and to many degrees a 'sham' (Kirk, 2013). Anti-psychiatric views such as these often focus on quantitative statistics rather than indepth rational inspection, e.g., that mental illness has grown, not shrunk, with about 20 per cent of American adults diagnosable as mentally ill in 2013 (Kirk, 2013).

1.7 The categorization of mental illness

The classification of mental disorders is essentially the holy grail of psychiatry. Creating a parsimonious, efficient and universal classification system is something that has only really begun to take shape in the last five decades. Pushed by the deinstitutionalization movement, the International Classification of Diseases (ICD) produced by the WHO and the Diagnostic and Statistical Manual of Mental Disorders produced by the American Psychiatric Association (APA) were the first comprehensive systems. Both systems list categories of disorders thought to be distinct types and have deliberately converged their codes in recent revisions so that the manuals are often broadly comparable, although significant differences remain.

The ICD is an international standard diagnostic classification for a wide variety of health conditions. One chapter focuses on 'mental and behavioural disorders' and consists of ten main categories:

1. Organic (including symptomatic) mental disorders.
2. Mental and behavioural disorders due to the use of psychoactive substances.

3. Schizophrenia, schizotypal and delusional disorders.
4. Mood (affective) disorders.
5. Neurotic, stress-related and somatoform disorders.
6. Behavioural syndromes associated with physiological disturbances and physical factors.
7. Personality and behaviour disorders in adults.
8. Mental retardation.
9. Disorders of psychological development.
10. Behavioural and emotional disorders with onset usually occurring in childhood and adolescence.

Within each group there are additional specific subcategories. The WHO is revising its classifications in this section as part of the development of the ICD-11, which is scheduled for 2014.

The *Diagnostic Statistic Manual – Version 4* (DSM-IV) consists of five axes (domains) on which disorder can be assessed. The five axes are as follows:

Axis I: clinical disorders (all mental disorders except personality disorders and mental retardation).
Axis II: personality disorders and mental retardation.
Axis III: general medical conditions (must be connected to a mental disorder).
Axis IV: psychosocial and environmental problems (for example, a limited social support network).
Axis V: global assessment of functioning (psychological, social and job-related functions are evaluated on a continuum between mental health and extreme mental disorder).

As with any competing enterprise, there are always ongoing scientific doubts concerning both validity and reliability (Baca-Garcia *et al*., 2007), but also and more importantly concerning boundaries of normality.

Studies reporting insignificant validities and reliability, while having important implications, need to be considered in light of what these manuals represent. Often mistaken for 'rule books', it is important to note that these are guidelines. Each person will experience mental illness in a slightly different way, with mental illness often being a vast combination of things that will never be fully understood. Thus, such studies may not always show such manuals to be useful. Their generalizability is of more importance. That being said, because there are no 'rules' as it were, natural boundaries between related syndromes or between a common syndrome and normality have failed. Many practitioners find this unacceptable as labelling inappropriately

cannot actually lead to mental illness, but can cause significant problems in all other areas of life.

When the fifth edition of the *Diagnostic and Statistical Manual of Mental Disorders* (DSM-V) was released at the American Psychiatric Association's Annual Meeting in May 2013, it marked the end of more than a decade of revising the criteria for the diagnosis and classification of mental disorders. DSM-V serves as the universal authority for the diagnosis of psychiatric disorders and most diagnosis and treatment of mental illness is based on the criteria and guidance set out in this manual. The publication of a revised and significantly altered version therefore has significant practical implications.

The manual is divided into three major sections: 1) introduction and clear information on how to use the DSM; 2) information and categorical diagnoses; 3) self-assessment tools as well as categories that require more research.

Whilst DSM-V has approximately the same number of conditions as DSM-IV, there have been some significant changes in specific disorders. A summary of these is as follows:

- Autism: there is now a single condition called autism spectrum disorder, which incorporates four previous separate disorders including autistic disorder (autism), Asperger's disorder, childhood disintegrative disorder and not otherwise specified pervasive developmental disorder.
- Disruptive Mood Dysregulation Disorder (DMDD): childhood bipolar disorder has a new name, which is 'intended to address issues of over-diagnosis and over-treatment of bipolar disorder in children'.
- ADHD: this disorder has been modified especially to emphasize that it can continue into adulthood. The one 'big' change is that you can be diagnosed with ADHD as an adult if you exhibit one less symptom than if you are a child.
- Bereavement exclusion removal: in DSM-IV, if you were grieving the loss of a loved one, technically you couldn't be diagnosed with a major depression disorder in the first two months of your grief. This exclusion was removed in DSM-V for a number of reasons. *First*, the implication that bereavement typically lasts only two months has been removed as most practitioners recognize that the duration is more commonly one to two years. *Second*, bereavement is recognized as a severe psychosocial stressor that can precipitate a major depressive episode in a vulnerable individual, generally beginning soon after the loss. *Third*, bereavement-related major depression

is most likely to occur in individuals with past personal and family histories of major depressive episodes. It is genetically influenced and is associated with similar personality characteristics, patterns of co-morbidity and risks of chronicity and/or recurrence as non-bereavement-related major depressive episodes. Finally, the depressive symptoms associated with bereavement-related depression respond to the same psychosocial and medication treatments as non-bereavement-related depression.

- PTSD: more attention is now paid to behavioural symptoms that accompany PTSD in DSM-V. It now includes four primary major symptom clusters: re-experiencing, arousal, avoidance and persistent negative alterations in cognitions and mood. The condition is now developmentally more sensitive in that diagnostic thresholds have been lowered for children and adolescents.
- Major and mild neurocognitive disorder: major neurocognitive disorder now subsumes dementia and amnestic disorder, but a new disorder – mild neurocognitive disorder – has also been added.
- Other new and notable disorders: both binge eating disorder and premenstrual dysphoric disorder are now official diagnoses in DSM-V (they were not prior to this, although there were commonly diagnosed by clinicians). Hoarding disorder is also now recognized as a real disorder separate from obsessive-compulsive disorder (OCD), 'which reflects persistent difficulty discarding or parting with possessions due to a perceived need to save the items and distress associated with discarding them. Hoarding disorder may have unique neurobiological correlates, is associated with significant impairment and may respond to clinical intervention'.

There are and will remain many criticisms of this manual, and the psychology and psychiatry community has come out in unison to highlight concerns about the changes. In a blog post in *Psychology Today* (2 December 2010), Frances lists the ten 'most potentially harmful changes' to DSM-V:

- DMDD being used to describe temper tantrums.
- Major depressive disorder being used to for normal grief situations.
- Minor neurocognitive disorder being used for normal forgetfulness in old age.
- Adult attention deficit disorder, which could lead to greater psychiatric prescriptions of stimulants.
- Binge eating disorder being used to describe excessive eating.
- Changes to autism diagnoses, thus reducing the numbers diagnosed.
- A risk that first-time drug users could be grouped with addicts.
- Behavioural addictions, making a 'mental disorder of everything we like to do a lot'.

- Generalized anxiety disorder being used to describe everyday worries.
- Changes to PTSD opening 'the gate even further to the already existing problem of misdiagnosis of PTSD in forensic settings'.

These criticisms are not new and are certainly not unique to DSM-V. Is the reliability of diagnosis improved? In other words, do psychiatrists and psychologists agree upon diagnoses? Is all this medicalization mainly for the benefit of the big pharmaceutical companies?

There is also the serious issue of cultural bias. It is argued that national culture affects the experience, expression, generation and management of symptoms. It also affects the management of symptoms. People in different cultures use different words and idioms to express their psychological distress and pain. National culture also reflects shame in different ways. Many cultures accept supernatural explanations for mental illness, while others try hard to medicalize it as soon as possible. What place does a universal diagnostic manual have in a multicultural and diverse world? And does it help to improve the mental health literacy of the general public?

1.8 Summary

Many groups have called for a change in attitude towards and an understanding of mental disorders which cost individuals, families and organizations a great deal. It seems that we have been much more successful at changing attitudes towards physical illness than mental illness. The sooner we are able to increase mental health awareness, the sooner we can help people in distress. There are a large number of self-help groups and societies dedicated to helping people and their relatives with a large range of psychological and physical problems. Each calls for the better education of the general public, particularly those in educational and organizational settings.

This is not only a humanitarian but also a business issue. The more mental health-literate manager should be able to make better hiring and managing decisions about people who are often the greatest asset but also the greatest cost to an organization.

chapter 2

The Basics: What is Mental Illness?

2.1 Introduction

Mental health problems can come in many shapes and sizes and take many forms. The terms used to diagnose them can sometimes be confusing as they have become words that we now use in everyday language to describe mood, e.g., 'I am depressed' or 'he is manic'.

On the one hand, this has helped bring mental health nomenclature into the daily language and has possibly helped to reduce the stigma of mental illness, but on the other hand, this brings with it a risk that we underestimate how severe and debilitating such conditions can be.

Mental health is also often used to describe a positive state of psychological well-being and attempts to describe mental health in positive terms can be traced back to the 1950s, when both psychoanalysts and social psychologists sought to bring greater clarity to the definition of mental health.

One of the difficulties of defining mental health, mental illness and mental disorder is the challenge of drawing a clear distinction between normal and abnormal behaviour.

Abnormal psychology is the study of abnormal behaviours. It looks at the origins, manifestations and treatments of disordered habits, thoughts or drives. These may be caused by environmental, cognitive, genetic or neurological factors. It is part but by no means the central part of psychology. Whilst it is relatively easy to spot people who are distressed or acting bizarrely, it is much more difficult to *define* abnormality.

Abnormal means departure from the norm. So, very tall and very short people are abnormal, as are very backward and very gifted people. Thus, strictly speaking, Einstein and Michaelangelo were abnormal, as were Bach and Shakespeare. For clinical psychology, the issue is not so much whether the behaviour is abnormal as whether it is *maladaptive*, causing a person distress and social impairment. If a person's behaviour seems irrational or potentially harmful to themselves and others, we tend to think of that as abnormal. For the psychologist, it is called psychopathology, while for the layperson, it is called madness or insanity.

We would all like the certainty and clarity of a clear distinction between normal and abnormal, yet we all know that history and culture often shape and determine what is considered abnormal. Psychiatric textbooks reflect this. Homosexuality was not that long ago considered a mental illness, while masturbation in the nineteenth century was thought of as an abnormal behaviour.

Socio-economic status, gender and race can all have an impact on abnormality. Women are more likely to have anorexia, bulimia or anxiety disorders than men, who, in turn, are more likely to be substance abusers. Poor people are more likely to be diagnosed schizophrenic than rich people. American children suffer a high incidence of disorders of *under-control* compared to *over-control*, but this is the other way around in the West Indies and Asia.

Early approaches to abnormality saw bizarre behaviour as 'spirit possession'. People then believed in animalism – the belief that we were very similar to animals and that madness was the result of uncontrolled regression. The Ancient Greeks saw abnormality and general malaise caused by bodily fluids or 'humours' (bile). As a result, humane treatment never really appeared until the nineteenth century.

NORMALITY VERSUS ABNORMALITY

Subjective: this is perhaps the most primitive idea that uses ourselves, our behaviour and our values as the criteria of normality. This is the stuff of idiom and adage (once a thief, always a thief; there's nowt so queer as folk). So people like us are normal, while those different from us are not. This approach also tends to think in simple categories or non-overlapping types: normal – abnormal – very abnormal.

Normative: this is the idea that there is an ideal, desirable state of how one should think and behave. This view of the perfect world is often developed by religious and political thinkers. Normality is perfection: the further from normality one is, the more abnormal. It's a more 'what ought to be' than a 'what is reasonably possible' state of affairs. Nothing is normal because nobody is perfect.

Cultural: culture dictates trends in everything from dress to demeanour, language to love. Culture prescribes and proscribes behaviours. Certain things are taboo, while other things are illegal. Again, the further away or different from cultural norms a person appears to be, the more they are judged as abnormal. However, as cultural beliefs and practices change, so do definitions of normality. The case of homosexual behaviour nicely illustrates this issue.

Statistical: all statisticians know the concept of the bell curve or the normal distribution. It has particular properties and is best known in the world of intelligence. Thus, a score of 100 is average and 66 per cent of the population score between 85 and 115, and around 97 per cent between 70 and 130. Thus, if you score below 70 and over 130, you are unusual: extreme, though the word 'abnormal' would not be applied. This model has drawbacks in that there is no guarantee that just because behaviour occurs frequently does not necessarily make it healthy or desirable. Also, whilst it may work for abilities which are reasonably straightforward to measure, it sits less easily with more subtle and multi-dimensional issues like personality or mental illness.

Clinical: social science and medical clinicians attempt to assess the effectiveness, organization and adaptiveness of a person's functioning. Much depends on which dimensions are being assessed. Clinicians also accept that the normal-abnormal distinctions are often grey areas and somewhat subjective, though they strive for reliable diagnosis. Abnormality is usually associated with poor adaptations, pain or bizarre behaviours.

2.2 Generally agreed-upon criteria

Today, psychological definitions of abnormality revolve around half-a-dozen or so 'generally agreed-upon' criteria. These have been called the 4Ds: distress,

deviance, dysfunction and danger. Abnormality generally involves *pain and suffering*. Acute and chronic personal suffering is one of these criteria. Another is *poor adaptation* – not being able to do the everyday things of life, such as hold down a job, maintain happy interpersonal relationships and plan for the future.

A very common criteria is *irrationality* – where people have bizarre, illogical beliefs about the physical or social world as well as sometimes the spiritual world. Their behaviour is often incomprehensible to others. Abnormal people are often *unpredictable*; they can be very volatile, changing from one extreme to another and are often quite unable to control their behaviour.

Almost by definition, abnormality is characterized by *unconventional*, rare and, usually undesirable behaviours. It is sometimes called vivid and eccentric. In addition, abnormality has a *moral* dimension. It is associated with breaking rules, violating moral standards and disregarding social norms. Illegal, immoral and undesirable behaviour is abnormal.

There is one other rather interesting criteria of abnormality: the discomfort that is generated in people around abnormality. Observers, be they friends, family or just onlookers, often feel uncomfortable around clear evidence of abnormality.

The problems with any definition of abnormality are clear. *First*, a healthy person in an unhealthy society is often labelled as abnormal. There have been many historical incidents where sick societies have been deeply intolerant of those who do not obey or concur with their narrow (unhealthy, maladaptive) standards of belief and behaviour. *Second*, of course, expert observers cannot agree on the categorization of normal vs. abnormal. Even when multiple criteria of abnormality are specified, there remains fundamental disagreement about whether a person is considered in some sense abnormal. *Third*, there is the actor-observer difference: who is to make the judgement? 'Actors' rarely think themselves abnormal: most of us are reasonably positive about ourselves and indeed have a great deal of information that others do not have. Yet there are well-known traps and hazards in making a self-diagnosis. It is easier to be observers and label others abnormal, particularly those different from us or threatening to us.

2.3 Biopsychosocial health and illness

An important point to make at the outset is that mental health affects physical health and vice versa. Nearly all those working in health now take a biopsychosocial perspective, which accepts that both health and illness are the consequence of physical/biological factors as well as psychological/mental factors and social/environmental factors. The biomedical approach assumes that ill health and disease are directly (and exclusively) caused by diseases and their specific pathological process. The biopsychosocial approach suggests that we will best understand a chronic condition by also understanding the person, the physical and the social context of both, and the healthcare system.

Historically, doctors have always taken a patient's psyche (personality, beliefs and values) and their social circumstances and context into consideration when treating them. Osler, a great nineteenth-century expert in internal medicine, noted: 'The good physician treats the disease but the great physician treats the patient who has the disease.' Whilst the biopsychosocial approach to health and illness has always been articulated in one form or another, the stunning success of pharmacotherapy over the last 20–30 years led to a resurgence of the biomedical model.

The biopsychosocial approach to health understands the nature/nurture interaction. It accepts conscious and unconscious influences on health and wellness. Most of all, it understands reciprocal determinism, which accepts that social factors may influence psychological factors which change the psychological factors. People choose how they live their lives and with whom they choose to live. Their psyche (personality, values and intellect) determines how they perceive their world and how others react to them. All of these have psychological and biological consequences. The biomedical approach is essentially *reductionist* and sometimes *exclusionist*. It underplays the role of social and emotional factors at work, trying to reduce everything to a strictly biological or neurological process and excluding the possibility that other factors play a part. The biopsychosocial approach sees the undissolvable nature of the mind-body line. Most of us know about somapsychic and psychosomatic illness where the body and mind interact.

The influence of psychosocial and biological factors is a two-way process. Physical conditions lead to 'sickness behaviour', which influences biological symptoms. Clearly, some conditions like chronic back pain present particular problems for those who favour either the medical model or the simply psychological model. Objective medical data provide little help to either to explain or treat many features of chronic pain. It is common sense and an empirical fact that social and psychological factors change health, yet it is by no means universally accepted. Clearly, there are economic, epistemological and political factors involved. Further, we have seen from historical studies that sometimes the psychosocial factors thought to be the

Social and psychological factors change health

primary causal agents in disease played a much smaller part than the biological factors once they were fully understood. Often, looking back shows how naïvely some were in trying to link social, moral and economic factors to the cause of a disease when it was later discovered how the disease really occurred.

The biopsychosocial model suggests disability first through a patient's illness beliefs and their consequent coping strategies, including their adherence to medical treatments and advice, and second through their emotional reactions, particularly fear and depression, with consequent catastrophizing and helplessness.

A biopsychosocial approach is one that incorporates thoughts, beliefs, feelings, behaviours and their social context and interactions with biological processes in order to better understand and manage illness and disability. The biomedical approach is a more linear approach that assumes that phenomena can be explained solely by biological processes. In reality, the processes are integrated and indivisible. For example, thoughts and feelings are impossible without a biological process occurring within the brain.

Despite all the advances in modern medicine, it remains important to recognize that all illness at work is caused and cured by biological, psychological *and* social factors. We hope for and constantly strive towards medical breakthroughs, such as a cure for cancer, understanding and therefore preventing the cases of some problems. There are tremendous advances in genetics, neurosciences and brain sciences. Our understanding of the neuro-anatomy, biology and genetics of medical conditions seems to be advancing exponentially. Maybe people said this too in the 1980s when looking forward to the forthcoming millennium. But to believe in magic bullets and miraculous discoveries would be naïve, as it is misplaced to think that these will always arise in the laboratory. We are social animals gifted with a complex will. Our lifestyle and our thoughts influence our health and vice versa.

We have learnt over the past 50 years to think about the medical profession and institutions differently. We know that the biopsychosocial message is fundamentally true in most cases. The challenge is to use its insights in the study and treatment of illness over the next decade.

2.4 The major categories of mental illness

Until the middle of the nineteenth century there was little attempt to categorize or systematize mental illness. All cultures and societies recognized that there were different kinds of mental illness, though they had very different ideas as to how they originated and how they should be cured, coped with or treated.

It was not until the turn of the twentieth century that Kraeplin, a German psychiatrist, tried to draw up the first psychiatric classification system. One disorder he called *dementia praecox*, which meant predictive deterioration, and he described various behavioural cues that we today would call schizophrenia. These included inappropriate emotional responses, repetitive motor behaviours, attention difficulties, illusory sensory experience, etc.

Today the DSM provides a common language and standard criteria for the classification of mental illness. It is relied upon by clinicians, researchers, psychiatric drug regulation agencies, health insurance companies, pharmaceutical companies, the legal system and policy makers. The next few pages will summarize some of the major categories of mental illness in further detail.

2.4.1 Schizophrenia

Most people are terrified by the prospect of meeting a schizophrenic. They are thought of as deranged, dangerous and demented, as well as unhinged, unpredictable and uncontrollable. Films and books have probably done more to perpetuate myths about them and this condition than to explain it. This is further exacerbated by the few cases where individuals suffering from schizophrenia have committed heinous crimes and the media has in turn demonized the illness and the individuals who suffer from it.

The diagnostic term 'schizophrenia' is a major cause of dispute and debate among psychiatrists, patient groups and the lay public. Over the years, doubts about the usefulness of the term have increased. The most common objection is that it is an unhelpful 'umbrella' term that covers a range of different disorders with different symptoms and different causes. Diagnosis is therefore unreliable. Some advocate the idea of *schizotypy*, which refers to a continuum of personality characteristics and experiences related to psychoses, particularly schizophrenia. This is different from the categorical view that you either have or do not have the condition.

It is assumed that schizophrenia affects one in 100 people and is the most serious of mental disorders. It has also been suggested that prognosis for the condition follows a pattern such as this: a third of people require long-term institutionalization, a third show remission and could be considered cured, while a third have periods of symptoms followed by 'normality'. They are different because of the symptoms that they do have (positive) and do not have (negative) compared to normal people. They tend to have various manifestations of thought disorders (disorganized, irrational thinking), delusions and hallucinations. However, they tend to lack energy, initiative and social contacts. They are emotionally very flat, have few pleasures and are withdrawn.

Schizophrenia is a psychotic illness characterized by a disorder of thoughts and perceptions, behaviours and moods. It is common to differentiate between *neuroses* and *psychoses*. Neurotics tend to be anxious, depressed, guilt-ridden or inhibited. They are often fearful, showing worry, tension distractibility, depression or fatigue or self-defeating coping behaviour like obsessive thoughts, compulsive rituals or excessive forgetting. *Psychoses* all show much more serious and disturbing symptoms. These include hallucinations, delusions, powerful disturbances of mood, obvious disturbances of thought, as well as acute and chronic relationship problems leading to isolation and social withdrawal. Whereas most neurotics have insight into their condition, psychotics do not.

There are many common misconceptions about schizophrenia:

- The *first* is that they are dangerous, uncontrollable and unpredictable, when in fact most are rather shy, withdrawn and concerned with their problems.
- The *second* is that they have a split Jekyll and Hyde personality, whereas what is split is the emotional (affective) and cognitive (thought) aspect of people with schizophrenia.
- *Third*, many people believe they do not and cannot recover, and that once a schizophrenic, always a schizophrenic.

The classification of schizophrenia remains complex because of the range of symptoms. These include delusion (odd, false beliefs), hallucinations (false sensory perceptions of sound, sight and smell), disorganized speech (incoherence, loose association, use of neologisms), disorganized behaviour (dress, body posture, personal hygiene), negative flat emotions (lack of energy, libido) as well as poor insight into their problems and depression.

Because of complications with the diagnosis, various subtypes for the condition have been created. Thus, there is *paranoid* and *catatonic* schizophrenia. Catatonics (from the Greek 'to stretch or draw tight') often adopt odd, stationary poses for long periods of time. Paranoid schizophrenics have delusions of control, grandeur and persecution, and are consistently suspicious of all around them. Disorganised schizophrenics manifest bizarre thoughts and language with sudden inappropriate emotional outbursts. Some mention *simple* or *undifferentiated* schizophrenia. Others have distinguished between *acute* (sudden onset and severe) versus *chronic* (prolonged and gradual). Another distinction is between Type I (mostly positive symptoms) and Type II (mostly negative symptoms).

There is still no complete agreement about the subtypes or the precise 'deficits' in functioning, although these usually come under four headings: cognitive or thinking; perceptual or seeing; motor or moving; and emotional or feeling. Researchers are also still continuing to seek out the source or cause of areas of 'vulnerability' that mean some people develop schizophrenia. So there are increasingly sophisticated genetic studies as well as those looking particularly at complications of pregnancy and traumatic childhood experiences, brain functioning and family and cultural influences.

It has been recognized that researchers and medical and laypeople tend to believe in or follow different approaches that describe the causes of and cures for schizophrenia. Essentially these are divided into biological models, stressing genetic, biochemical or brain structure causes, and the sociopsychological models, which focus on problems of communication, distress and punishment in early life. Certainly, development in behaviour genetics and brain science has led to more interest in the biological approach to cause and cure. The popularity of different approaches waxes and wanes, but they are still identifiable in how various groups of people approach schizophrenia.

According to DSM-IV-TR, in order to be diagnosed with schizophrenia, three diagnostic criteria must be achieved:

1. *Characteristic symptoms*: two or more of the following must be present for much of the time during a one-month period (or less, if symptoms relapse with treatment):
   - Delusions.
   - Hallucinations.
   - Disorganized speech, which is a manifestation of formal thought disorder.
   - Grossly disorganized behaviour (dressing inappropriately, crying frequently) or catatonic behaviour.
   - Negative symptoms: blunted emotions (lack or decline in emotional response), alogia (lack or decline in speech) or avolition (lack or decline in motivation).

   If the delusions are bizarre or the hallucinations consist of hearing one voice of a running commentary of the person's actions, or of hearing two or more voices conversing with each other, only that symptom is required for diagnosis.

2. *Social or occupational dysfunction*: for a significant amount of time since the onset of the disturbance, one or more major areas of functioning such as work, interpersonal relations or self-care are markedly below the level achieved prior to the onset. In short, the person seems unable to cope.
3. *Significant duration*: continuous signs of the disturbance persist for at least six months, which must include at least one month of symptoms (or less, if symptoms relapsed with treatment). Symptoms lasting less than a month may be diagnosed as brief psychotic disorder.

2.4.1.1 *Consequences of schizophrenia in the workplace*

Regardless of the definition or model one chooses to favour, one thing is certain: we tend to shy away from engaging with individuals who suffer from schizophrenia. The reality, however, is that many individuals manage to function in society and around 10–27 per cent of schizophrenics are in employment. Although attempting to find new work after a diagnosis of schizophrenia can be particularly difficult, it has become easier with the increased awareness of and reduced stigma associated with the condition in recent years.

Schizophrenia is usually not diagnosed until a person has their first psychotic episode and this is usually quite severe in terms of symptoms and will, more often than not, require hospitalization. For men, onset will typically occur at some point in late adolescence or in their early twenties, around about the time when they are finishing school, starting university or entering the workplace. For women, the onset of the illness is usually a little later and will occur during their mid-twenties to early thirties. They are therefore more likely to have completed their education and will be established in the workplace. This presents a different set of challenges as returning to work after diagnosis can be very difficult.

For both men and women, the effectiveness of initial and ongoing treatment will play a major part in the success of returning to work or education. The environment will also have an impact in terms of how stressful it is and how likely it is to increase the chances of relapse. For someone with schizophrenia, there are numerous pros and cons to working: the ability to hold down a job is often critical to their ability to function socially, while work provides important connections to other people, improves self-esteem and provides a focus outside of the illness. In some instances, however, the work environment can be too stressful and the risk of a relapse outweighs any potential benefits. The situation therefore must be carefully monitored and managers and colleagues should be alert to certain red flag behaviours and signs that an individual's condition could be worsening.

It seems that whether a schizophrenic can work or not depends upon the severity of the illness and the nature of the symptoms. Studies such as that by Rosenheck *et al*. (2006) have found that symptoms, such as hallucinations and delusions, are less of a barrier to employment, partly due to them being controllable to some degree and partly because they do not cause long-term issues. On the other hand, negative symptoms and cognitive deficits such as the absence or reduction of mental processes, e.g., executive functioning (making plans, delegating, etc.), enjoying pleasurable activities and sociability, are all far more detrimental in the long term. Cognitive deficits are problems with planning and organizing, remembering things and paying attention.

Two interesting case studies can help to highlight how schizophrenics can indeed thrive regardless of the barriers. What hopefully becomes evident in both instances is that it is the willpower to reject the prognosis and work hard that makes them successful.

The first case study relates to Frank Baron. He lives with schizophrenia and although he has not returned to regular employment since his diagnosis, he is still very much active: 'In my case, medications stop the delusions, but they do not manage the cognitive deficits.' He says that the cognitive issues prevent him from working: 'Before, I was a civil engineer, but now I don't have the concentration.' He now serves on the Institutional Review Board for the Los Angeles County Mental Health Commission and undertakes public speaking on mental illness issues.

The second case study is Elyn R. Saks. Thirty years ago, she was given a diagnosis of schizophrenia. Her prognosis was 'grave', but she made a decision to write the narrative of her life. Today she is a chaired professor at the University of Southern California Gould School of Law, has an adjunct appointment in the Department of Psychiatry at the medical school of the University of California, San Diego, and is on the faculty of the New Center for Psychoanalysis. The MacArthur Foundation also gave her a genius grant. She comments: 'Although I fought my diagnosis for many years, I came to accept that I have schizophrenia and will be in treatment the rest of my life. Indeed, excellent psychoanalytic treatment and medication have been critical to my success. What I refused to accept was my prognosis.'

Schizophrenia does not necessarily predispose people to a specific type of work. The right job for a person with schizophrenia depends upon the severity of the illness and on that person's skills and interests. A few people with schizophrenia have been very successful professionally: Fred Frese earned his doctorate in psychology after a diagnosis of schizophrenia and, as stated above, Elyn R. Saks earned a law degree after her diagnosis and is a professor of law at the University of Southern California. Even though some people are the exception, the majority of sufferers end up with work in entry-level and part-time positions. This is for a number of reasons, primarily relating to the barriers mentioned above. Moreover, statistics have shown that only 30 per cent of working people with psychiatric disorders such as schizophrenia have been promoted from entry-level positions. Discriminatory? Yes, but a vicious cycle it unfortunately is.

With the statistics clearly showing a bias against the "sufferers", entry-level positions are problematic for a variety for reasons. Health insurance and other benefits are an important issue for people with schizophrenia to consider when choosing a job and even when deciding how many hours to work. While increasing one's income seems appealing, the reality for people with schizophrenia is somewhat more complicated. The entry-level positions that people with schizophrenia most often obtain rarely include benefits. This is of course not such an issue in countries like the UK, where there is a universally available funded healthcare system. That being said, there are other challenges to consider in relation to even getting a job. For instance, it can be difficult to explain gaps in a CV to a potential employer without revealing one's mental illness status, and discrimination against people with mental illness still exists. On an individual level, however, employment programmes do exist to help people with psychiatric disabilities prepare for, find and maintain competitive employment.

Early signs of schizophrenia will often manifest themselves as extremely abnormal behaviours, for example, hallucinations (hearing voices or feeling or seeing things that don't exist). Sufferers may have delusional, paranoid thoughts and fear that others are out to get them. Disorganized thoughts may lead to speech patterns that do not make sense to others. However, these typical behaviours are often preceded by less obvious warning signs and some of these symptoms, such as lack of enjoyment in everyday life, can mimic depression. Signs to watch out for in the workplace include:

- deteriorating work performance;
- change in personality;

- change in personal hygiene and appearance;
- trouble concentrating for prolonged periods of time;
- withdrawal from social activities;
- appearing emotionally distant or detached;
- decreased motivation and interest in work.

Managers and co-workers should be alert to these signs, and later in this book we will explore some of the practical things that can be done to help the individual to manage their illness effectively at work.

2.4.2 Stress

The word 'stress' is derived from the Latin word *stringere*, which means 'to draw tight'. It is such an overused and elusive term that many have agreed that it should be completely abandoned. Many definitions exist: some believe stress can and should be *subjectively* defined (i.e., what I say about how I feel), while others feel that an *objective* definition (perhaps physical measures of saliva, blood or heartbeat) is required. Some researchers believe that a *global* definition is appropriate (there is one general thing called stress), while others emphasize that stress is *multi-dimensional* (i.e., it is made up of very different features) Moreover, should it be defined by the outside stimulus factors that *cause* it or rather by how *people respond* to it? In other words, if somebody does not experience something as stressful, can we really call it a stressor?

Lots of questions remain in relation to stress and are often discussed in the popular press. Many 'scare' statistics are quoted about how much stress causes mental and physical illness, resulting in absenteeism and thus cost to the economy of the country as a whole. There are debates about which jobs are most or least stressful and what one could do about them. Is work stress primarily a function of the person or the job? In other words, does it arise because some are (neurotically) vulnerable to stress, whereas others are hardy and resistant? These days, most people speak as if stress is imposed on them by work conditions, yet in earlier times, people spoke about 'having nerves', implying nervous dispositions. Other questions include the following. Is there the possibility that moderate amounts of stress may be good for one? Should people be taught coping skills to overcome inevitable work stress? And because there is a stress industry committed to finding work stress, is it frequently misdiagnosed?

2.4.2.1 Demands and control

There are various models or theories that try to describe and understand stress. The simplest perhaps is the demand-control theory, which looks at the various psychological and physical demands put on the person to behave in a particular way and the control or decision latitude that they have. High-demand, low-control situations are most likely to cause stress. Another way of describing this is challenge and support.

In most management jobs, leaders are both supported and challenged. They are supported by peers, subordinates and superiors, who also challenge them to work harder and 'smarter'. Thus, it is possible to think of the average manager in terms of support and challenge as follows:

Much support, little challenge: managers in this role are in the fortunate position of good technical and social support, but the fact they are underchallenged probably means that they underperform. They may actually be stressed by boredom and monotony.

Much support, much challenge: this combination tends to get the most out of managers as they are challenged by superiors, subordinates, shareholders and customers to 'work smarter', but are given the appropriate support to succeed.

Little support, much challenge: this unfortunate but very common situation is a major cause of stress for any manager because they are challenged to work consistently hard, but are only offered minimal emotional, informational (feedback) and physical (equipment) support.

Little support, little challenge: managers in some bureaucracies lead a quiet and unstressed life because they are neither challenged nor supported, which usually means neither they nor their organization benefits. They belong to the 'psychologically quit but physically stay' category of employee.

Most of the models and theories about stress consider how three factors lead to stress. *First*, there are essentially things about the *make-up of the individual*, particularly their personality, ability and background. *Second*, there are features about the *environment* (job, family, organization), usually but not exclusively considered in terms of the work environment. *Third*, there is how the individual and the environment perceive, define and, more importantly, try to *cope* with stress, strains and pressures. The argument is that there are individual, environment and coping factors that, considered together, determine whether, when and why individuals and group experience stress.

2.4.2.2 *Optimism: a buffer against stress*

One personal factor that seems to play an important role in determining resistance to stress is the familiar dimension of optimism/pessimism. Optimists are hopeful in their outlook on life, interpret a wide range of situations in a positive light and tend to expect favourable outcomes and results. Pessimists, by contrast, interpret many situations negatively and expect unfavourable outcomes and results. Optimists are much more stress-resistant than pessimists.

Optimists and pessimists adopt sharply contrasting tactics for coping with stress. Optimists concentrate on problem-focused coping – making and enacting specific plans for dealing with sources of stress. In addition, they seek social support – the advice and help of friends and others – and refrain from engaging in other activities until current problems are solved and stress is reduced. Pessimists tend to adopt rather different strategies, such as giving up in their efforts to reach goals with which stress is interfering, and denying that the stressful events have even occurred. Furthermore, they have different attributional styles: the optimist attributes success internally and failure externally, and vice versa. Indeed, that is how optimism and pessimism are both measured and maintained.

2.4.2.3 Hardiness: viewing stress as a challenge

Another individual difference factor that seems to distinguish stress-resistant people from those who are more susceptible to its harmful effects is hardiness or resilience. This term refers to a cluster of characteristics rather than just one. Hardy people appear to differ from others in three respects. They show higher *level of commitment* (deeper involvement in their jobs and other life activities), *control* (the belief that they can, in fact, influence important events in their lives and the outcomes they experience) and *challenge* (they perceive change as a challenge and an opportunity to grow rather than as a threat to their security).

Together, these characteristics tend to arm hardy persons with high levels of resistance to stress. People classified as high in hardiness report better health than those with low hardiness, even when they encounter major stressful life changes.

2.4.2.4 Consequences of stress in organizations

One can often recognise stress by its consequences in the workplace. The list is long, but can usually be categorized under three headings:

- *Physiological symptoms*: a noticeable decline in physical appearance, chronic fatigue and tiredness, frequent infections, health complaints such as headaches, backache, stomach and skin problems, and change in weight or eating habits.

- *Emotional symptoms*: boredom or apathy, lack of affect and hopelessness, cynicism and resentfulness, depressed appearance (sad expressions, slumped posture), and expressions of anxiety, frustration and tearfulness.
- *Behavioural symptoms*: absenteeism, accidents, increase in alcohol or caffeine consumption, increased smoking; obsessive exercising, being irrational or quick to fly off the handle and reduced productivity (inability to concentrate or complete a task).

Individuals often try to cope with their stress through lifestyle changes, such as attempting relaxation or mediation techniques or by signing up for therapy. There are also organizational symptoms of stress, such as high levels of absenteeism and staff turnover. Some organizations attempt to reduce a worker's stress by job redesign, organizational restructuring and introducing stress management programmes.

2.4.2.5 Burnout

Burnout is the outcome of physical, psychological and emotional exhaustion. Boredom, the opposite of a heavy workload, may cause it. At work, poor communication between supervisors, peers, subordinates and clients is a common cause of this. Too much responsibility with too little support is also found to contribute to it. Having to acquire new and specialized skills too frequently to do quite different and important but meaningless tasks is yet another cause.

Classic causes and consequences of burnout are the following well-established facets of alienation: first, *meaninglessness* – the idea that there seems to be no purpose, inherent worth or meaning in day-to-day work; second, *estrangement* from the goals of the organization – a person assigning low value to those things the organization values highly; third, *powerlessness* – the expectancy that, whatever one does, it will not relate to success or happiness.

These casuses and consequences arise for a number of reasons. Victims of burnout complain about physical exhaustion. They have low energy levels and feel tired much of the time. They report many symptoms of physical strain, such as frequent headaches, nausea, poor sleep and changes in eating habits. Furthermore, they experience emotional exhaustion. Depression and feelings of helplessness and of being trapped in one's job are all part of the syndrome. People suffering from burnout also often demonstrate a pattern of mental or attitudinal exhaustion, often known as depersonalization. They become cynical about others, tend to treat them as objects rather than as people and hold extremely negative attitudes towards their organization. In addition, they tend to derogate themselves, their jobs, their managers and even life in general. Finally, they often report feelings of low personal accomplishment. They conclude that they have not been able to accomplish much in the past and assume that they probably will not succeed in the future. Burnout is a syndrome of emotional, physical and mental exhaustion, coupled with feelings of low self-esteem or low self-efficacy, resulting from prolonged exposure to intense stress. Not much fun really.

2.4.3 Depression

Depression is a state of low mood and aversion to activity that can affect a person's thoughts, behaviour, feelings and sense of well-being (Salmans, 1997). As with our everyday feelings of low mood, there will sometimes be an obvious reason for becoming depressed and sometimes no reason. It can be a disappointment, a frustration, or the fact that the person has lost something – or someone – important to them. There is often more than one reason and these will be different for different people. For instance, it is normal to feel depressed after a distressing event, such as a divorce or losing a job. The person involved may well spend a lot of time over the next few weeks or months thinking and talking about it. After a while, they will come to terms with what has happened, but they may get stuck in a depressed mood, which doesn't seem to lift. Other factors include social loneliness, genetics, gender and even personality. While some people see it as a form of weakness or 'giving in', once a depressive spiral begins, it is considered far more akin to an illness.

There is a set of symptoms that are associated with depression and help to clarify the diagnosis. These are essentially persistent sadness, gloominess or low mood. This may be accompanied by frequent crying and weeping. Next there is marked loss of interest or pleasure in activities that were previously enjoyed. Other common symptoms include the following:

- Disturbed sleep compared to usual pattern: difficulty in getting to sleep, waking early and being unable to get back to sleep or sleeping too much.
- Change in appetite: poor appetite and weight loss or comfort eating and weight gain.
- Fatigue (tiredness) or loss of energy and libido.
- Agitation and anxiety or slowing of movements as well as speech.
- Poor concentration or indecisiveness, making simple tasks seem difficult and requiring considerable effort.
- Feelings of worthlessness and pointlessness, as well as excessive or inappropriate guilt about past actions.
- Recurrent thoughts of death of oneself or that of others.

Depression is not a single experience, but has three typical features (Middleton *et al.*, 2005): *first*, there is a change in mood so that the person experiences continuous sadness, irritability and loss of pleasure; *second*, there is a high level of negative thinking, often of a severely self-critical nature; *third*, activity levels are reduced so that normal routine activities may not be carried out. What characterizes depression as different from everyday experience is the persistence of these changes over days and weeks.

Various people have argued there are (subtly) different types of depression. The list is certainly not agreed upon or exhaustive:

1. *Major depressive disorder*: one of the key criteria for diagnosing a major depressive disorder is the experience of acute and chronic depressive episodes. Major depressive disorder can also be broken down into a few subtypes: *atypical depression* (which revolves around feelings of social rejection and is often accompanied excessive tiredness); *postnatal depression* (a type of major depression experienced by some after childbirth); *catatonic depression* (an extreme type of depression in which the sufferer cannot speak and often has very limited control over his or her body movements); *seasonal affective disorder* (which includes essentially the same symptoms as major depressive disorder, except it only affects the sufferer during certain seasons, usually autumn and winter); and *melancholic depression* (characterized by feelings of grief or guilt, the loss of ability to feel enjoyment or pleasure, and often accompanied by weight loss).
2. *Manic depression (bipolar disorder)*: bipolar disorder is an affective disorder involving a cyclical pattern of extreme moods known as 'episodes'. Episodes can be classed as 'depressive', 'manic' or 'mixed', and are interspersed by periods of 'euthymia' (normal mood). Depressive episodes are characterized by a depressed mood, abnormal sleeping and eating patterns (e.g., insomnia or loss of appetite), psychomotor retardation and recurrent thoughts of death. Conversely, mania is characterized by a euphoric mood, racing thoughts, a reduced need for sleep, increased productivity and reckless behaviour (e.g., impulsive spending and sexual indiscretions). Mixed episodes contain mood, motor and cognitive features from both mania and depression. Severe episodes may also contain delusions and hallucinations. 'Psychosocial' theories of aetiology include stressful life events and dysfunctional attempts to avoid depression. A dysregulation of self-esteem has been proposed and childhood trauma and abuse have also been linked with bipolar disorder. Generally, however, it is believed that bipolar disorder is caused by a complex interaction of genetic, biological and psychosocial factors, which is known as the 'diathesis-stress' model.

3. *Dysthymic depression*: dysthymia is a serious state of chronic depression which persists for at least two years but it is less acute and severe than major depressive disorder. People may experience symptoms for many years before it is diagnosed (if it is diagnosed at all) and may believe that depression is a part of their character. It often co-occurs with other mental problems. 'Double depression' is the occurrence of episodes of major depression in addition to dysthymia and cyclothymia.
4. *Situational depression*: this is only experienced in particular situations, such as perhaps going to weddings or funerals, and the sufferer experiences no symptoms in most other settings.
5. *Psychotic depression*: this is an extreme form of depression in which the low mood states are often accompanied by delusions or even complete hallucinations.
6. *Endogenous depression*: this is the result of a person's make-up or personality, such as being an unstable introvert or extravert, choleric or melancholic. This is contrasted with exogenous depression, which is caused by external factors like being sexually abused or involved in a terrible accident.

Worldwide, depression is the most commonly reported cause of living with a long-term disability (Ustün *et al.*, 2004). It can affect many aspects of life, including work. In fact, the impact of depression on job performance has been estimated to be greater than that of chronic conditions such as arthritis, hypertension, back problems and diabetes.

2.4.3.1 *Consequences of depression in the workplace*

Although the symptoms and conditions associated with depression may make it difficult to find and keep a job, many people who have had a recent depressive episode are holding down positions in the workplace. In 2002, the majority (71 per cent) of 25–64 year olds who had had a major depressive episode in the previous 12 months were employed and thus were potentially dealing with the interference of depressive symptoms on their ability to do their jobs.

Depression has been associated with both absenteeism and decreased productivity (presenteeism). Estimates for the USA have placed the cost of depression at $83.1 billion a year (2000 figure) (Greenberg *et al.*, 2003).

Literary and academic reviews have found greater self-reported work impairment among depressed workers, but on the other hand, treatment studies have found reduced work impairment with successful treatment, therefore highlighting that treatment is essential. Observational data has also suggested that productivity gains following effective depression treatment could far exceed direct treatment costs (Simon *et al.*, 2001).

It can be difficult to know the best way to handle depression in the workplace. Although we know that employers should be kind, caring and only have our best interests at heart, it is perhaps fair to say that this is not always the case. However, it is very important that both the employee's and the employer's expectations are realistic and that there is an agreed understanding of the practicalities surrounding depression in the workplace. It is worth noting that at least one in ten of us will suffer from depression at some point in our working lives, so this is an issue that should be considered by all managers and organizations.

That being said, while depression is not surrounded by the 'fear of the unknown' to the same degree as schizophrenia, there are many reasons to be cautious about how we deal with depression in the workplace because there is no doubt that it is not a positive attribute to add to your personnel files. If you work for a large company or have a particularly effective HR department, there may be a system in place to support you through your depression, but unless people are aware of these services, they may not choose to speak to their employers about it.

For most of us, work provides structure to our day, the opportunity to socialize, a sense of accomplishment and a source of happiness. In other words, work can reduce the likelihood of becoming depressed. There are many other things one can do to achieve satisfaction in work. These can be discussed with sufferers or assessed via intermittent 'well-being' surveys. Likewise, encouraging a culture of openness and well-being can help alleviate any apprehension from the sufferer with regard to talking about their problems. The longer the issue goes on, the more detrimental the effects to the organization will be.

Depressive illnesses can affect an employee's productivity, judgement, ability to work with others and overall job performance. The inability to concentrate fully or make decisions may lead to costly mistakes or accidents. Changes in performance and on-the-job behaviours that may suggest an employee is suffering from a depressive illness include:

- decreased or inconsistent productivity;
- absenteeism, tardiness, frequent absence from work station;
- increased errors, diminished work quality;
- procrastination, missed deadlines;

- withdrawal from co-workers;
- overly sensitive and/or emotional reactions;
- decreased interest in work;
- slower thought processes;
- difficulties in terms of learning and remembering;
- slow movement and actions;
- frequent comments about being tired all the time.

You will know whether or not to help someone if you notice that their depressed mood continues unabated for weeks, they don't appear to enjoy their usual interests or they have a sense of gloom about them.

2.4.4 Anxiety disorders

Anxiety disorders are amongst the most common mental disorders, with high prevalence rates ranging from 13.6 per cent to 28.8 per cent in the West (Michael, Zetsche and Margraf, 2007). Michael, Zetsche and Magraf (2007) provided an overview of results from 14 mental health surveys, including that of Kessler *et al.* (2005), who reported anxiety disorders as the most prevalent class of disorders at 18.1 per cent. These studies also report that specific phobias and social phobia (or Social Anxiety Disorder) are the most common of anxiety disorders. Similarly, Merikangas *et al.* (2010) reported that specific phobias, social phobias and separation anxiety are the most common disorders in US adolescents, and their research reports an even higher prevalence rate of 39.1 per cent for anxiety disorders overall. Other than those mentioned anxiety disorders also referenced in the DSM-IV-TR (American Psychiatric Association, 2000) include generalized anxiety disorder (GAD), panic disorder with and without agoraphobia, OCD and PTSD.

According to DSM-V, there are 12 different anxiety disorders: acute stress disorder; social phobia; GAD; panic attacks; specific phobias; OCD; PTSD; anxiety disorder due to general medical conditions; agoraphobia; agoraphobia without history of panic disorder; panic disorder without agoraphobia and panic disorder with agoraphobia; and anxiety disorder not otherwise specified. These can be further grouped under seven different headings:

1. *Panic disorder with or without agoraphobia*: the main characteristic of panic disorder is the occurrence of a panic attack linked with the fear of another attack. Agoraphobia is not, within a clinical setting, categorized as a disorder, but is usually associated in some way with panic disorder.
2. *Phobias*: a phobia is described as an intense and irrational fear of a specific object or situation that is so intense that it can cause the individual to be

compelled to go to great lengths to avoid it. Phobias can relate to harmful things or situations that present a risk, but they can also relate to harmless situations, objects or sometimes animals. Social phobia can include a fear of being judged, scrutinized or humiliated in some way.

3. *OCD*: this condition is characterized by unwanted, intrusive, persistent or repetitive behaviours. These will reflect a person's attempts to control them and the anxiety caused by them. OCD effects around two to three per cent of the population, making it far more common than it was previously considered to be.
4. *Stress disorders*: this includes PTSD and acute stress disorders. These are categorized as being a symptomatic response to a traumatic experience that the individual has experienced.
5. *GAD*: this is the most commonly diagnosed anxiety disorder and usually affects young adults.
6. *Anxiety disorders due to a known physical cause*: this includes medical conditions and symptoms caused by drug misuse.
7. *Anxiety disorder not otherwise specified*: this is not a separate type of disorder, but is included in order to cover symptoms that do not meet the criteria for any of the other anxiety disorders.

The anxiety disorder has to be severe enough to be classed as interfering with an individual's life. This includes work commitments, social activities, educational commitments and any other activities they take part in.

2.4.4.1 GAD

GAD is an anxiety disorder that is characterized by excessive, uncontrollable, unexplained and often irrational worry about everyday things in a manner that is disproportionate to the actual source of worry. For diagnosis of this disorder, symptoms must last at least six months (Torpy, Burke and Golub, 2011). This excessive worry often interferes with daily functioning, as individuals suffering GAD typically anticipate disaster and are overly concerned about everyday matters such as health issues, money, death, family problems, friendship problems, interpersonal relationship problems or work difficulties (National Institute of Mental Health, n.d. a).

Individuals often exhibit a variety of physical symptoms, ranging from fatigue to numbness in the hands and feet. For a formal diagnosis of GAD to be introduced, these symptoms must be consistent and ongoing, persisting for at least six months. In any given year, approximately 6.8 million American adults and two per cent of European adults experience GAD (National Institute of

Mental Health, n.d. b), with GAD subtypes (social phobia and agoraphobia) being the most common cause of disability in the workplace in the USA (Ballenger *et al.*, 2001).

2.4.4.2 *Social phobia*

Social anxiety disorder is also commonly known as social phobia and is the most common anxiety disorder (Stein and Stein, 2008). It is one of the most common psychiatric disorders, with a lifetime prevalence of 12 per cent (Schneier, 2006). It is characterized by intense fear in social situations, causing considerable distress and impaired ability to function in at least some parts of the sufferer's daily life. These fears can be triggered by perceived or actual glances, gazes or even more intensely, staring from others. While the fear of social interaction may be recognized by the person as excessive or unreasonable, overcoming it can be quite difficult. Some people suffering from social anxiety disorder fear a wide range of social situations, while others may only show anxiety in performance situations, which understandably has direct implications in the workplace. The workplace, a socially buzzing environment, can often become a 'nightmare' for people suffering from social phobia. There is an early-age onset in most cases, with 80 per cent having developed it by the age of 20, making this disorder particularly significant in a sufferer's whole work history. This early age of onset also increases the susceptibility of the sufferer to depressive illnesses, drug abuse and other psychological conflicts (Stein and Stein, 2008) which have been shown to lead to even more problems.

There are various signs that teenagers and adults may exhibit which point to them being a sufferer of this condition. These include *evident dread towards everyday activities*, such as meeting new colleagues, talking in social situations or giving presentations, telephone conversations, talking to leaders/managers, and working and participating in social activities. Sufferers tend to have low self-esteem and feel insecure about their relationships, fear being criticized, avoid eye-to-eye contact and can misuse drugs or alcohol to try to reduce their anxiety.

It may be the case that sufferers may fear only one particular situation, such as speaking on the phone, but what will be noticeable is the fear and avoidance of such situations, something that co-workers and managers can look out for. In the worst-case scenario, the fear and anxiety in relation to a social situation can build up into a panic attack, a period of usually just a few minutes when the person feels an overwhelming sense of fear, apprehension and anxiety.

2.4.4.3 Agoraphobia

Agoraphobia and social phobia are two very closely related phobias. The differences between the two, however, are worthy of consideration. Agoraphobia can be termed as a fear of being in a crowded place or open space, while social phobia can be termed as a fear of facing groups of people – a fear that is characterized by excessive shyness in social situations. One of the main differences between the two phobias is in the nature of the fear that sufferers experience. Individuals suffering from social phobia are afraid of settings involving crowds or groups of people. Social phobia involves the fear of interacting in a social setting. People suffering from social phobia are very much shy to face society and they are content with their own company.

On the other hand, agoraphobia is the fear of public or open spaces, or being in the company or absence of other people. People with agoraphobia conditions try to avoid crowds or situations where they fear having a panic attack and getting embarrassed. Unlike people with social phobia, people with agoraphobia are afraid of walking alone in a secluded place and this is because of the fear of not being able to get any help if a panic situation arises. A long hallway, a crowded building and an exposed place are very disturbing to people with agoraphobia issues. These people feel like they are in unfamiliar territory. Once they return to familiar territory, their symptoms will usually subside.

Symptoms of agoraphobia typically include the following: a rise in anxiety when away from places of perceived safety; breathlessness, dizziness, sweating, nausea and increased heart rate – all of which are common symptoms of anxiety; increased anxiety in anticipation of having to leave a safe environment; low self-esteem and confidence; reluctance to leave familiar surroundings and a fear of being embarrassed or humiliated.

Agoraphobia can often be very debilitating and difficult to overcome. It can greatly affect a person's normal way of living as it may restrict them from going to public places or being able to go to their workplace. In extreme cases, a person with agoraphobia can even become a prisoner in their own home as they may feel it is the only safe haven for them. Treatment for agoraphobia is often long term and requires a sensitive approach by the therapist. Cognitive behavioural therapy (CBT) is frequently used and helps by teaching a person with agoraphobia how to deal with difficult situations or public events by using the following:

1. *Cognitive therapy*: helping to change a person's thinking patterns and attitudes towards a situation.

2. *Behavioural therapy*: helping to change a person's fear response by strategically and systematically supporting them to safely face the feared situation and in turn allow them to learn new coping strategies to deal with it.

In addition to CBT, other approaches to treating agoraphobia include exposure therapy and the use of pharmaceuticals such as DCS (D-cyclocserine). While somewhat different from social phobia, the two go largely hand in hand, both combining to form the previous mentioned workplace phobia. Treatment options and considerations are the same in both cases and symptoms of both disorders can occur together.

2.4.4.4 Consequences of agoraphobia and social phobia in the workplace

In terms of the workplace directly, social phobia can manifest itself either as a more general condition but also more specifically as a workplace phobia where it is the fear associated with interacting with people in a work setting that causes the anxiety. Those with overall social phobia will experience the same 'symptoms' as with workplace phobia, while some workplace-phobics find the work environment particularly difficult. Workplace phobia can be defined as 'actual or imagined confrontations with the workplace or certain stimuli at the workplace (e.g. persons, objects, situations, and events) that cause a prominent anxiety reaction in a person' (Kessler *et al.*, 1998). This psychological fear is coupled with more visible signs of physiological arousal, such as accelerated heartbeat, sweating, trembling, hot flushes and chest pains, which can lead to negative behaviour towards the person in charge.

When avoiding or leaving the feared workplace, arousal and anxiety decrease. This functions as a classical negative reinforcement, with the avoidance reaction essentially being rewarding as it reduces anxiety and relieves symptoms. Over a period, avoidance behaviour is being reinforced again and again as the individual takes more 'sick leave'.

The workplace is especially challenging and has very significant impacts for social phobics for a variety of reasons. For instance, the workplace is not a simple stimulus like a train or a spider. In contrast, it is a very complex stimulus containing both situational as well as interactional elements. Some of the main workplace stressors as reported by sufferers include deadlines (55 per cent), interpersonal relationships (53 per cent), staff management (50 per cent) and dealing with issues/problems that arise (49 per cent) (ADAA, 2006).

Moreover, one cannot simply choose when to arrive at work; one has to be there on time, thus forcing the sufferer to avoid it to an even greater degree. Avoiding the workplace regularly means negative consequences for the development of the concerned person (long-term sick leave, loss of employment, endangerment of work ability and early retirement). This, coupled with the early onset of the disorder, often results in a fragmented CV with multiple entries and a multitude of entry-level jobs.

The survey also indicated that employees said that stress and anxiety most often impacts their workplace performance (56 per cent), their relationships with co-workers and peers (51 per cent), their quality of work (50 per cent) and their relationships with superiors (43 per cent). Essentially, these are all traits that make a good employee, so not being able to fulfil the majority of these requirements limits an employee's work options.

For agoraphobics, the first hurdle that they must often overcome is the very act of physically getting to work in the first place. Agoraphobia can make commuting to work very difficult and can also be a barrier to any work-related travel or maintaining employment in a large open area or a crowded work environment. The fear, worry and avoidance associated with agoraphobia can at times make it difficult to find and maintain employment. All too often, the condition results in unemployment or underemployment and serious financial pressures. This can in turn lead to increased stress, panic and the symptoms of agoraphobia being exacerbated.

2.4.5 PTSD

PTSD affects many individuals around the world and it can be a debilitating illness that inhibits the individual's life. It can develop after a traumatic event has occurred and thus is most commonly found in war veterans and roles revolving around the emergency services. One of the drawbacks that some people face in their diagnosis is the lack of disclosure of certain events. For instance, childhood sexual abuse is often repressed and thus PTSD can develop without a seemingly causal root.

The components of PTSD can be broken down into three main areas: *intrusive, arousal* and *avoidance* symptoms. These exist in a harmonious triad, having a symbiotic relationship with each other in which all three feed off and interact with each other. This forms a cyclical cycle which sustains the existence of PTSD. However, it must be noted that not every trauma survivor experiences all three symptoms – some may experience one symptom more than another and others may experience a different cycle.

Intrusive symptoms are things that literally 'intrude' into a survivor's life. They can be thoughts, feelings or body memories, and these differentiate PTSD from anxiety disorders. The individual experiencing these may feel as if the trauma is happening all over again. They may also experience similar feelings or reactions as they did when the trauma originally occurred. Examples of intrusive symptoms include flashbacks, nightmares, body memories and frightening thoughts.

Arousal symptoms literally 'arouse' the body to get into a heightened state of alert. When a survivor is having intrusive thoughts or feelings that the event is happening again, it is natural for the body to respond with anxiety. Examples of arousal symptoms are: feeling tense, hyper-vigilance, excessive anxiety or worry, anger outbursts, being startled easily/jumpiness and over-reacting to others' emotions and outbursts.

In contrast, *avoidance symptoms* are when the sufferer has unwanted thoughts and feelings intruding into their life. Their body is in a heightened state of arousal to guard themselves against harm with the natural tendency to want to escape. This phenomenon is part of what brings on avoidance symptoms. Avoidance symptoms are just that – they are symptoms that allow the individual to avoid their feelings and what they are experiencing at that point in time. Examples of avoidance symptoms are avoiding places and people associated with the trauma, loss of memory, loss of interest in once-important activities, difficulty falling asleep, feeling distant and self-harming.

One of the many areas in which PTSD has an effect is the workplace. There are many individuals with PTSD who are able to work and are functioning at a level where they are able to hold a job – some successfully and some just barely. The level of success the individual has at their place of employment depends on many factors, including the level of impairment and support inside and outside the work environment. PTSD can manifest itself in various ways in the workplace following the symptoms listed above. Some examples of problems associated with the workplace for those who have PTSD are as follows: memory problems; lack of concentration; difficulty retaining information; feelings of fear or anxiety; physical problems; poor interactions with co-workers; unreasonable reactions to situations that trigger memories; absenteeism; interruptions if the employee is still in an abusive relationship (harassing phone calls, etc.); and trouble staying awake and panic attacks.

In many instances, these behaviours will be relatively noticeable and thus a solution will have to be found. That being said, accommodating an employee with PTSD can be complex and is a unique process for each individual – what may be helpful for one individual may not be helpful for the next. First, though, it is important for the employer to be educated about PTSD and its symptoms. Knowledge can lead to understanding reactions which may seem out of the ordinary and can also provide a framework for adapting the work environment to suit the needs of the individual with PTSD.

Some things that a manager can do to assist the employee with PTSD are as follows:

1. Listening to the employee's limitations relating to their job performance. For instance, if a woman has a history of sexual assault that occurred during the night and fears walking alone, she may request to have someone walk her to her car at night or may even request not to work after dark.
2. Identifying which specific tasks may be challenging. At times, PTSD symptoms may manifest themselves in cognitive challenges. An employee may need more time to finish a task or require an office which has fewer distractions.
3. Identifying specifically how assistance can be provided. The best way to find out how to assist someone is to ask them. This may be something that develops over time as the employee may not be aware of limitations until they run into them. An open dialogue about how the employer can assist would be helpful from the beginning. Some survivors of abuse will feel embarrassed to admit they need help, so it is important to keep asking. It may be necessary to balance this and ensure that the employer makes themself available versus being overly persistent and aggressive.
4. Evaluating the effectiveness of the environment and the employee. If there are times when the employee is having a hard time or producing output that is not up to standard, speak directly to that employee about how they can be assisted. Providing gentle and immediate feedback will allow the employee to determine what is needed to get the task back up to the necessary standard. This is not to say that all substandard work is due to PTSD symptoms, but it is helpful to know the origins of the problem.
5. Providing training for co-workers and supervisors. By providing training on PTSD and related symptoms, the other staff members can also be educated on how to help the individual. Sensitivity training may be needed on topics relating to PTSD.

If you are a PTSD sufferer yourself, there are various things you can also do to help reduce the impact that this condition may have on you at work.

Likewise, as a co-worker you can help the person suffering from PTSD through their symptoms and can aid the process a great deal. Work is after all a 'team' effort:

1. Deal with your concentration problems. A common complaint of PTSD survivors is difficulty concentrating because of the heightened state of arousal, stress levels or even fatigue. Reducing distractions such as noise and having a clean workspace will enhance the ability to concentrate. Making lists and creating small, goal-oriented tasks will help create a sense of accomplishment. Also, it may be helpful to ask to work at a time when concentration is at its peak (i.e., earlier in the morning before everyone gets there).
2. Dealing with fallible memory. There are often blocks to memory when there is so much happening in the mind of someone with PTSD. Common tricks to tackle this include making lists, decreasing distractions and increasing the ability to concentrate on tasks which will assist with the ability to remember things. Other ideas include setting reminders in a phone or on a computer, using a calendar, taking notes during a meeting or asking for written instructions to given tasks.
3. Flashbacks can be some of the most stressful symptoms experienced by sufferers at work. At a time when the sufferer is supposed to be managing the environment, the environment starts to try and manage the sufferer survivor. As the symptoms relate to work, reaching out to the outside world can help, for example, having someone available outside the office to take their phone calls if necessary. If possible, perhaps there is someone within the office that the sufferer feels safe going to. Have a safe place within the workplace or outside the building that can be used in the event of a flashback and have a pre-existing understanding with your employers and co-workers that, in the event that it is necessary, the sufferer may excuse themself and take a phone call or go to that safe place. It is important to have a well-established protocol prior to a flashback occurring.
4. Finding the triggers to the anxiety or the startle responses is a starting point for addressing them. Many sufferers have a difficult time when someone walks up behind them. In such a case, asking for a desk to be physically positioned perhaps with the occupier's back against the wall or even having a mirror on it so that the occupier can see what is coming up behind them would be empowering. Keeping oneself in a calm state throughout the day is important and taking care of one's anxiety will be necessary on an ongoing basis. This will take effort on the individual's

part, such as listening to soothing music or just taking short breaks several times a day to do some deep breathing. By keeping one's resting state calm, the sufferer can decrease the level of anxiety experienced. Again, how to maintain a calm work environment would be something to address with the employer as a preventative technique versus undertaking damage control in an anxious state.

5. Dealing with co-workers at times can be stressful in any work environment. Open communication is the key here. This does not mean that the sufferer needs to share the fact that they are experiencing PTSD, although it would help with understanding. In some cases, it simply means that there needs to be open communication among co-workers and employers. If there is a negative interaction with another co-worker, address it with your employer. In addition, the sufferer should allow themself to experience the broad range of emotions that this co-worker might elicit, knowing that it may 'strike a chord'. Through processing these thoughts and feelings, the sufferer can gain a better understanding of what bothers them and how to best address it. Answers may come in the form of working through the issue with the individual or perhaps in a request to work part-time from home.
6. Stress management is often a difficult task at work for most employees. With PTSD, it becomes even harder. Stress management can come in many forms. The key is to practise coping mechanisms with consistency. Coping at work may mean having a longer work day because the individual may need more breaks during the day. A flexible schedule may be necessary as counselling may be required. Sometimes a difficult home environment may also necessitate a flexible work schedule. Predictability is the key to safety and reduces stress. The more predictable the sufferer's schedule can be, the less stress will be generated. Creating a strategy at the beginning of the day to tackle the day's work will help, as will planning for breaks to take care of anxiety from PTSD and additional work-related needs that arise.

As a co-worker, it may be difficult for you to help. After all, the person many not want it. That being said, many of the symptoms will be clearly visible and thus where one can help, doing so would be beneficial for the whole team. The ways in which you can help are varied and include the following:

1. You can assist by educating yourself on PTSD. Having an overview of the symptoms of PTSD is a starting point to supporting someone struggling with it. Of course, also ask how you can assist. It is always helpful to ask the individual what they need. Practical assistance, such as walking them to their car at night or being a safe person to talk to, can prove to be invaluable to a individual experiencing PTSD.

2. Listen to what the individual has to say. So often, assumptions are made when people are speaking. We feel as if we are helping by 'filling in the blanks' when people are talking when what we are really doing is interrupting them. Listening to an individual can sometimes be all that is needed at the time. Listening without interruption, without an agenda and without the need to steer the conversation can prove to be very supportive to individuals. If the employee has difficulty verbalizing, permit them to communicate their needs in writing.
3. Be open to communication about any necessary accommodations that need to be made – being open to a dialogue about the specific accommodations necessary will enhance everyone's understanding of what is expected. It will also give the individual the opportunity to clarify what specifically will be helpful.

As with physical disabilities, through gaining an understanding and providing the necessary accommodations, we can cast a wide net of support for those suffering from mental illness. It starts with education and continues through making the necessary modifications to create a successful experience. It benefits the individual as well as the company when people come together for the betterment of one person. A place of employment is where individuals work together towards a common goal. As such, supporting the individual with PTSD should be a common goal for everyone.

2.5 Summary

In this chapter we have tried to outline some of the more common mental illnesses that people might experience in the workplace. Which conditions we chose to include and exclude is open for debate and we do consider more later on in the next chapter of the book. The aim here was to try to introduce in non-technical terminology the description of the symptoms of these disorders as well as their consequences in the workplace. Later chapters will provide further insight into the steps that can be taken to support these conditions in an effective way.

chapter 3

The Personality Disorders

3.1 Introduction

Most of the attempts to categorize and describe mental illness tend to have a long list of very specific disorders like eating, sleep or sexual disorders. Some are more common in certain groups than others (i.e., anorexia in adolescent girls), whilst others are comparatively rare.

This chapter concentrates on the personality disorders. Psychiatrists and psychologists share many common assumptions with respect to personality. Both argue for the stability of personality over time. They talk of an 'enduring pattern' that is 'inflexible and pervasive' and 'stable and of long duration'. The pattern of behaviour is not a function of drug use or some other temporary medical condition. Furthermore, the personality pattern is not a manifestation or consequence of another mental disorder. Personality traits and personality disorders are stable over time and consistent across situations. In this sense, there should be obvious biographical clues to an individual's make-up.

Both psychologists and psychiatrists believe that personality factors relate to cognitive, affective and social aspects of functioning. Both disorders and traits affect how people think, feel *and* act. It is where a person's behaviour 'deviates markedly' from the expectations of an individual's culture that personality disorders are manifest. 'Odd behaviour' is not simply an expression of habits, customs or religious or political values professed or shown by a people of particular cultural origin.

Psychologists and psychiatrists have disagreed about one very important issue here. This is referred to as the categorical versus dimensional debate.

Traditionally, psychiatrists have favoured a cut-off criteria by which you can say 'he is a psychopath' or 'she is passive aggressive'. You either have or do not have a disorder – there is no grey area. Psychologists have always argued for the dimensional approach whereby you could say 'he was subclinically narcissistic', inferring that the person was a 'functioning narcissist'. Psychologists have talked about the dark side of personality, meaning the disorders which they think of as ways of coping when under stress (Hogan, 2007). This remains a highly contentious area of research and theorizing.

3.2 The distinction between personality disorder and mental illness

Another question that is often up for debate is whether or not personality disorders should be classified as mental illness and whether they should in turn be represented in the *Diagnostic and Statistical Manual* (DSM). The work by Bernstein, Iscan and Maser (2007) aimed to survey the opinions of personality disorder experts on possible revisions in the classification system for personality disorders in DSM-V. Of the 96 experts who completed their survey, 80 per cent felt that personality disorders are better conceived of as personality dimensions or illness spectra rather than categories. What was concluded from this was that currently the classification system is not adequate enough to diagnose personality disorders effectively.

The DSM manuals note that personality disorders all have a long history and have an onset no later than early adulthood. There are some gender differences: anti-social personality disorder is more likely to be diagnosed in men, whereas the borderline, histrionic and dependent personality is more likely to be diagnosed in women. Some personality disorders have similar symptoms to other disorders – anxiety, mood, psychotic, substance-related, etc. – but have unique features.

The essence of the difference between normal traits and disorders is as follows: 'Personality Disorders must be distinguished from personality traits that do not reach the threshold for a Personality Disorder. Personality traits are diagnosed as a Personality Disorder only when they are *inflexible, maladaptive* and *persisting* and cause significant functional impairment or subjective distress' (American Psychiatric Association, 1994: 633). In this sense, disorders can be seen as extreme traits. Indeed, there is a hypothesis called the spectrum hypothesis which believes that disorders are extreme traits, between one and two standard deviations away from the norm (Furnham, 2006). Thus, psychopaths/anti-social individuals are extremely low on agreeableness (or psychoticism in Eysenck's terminology), while histrionic types are extremely neurotic and obsessive-compulsives are extremely conscientious.

DSM-IV provides a clear summary:

General diagnostic criteria for a Personality Disorder

A. An enduring pattern of inner experience and behaviour that deviates markedly from the expectations of the individual's culture. This pattern is manifested in two (or more) of the following areas:

   1. cognition (i.e., ways on perceiving and interpreting self, other people, and events)
   2. affectivity (i.e., the range, intensity, liability, and appropriateness of emotional response)
   3. interpersonal functioning
   4. impulse control.

B. The enduring pattern in inflexible and pervasive across a broad range of personal and social situations.

C. The enduring pattern leads to clinically significant distress or impairment in social, occupational or other important areas of functioning.

D. The pattern is stable and of long duration and its onset can be traced back at least to adolescence or early childhood.

E. The enduring pattern is not better accounted for as a manifestation or consequence of another mental disorder.

F. The enduring pattern is not due to the direct physiological effects of a substance (e.g., a drug of abuse, a medication) or a general medical condition (e.g., head trauma). (DSM-IV: 633)

There are a number of defined and distinguishable personality disorders, which will be considered in due course:

- *Paranoid Personality Disorder* is a pattern of distrust and suspiciousness such that others' motives are interpreted as malevolent.
- *Schizoid Personality Disorder* is a pattern of detachment from social relationships and a restricted range of emotional expression.
- *Schizotypal Personality Disorder* is a pattern of acute discomfort in close relationships, cognitive or perceptual distortions, and eccentricities of behaviour.

- *Anti-social Personality Disorder* is a pattern of disregard for, and violation of, the rights of others.
- *Borderline Personality Disorder* is a pattern of instability in interpersonal relationships, self-image and affects, and marked impulsivity.
- *Histrionic Personality Disorder* is a pattern of excessive emotionality and attention seeking.
- *Narcissistic Personality Disorder* is a pattern of grandiosity, need for admiration and lack of empathy.
- *Avoidant Personality Disorder* is a pattern of social inhibition, feelings of inadequacy and hypersensitivity to negative evaluation.
- *Dependent Personality Disorder* is a pattern of submissive and clinging behaviour relating to an excessive need to be taken care of.
- *Obsessive-Compulsive Personality Disorder* is a pattern of preoccupation with orderliness, perfectionism and control.
- *Personality Disorder Not Otherwise Specified* is a category provided for two situations: 1) the individual's personality pattern meets the general criteria for personality disorder and traits of several different personality disorders are present, but the criteria for any specific personality disorder are not met; or 2) the individual's personality pattern meets the general criteria for a personality disorder, but the individual is considered to have a personality disorder that is not included in the classification (e.g., Passive-Aggressive Personality Disorder) (DSM-IV: 629).

These disorders have been given different names by different writers. One attempt by a work psychologist eager to help people in the workplace spot the disorders described them thus:

- *Arrogance*: they are right and everybody is wrong.
- *Melodrama*: they want to be the centre of attention.
- *Volatility*: their mood swings create business swings.
- *Excessive caution*: they cannot make important decisions.
- *Habitual distrust*: they focus on the negatives all the time.
- *Aloofness*: they disengage and disconnect with staff.
- *Eccentricity*: they think it is fun to be different just for the sake of it.
- *Passive resistance*: their silence is misinterpreted as agreement.
- *Perfectionism*: they seem to get the little things right even if the big things go wrong.
- *Eagerness to please*: they stress being popular matters most.

Table 3.1 below provides an opportunity to compare the terminology of different authors.

Table 3.1 Different labels for traits associated with similar disorders

DSM-IV Personality Disorder		Hogan and Hogan (1997) HDS themes		Oldham and Morris (1991)	Miller (2008)	Dotlich and Cairo (2003)
Borderline	Inappropriate anger; unstable and intense relationships alternating between idealization and devaluation.	Excitable	Moody and hard to please; intense but short-lived enthusiasm for people, projects or things.	Mercurial	Reactors	Volatility
Paranoid	Distrustful and suspicious of others; motives are interpreted as malevolent.	Sceptical	Cynical, distrustful and doubting others' true intensions.	Vigilant	Vigilantes	Habitual
Avoidant	Social inhibition; feelings of inadequacy and hypersensitivity to criticism or rejection.	Cautious	Reluctant to take risks for fear of being rejected or negatively evaluated.	Sensitive	Shrinkers	Excessive caution
Schizoid	Emotional coldness and detachment from social relationships; indifferent to praise and criticism.	Reserved	Aloof, detached and uncommunicative; lacking interest in or awareness of the feelings of others.	Solitary	Oddballs	Aloof
Passive-aggressive	Passive resistance to adequate social and occupational performance; irritated when asked to do something he/she does not want to.	Leisurely	Independent; ignoring people's requests and becoming irritated or argumentative if they persist.	Leisurely	Spoilers	Passive resistance
Narcissistic	Arrogant and haughty behaviours or attitudes, grandiose sense of self-importance and entitlement.	Bold	Unusually self-confident; feelings of grandiosity and entitlement; over-valuation of one's capabilities.	Self-confidence	Preeners	Arrogance

Anti-social	Disregard for the truth; impulsivity and failure to plan ahead; failure to conform.	Mischievous	Enjoying risk taking and testing the limits; needing excitement; manipulative, deceitful, cunning and exploitative.	Adventurous	Predators	Mischievous
Histrionic	Excessive emotionality and attention seeking; self-dramatizing, theatrical and exaggerated emotional expression.	Colourful	Expressive, animated and dramatic; wanting to be noticed and needing to be the centre of attention.	Dramatic	Emoters	Melodramtic
Schizotypal	Odd beliefs or magical thinking; behaviour or speech that is odd, eccentric or peculiar.	Imaginative	Acting and thinking in creative and sometimes odd or unusual ways.	Idiosyncratic	Creativity and vision	Eccentric
Obsessive-compulsive	Preoccupations with orderliness; rules, perfectionism and control; over-conscientious and inflexible.	Diligent	Meticulous, precise and perfectionistic, inflexible about rules and procedures; critical of others.	Conscientious	Detailers	Perfectionistic
Dependent	Difficulty making everyday decisions without excessive advice and reassurance; difficulty expressing disagreement out of fear of loss of support or approval.	Dutiful	Eager to please and reliant on others for support and guidance; reluctant to take independent action or to go against popular opinion.	Devoted	Clingers	Eager to please

It should be noted that these personality disorders are grouped along different axes or different clusters. When clustering, the following groups are usually formed:

a. Odd and eccentric (paranoid, schizoid, schizotypal).
b. Dramatic, emotional and erratic (anti-social, borderline, histrionic, narcissistic).
c. Anxious and fearful (avoidant, dependent and obsessive-compulsive).

This classification echoes the work of Horney over 60 years ago when she classified people into the following groups:

- Moving away from others: with a need for independence.
- Moving against others: with a need for power.
- Moving towards others: with a need for love.

One of the most important ways to differentiate between a particular personal trait and a personality disorder is *flexibility*. There are lots of difficult people at work, but relatively few whose rigid, maladaptive behaviours mean that they continually have disruptive, troubled lives and cause problems for those around them. It is their inflexible, repetitive, poor stress-coping responses that are the marks of many disorders. There are two simple and abiding characteristics of all these disorders: first, the ability to establish and maintain healthy relationships outside and inside the workplace; and, second, a realistic self-perception.

Personality disorders influence the sense of self – the way people think and feel about themselves and how other people see them. The disorders often powerfully influence interpersonal relations at work. They reveal themselves in how people 'complete tasks, take and/or give orders, make decisions, plan, handle external and internal demands, take or give criticism, obey rules, take and delegate responsibility, and co-operate with people' (Oldham and Morris, 1991: 24). The anti-social, narcissistic, histrionic, obsessive-compulsive, passive-aggressive and dependent types are particularly problematic in the workplace.

Personality disorders influence the sense of self

People with personality disorders have difficulty expressing and understanding emotions. It is the intensity with which they express them and their variability that makes them odd, difficult and prone to derailment. More importantly, they often have serious problems with self-control.

There are various ways in which experts have tried to classify the disorders themselves, but of most relevance to this chapter is the work of researchers who have understood the impact of personality disorders of those at work. Without doubt, it goes as far back as the work of Hogan and Hogan (1997), who note that a 'view from the dark side', as they call the personality disorders, gives an excellent understanding of the causes of management derailment. They argue that there are obviously many dysfunctional managers in organizations and that helping people to identify potentially bad or derailed managers can help to alleviate a great deal of suffering. They also note from their reading of the literature that derailment is more about *having* undesirable qualities rather than *not having* desirable qualities. This results from people at work being more concerned with select-in rather than select-out criteria; in other words, they rarely look for what they don't want as opposed to what they do want. There is frequently no mechanism for, interest in or ability to look for potential signs of derailment, including the personality disorders.

This chapter will examine the specific personality disorders ranked by prevalence and power to disrupt social functioning in the workplace.

3.3 The disorders

3.3.1 Paranoid (argumentative, vigilant)

It is thought that between 0.5 and 2.5 per cent of the population have this disorder, which must not be confused with the paranoid delusions of schizophrenics. Paranoids are *super-vigilant*: nothing escapes their notice. They seem tuned into mixed messages, hidden motives and secret groups. They are particularly sensitive to authority and power and are obsessed with maintaining their own independence and freedom.

Distrust and suspiciousness of others at work is their abiding characteristic. The motives of all sorts of colleagues and bosses are interpreted as malevolent all the time. The 'enemy' is both without and within.

They suspect (without much evidence) that others are exploiting, harming or deceiving them about almost everything, both at work and at home. They are preoccupied with unjustified doubts about the loyalty or trustworthiness of subordinates, customers, bosses, shareholders, etc. on both big and small matters. They are reluctant to confide in others (e.g., peers at work) because of the fear that the information will be used against them, kept on file or used to sack them. They may even be wary of using email. They read hidden or threatening meanings into the most benign remarks or events from emails to coffee-room gossip, and then remember them. They are certainly *hypersensitive* to criticism. They persistently bear grudges against all sorts of people going back many years and can remember even the smallest slight. They perceive attacks on their character or reputation that others do not see and are quick to react angrily or to counter-attack. They seem *hyper-alert and sensitive*. They are slow to commit and trust, but once they do so are loyal friends. They are very interested in others' motives and prefer 'watchdog' jobs. They like being champions of the underdog, such as whistleblowers on corruption. They are courageous because they are certain about their position. They are on the side of right: idealists striving for a better world. However, they can be overly suspicious or fearful of certain people, which can manifest itself in an irrational hatred towards certain groups.

Many of their characteristics can make them excellent managers: *alert*, *careful*, *observant* and *tactical*. But they can have problems with authority and in dealing with those who hold different opinions from their own. However, they are more sensitive to the faults in others than the faults in themselves. The business world, they believe (sometimes correctly), is full of danger, dishonest people and those who are untrustworthy and will let them down. Because they believe that others are out to harm them, they can be over-argumentative, bellicose, belligerent, hostile, secretive, stubborn and consumed with mistrust. They do not disclose, are suspicious of others and are experts on projecting blame onto others.

Psychoanalysts believe the paranoid feel weak and dependent but yet are sensitive to weakness in others and renounce them for it. They yearn for dependency but fear it. Instead of showing personal doubt, they doubt others.

Hogan and Hogan (2001) call these people 'argumentative'. Individuals with this type of disorder, they argue, expect to be wronged, to be betrayed, to be set up, to be cheated or to be deceived in some way. They see the world as a dangerous place, full of potential enemies, they enjoy conspiracy theories and are keenly alert for signs of having been mistreated. When they think they have been unfairly treated, they retaliate openly and directly. This may involve physical violence, accusations, retaliation or litigation. Retaliation is designed to send the signal that they are prepared to defend themselves. They are known for their suspiciousness, their argumentativeness and their lack of trust in others. They are hard to deal with on a continuing basis because they are always prone to being offended by something (unpredictability) and because they are so focused on their own private agenda that they do not have much time for others (unrewarding).

To work with them, colleagues have no alternative but to agree with them because they will defeat others' objections in a way that makes sense to them. Those who work for them will not be able to persuade them that they are wrong and risk alienating them by challenging them, and once they decide people cannot be trusted, the relationship will be over.

According to Oldham and Morris (1991: 151–2), the following six traits and behaviours are clues to the presence of what they term the 'vigilant' disorder:

1. *Autonomy.* They possess a resilient independence. They keep their own counsel, they require no outside reassurance or advice, they make decisions easily and they can take care of themselves.
2. *Caution.* They are careful in their dealings with others, preferring to size up a person before entering into a relationship.
3. *Perceptiveness.* They are good listeners, with an ear for subtlety, tone and multiple levels of communication.
4. *Self-defence.* They are feisty and do not hesitate to stand up for themselves, especially when they are under attack.
5. *Alertness to criticism.* They take criticism very seriously, without becoming intimidated.
6. *Fidelity.* They place a high premium on fidelity and loyalty. They work hard to earn it and they never take it for granted.

3.3.2 Schizoid (solitary)

These are the cold fish of the personality disordered world: distant, aloof and emotionally flat, often preferring the affection of animals to that of people. They are very self-contained: they do not need others to admire, entertain, guide or amuse them. They seem completely dispassionate. They are doers and observers, not feelers. They seem stoical in the face of pain and passion. They can take or leave relationships and they don't really understand emotions.

They often have a restricted range of emotions to express in interpersonal settings and they can seem more emotionally flat than is necessary. They are thought of as unresponsive and low in emotional intelligence.

They neither desire nor enjoy close relationships at work, including being part of a family. They are never team players and hate the idea of being so. They often choose solitary activities, feeling uncomfortable even in informal gatherings. They take pleasure in few if any activities. They seem joyless, passionless and emotionless. They lack close friends or confidants other than first-degree relatives. They are isolated at work but are apparently not unhappy with their lack of friends. They appear indifferent to the praise or criticism of others. Absolutely nothing seems to get them going. They show emotional coldness, detachment or flattened emotionality.

Schizoid people are not team players, nor are they sensitive or diplomatic. They are not aware of office politics. Hence, they may be more successful in solitary careers. They are not anti-social but asocial. They are the 'hollow man': empty, flat, emotionally unmovable. They may have a rich fantasy life, but a very poor emotional life.

Hogan and Hogan (2001) call these people self-absorbed, self-focused and indifferent to the feelings or opinions of others – especially their staff. They are introverted, misanthropic, imperceptive and lacking in social insight. They appear thick-skinned and indifferent to rejection or criticism. They prefer to work alone and are more interested in things like data than in people. They tend to work in finance, accounting, programming and information technology where their progress will depend on their technical skills and not their social insight. They are often uncommunicative and insensitive, which makes them unpredictable and unrewarding, and they have trouble building or maintaining a team.

They can be very tough in the face of political adversity, they have a hard surface and they can take criticism and rejection where others would tremble. They can also stay focused and on task, and not be distracted by tumult, emotional upheavals and stressful meetings; through it all, they will continue to do their jobs. They are indifferent to the needs, moods or feelings of others and can be rude, tactless, insensitive and gauche. They are therefore very poor managers. They are unperturbed by daily stress and heavy workloads; however, at the same time, they are insensitive or indifferent to the stress levels of their staff. When the pressure is really on, they retreat into their office, begin handling matters themselves and stop communicating, which leaves others at a loss to know what they want or need. Always extremely self-centred and self-reliant, they do not need emotional support from others and they do not provide any to others. They primarily do not want to be bothered by other people's problems – they just want to get on with their own work.

To work with these people, colleagues should stay task-orientated and keep questions and comments job-related. Such people will ignore requests for more and better communication and will tend to work by themselves. Those who work for them should observe what they do so that they do not act that way themselves and develop lines of communication with other people in the organization so that they have an alternative source of advice during times of trouble.

Oldham and Morris (1991: 264–5) note that the following five traits are clues to the presence of what they call the 'solitary' style of behaviour disorder:

1. *Solitude*. Individuals with the Solitary personality style have little need of companionship and are most comfortable alone.
2. *Independence*. They are self-contained and do not require interaction with others in order to enjoy their experiences or to get on in life.
3. *Sangfroid*. Solitary men and women are even-tempered, calm, dispassionate, unsentimental and unflappable.
4. *Sexual composure*. They are not driven by sexual needs. They enjoy sex but will not suffer in its absence.
5. *Feet on the ground*. They are unswayed by either praise or criticism and can confidently come to terms with their own behaviour.

Again, there may be jobs where detached, solitary ways of behaving may be adaptive: research and development (R&D) scientists. meteorologists on an uninhabited island and artistic craftspersons may work very well alone. It is when they are promoted to the position of managing teams that the problem arises.

3.3.3 Schizotypal (imaginative, idiosyncratic)

This disorder, which is more common in men than in women, has been estimated to affect about three per cent of the population. In a sense, such people are mild schizophrenics, but do not show the same gross disorganization in thinking and feeling or severe symptoms as the latter. However, they all appear to be pretty idiosyncratic and often creatively talented and curious. They often hold very strange beliefs and have odd habits, eccentric lifestyles and a rich inner life, often seeking emotional experience. Hence, they are drawn to religion and pharmacological techniques that promise to 'test the limits'. They seek rapture and nirvana.

This disorder is marked by acute discomfort with and reduced capacity for close relationships. Schizotypal people show many eccentricities of behaviour. They may look odd and have a reputation for being 'peculiar'.

They often have very odd ideas about business: how to succeed, whom to hire and what controls what. They can have very odd beliefs or magical thinking that influences behaviour and is inconsistent with business norms (e.g., superstitiousness or belief in clairvoyance and telepathy). They can have odd thinking and speech styles, being very vague or very elaborate. They can seem 'other-worldly' and may be very difficult to follow. They can have unusual perceptual experiences, seeing things that are not there, and can smell and taste things differently. Some are very suspicious or paranoid around the home and the office. They show inappropriate or constricted affect: they react oddly emotionally in various contexts. In other words, they may become very emotional in response to some trivial issues, but strangely and unpredictably cold to others.

Many organizations do not tolerate the odd behaviours of these idiosyncratic types. They dress oddly and work odd hours. They are not very loyal to their companies and do not enjoy the corporate world. They do not 'connect' with their staff, customers and bosses. Their quirky quasi-religious beliefs estrange them yet further from the normal world of the other people. They are often loners.

Hogan and Hogan (2001) call these people 'imaginative' and describe them as follows: they think about the world in unusual and often quite interesting ways. They may enjoy entertaining others with their unusual perceptions and insights. They are constantly alert to new ways of seeing, thinking and expressing themselves, and unusual forms of self-expression. They often seem bright, colourful, insightful, imaginative, very playful and innovative, but also eccentric, odd and flighty.

These people are curiously interesting and may be fun to be around, but they are distractible and unpredictable, and as managers they often leave people confused regarding their directions or intentions. They tend to miscommunicate in idiosyncratic and unusual ways. At their best, these people are imaginative, creative, interesting and amazingly insightful about the motives of others, but at their worst, they can be self-absorbed, single-minded, insensitive to the reactions of others and indifferent to the social and political consequences of their single-minded focus on their own agendas.

Under the pressure of stress and heavy workloads, they can become upset, lose focus, lapse into eccentric behaviour and not communicate clearly. They can be moody and tend to get too excited by success and too despondent over failure. They want attention, approval and applause, which explains the lengths that they are willing to go to in order to attract it.

To work with the 'imaginative' individual, one needs primarily to be a good audience, to appreciate their humour, creativity and spontaneity, and to understand that they do not handle reversals very well. They will not mind suggestions and recommendations regarding important decisions, and in fact may even appreciate them. Colleagues should study their problem-solving style, listen to their insights about other people and model their ability to 'think outside the box'.

Oldham and Morris (1991: 242–3), who call these people 'idiosyncratic', note that the following six traits and behaviours are clues to the presence of this disorder:

1. *Inner life.* Idiosyncratic individuals are tuned into, and sustained by, their own feelings and belief systems, whether or not others accept or understand their particular worldview or approach to life.
2. *Own world.* They are self-directed and independent, requiring few close relationships.
3. *Own thing.* Oblivious to convention, Idiosyncratic individuals create interesting, unusual, often eccentric lifestyles.
4. *Expanded reality.* Open to anything, they are interested in the occult, the extrasensory and the supernatural.
5. *Metaphysics.* They are drawn to abstract and speculative thinking.
6. *Outward view.* Though they are inner directed and follow their own hearts and minds, Idiosyncratic men and women are keen observers of others, particularly sensitive to how other people react to them.

The imaginative, idiosyncratic person is unlikely to reach a very high position in organizations, though they may be promoted in the fields of advertising or academia. The absent-minded, nutty professor and the creative advertising genius may share many schizotypical behaviours. If they are talented, they may do well, but rarely as managers of others.

3.3.4 Anti-social (mischievous)

The terms 'psychopath' or 'sociopath' were used to describe anti-social personality types whose behaviour is amoral or asocial, impulsive and lacking in remorse and shame. Indeed, perhaps for obvious reasons, this is the most studied of all the personality disorders. Once called 'moral insanity', it is found more commonly among lower socio-economic groups, no doubt because of the 'downward drift' of these types of people. Since the 1940s it has been shown that the characteristics defining this disorder – self-centredness, irresponsibility, impulsivity and insensitivity to the needs of others – are found in many professions.

These people show a disregard for and often violate the rights of others. They often have a history of being difficult, delinquent or dangerous. They show a failure to conform to social norms with respect to lawful behaviours (repeatedly performing acts that are grounds for arrest, imprisonment and serious detention), including lying, stealing and cheating. They are always deceitful, as indicated by their repeated lying, use of aliases or conning others for personal profit or pleasure. They are nasty, aggressive, con artists ... the sort who often get profiled on crime programmes. They are extremely impulsive and fail to plan ahead.

These people live only in, and for, the present. They show irritability and aggressiveness, as indicated by repeated involvement in physical fights or assaults. They cannot seem to keep still – ever. They manifest a terrifying reckless disregard for the physical and psychological safety of themselves or others, or the business in general. They are famous for being consistently irresponsible. A repeated failure to maintain consistent work behaviour or to honour financial obligations are their hallmark. Most frustratingly of all, they show a lack of remorse. They are indifferent to or rationalize having hurt, mistreated or stolen from another. They never learn from their mistakes. It can seem like labelling them as anti-social is a serious understatement.

Anti-social, adventurous challengers are not frightened by risk; indeed, they thrive on it. They love the thrill of adventure and are happy to put others' lives at risk as well as their own. They tend to be self-confident and not overly concerned with the approval of others. They live for the moment: they are neither guilty about the past nor worried about the future. They can be seriously reckless and they tend not to tolerate frustration well. They resist discipline and ignore rules. They have poor self-control and think little about the consequences of their actions. They need excitement all the time and are very easily bored. They can be successful entrepreneurs, journalists, bouncers and lifeguards.

Anti-social adventurers do not hide their feelings and do not experience stress unless confined or frustrated. They are adolescents all their life: careless, irresponsible, hedonistic, forever sowing their wild oats. They like outwitting the system, opportunistically exploiting who and what they can. They are rolling stones that gather no moss. They hate routine and admin, which they see as drudgery.

Anti-social adventurers often make bad bosses and bad partners because they are egocentric, continuing a relationship as long as it is good for them. They rarely have long-lasting, meaningful relationships. They have two human ingredients missing which are pretty crucial: *conscience* and *compassion*. Hence, they can be cruel, destructive, malicious and criminal. They are unscrupulous and exploitatively self-interested with little capacity for remorse. They act before they think and are famous for their impulsivity.

Hogan and Hogan (2001) call these people 'mischievous'. They note that these types of people expect that others will like them and find them charming, and expect to be able to extract favours, promises, money and other resources from other people with relative ease. However, they see others as merely to be exploited, so have problems maintaining commitments, and are unconcerned about violating expectations. They are self-confident to the point of feeling invulnerable and have an air of daring and sangfroid that others often find attractive and even irresistible.

Such people are highly rewarding to deal with, but unpredictable. They can be charming, fun, engaging, courageous and seductive; however, they are also impulsive, reckless, faithless, remorseless and exploitative. Moreover, they have problems with telling the truth. Their self-deception, self-confidence and recklessness leads to lots of conflicts, but they have almost no ability to learn from experience. According to Hogan and Hogan (2001: 49):

> They tend to be underachievers, relative to their talent and capabilities; this is due to their impulsivity, their recklessness, and their inability to learn from experience. These people handle stress and heavy workloads with great aplomb. They are easily bored, and find stress, danger, and risk to be invigorating – they actively seek it. As a result, many of these people become heroes – they intervene in robberies, they rush into burning buildings, they take apart live bombs, they volunteer for dangerous assignments, and they flourish in times of war and chaos. Conversely, they adapt poorly to the requirements of structured bureaucracies.

To work with them, their employees must be prepared to help them follow through with commitments and pay attention to details, and to encourage them to think through the consequences of their actions. They should not expect a lot of gratitude or even loyalty, but at the same time those who work for them can can learn a lot by watching how they handle people and how they are able to achieve their goals through charm and persuasion.

Oldham and Morris (1991: 218), who call these types of people 'adventurous', note that the following 11 traits are clues to the presence of this disorder:

1. *Nonconformity.* Men and women who have the Adventurous personality style live by their own internal code of values. They are not strongly influenced by other people or by the norms of society.
2. *Challenge.* To live is to dare. Adventurous love the thrill of risk and routinely engage in high-risk activities.
3. *Mutual independence.* They do not worry too much about others, for they expect each human being to be responsible for himself or herself.
4. *Persuasiveness.* They are silver-tongued, gifted in the gentle art of winning friends and influencing people.
5. *Sexuality.* Adventurers relish sex. They have a strong sex drive and enjoy numerous, varied experiences with different partners.
6. *Wanderlust.* They love to keep moving. They settle down only to have the urge to pick up and go, explore, move out, move on.
7. *Freelance.* Adventurous types avoid the nine-to-five world. They prefer to earn an independent, free-lance living, do not worry about finding work, and live well by their talents, skills, ingenuity, and wits.
8. *Open purse.* They are easy and generous with money, believing that money should be spent and that more will turn up somewhere.
9. *Wild oats.* In their childhood and adolescence, people with the Adventurous personality style were usually high-spirited hell-raisers and mischief makers.
10. *True grit.* They are courageous, physically bold and tough. They will stand up to anyone who dares to take advantage of them.
11. *No regrets.* Adventurers live in the present. They do not feel guilty about the past or anxious about the future. Life is meant to be experienced now.

In many ways, these types of people are the most common in the business world because if they are bright and good looking, their pathology may benefit them. They can be found in all sectors, but are perhps most attracted to those jobs that involve persuading others, such as the media, politics and religion.

3.3.5 Borderline (excitable, mercurial)

These are people 'living on the edge'. Apparently about two per cent of the population have this disorder, which is more common in women than men. The term 'borderline' originally referred to the border between neuroses and psychoses. There are often signs of other disorders: mood, depression and histrionic. People like Marilyn Monroe, Adolf Hitler and Lawrence of Arabia have been diagnosed as having this disorder, being impulsive, unpredictable and reckless. Most of all, they tend to have problems with their self-image, often 'splitting' their positive and negative views of themselves. They can vacillate between self-idealization and self-abhorrence.

These individuals show chronic instability in relation to interpersonal relationships, self-image and emotions. They are also marked by impulsivity in their daily behaviour. Sometimes they make frantic efforts to avoid real or imagined abandonment by managers, their staff, etc. They can become dependent and clingy. They often show a pattern of unstable and intense interpersonal relationships characterized by alternating between extremes of love and hate, worship and detestation. Most have identity disturbance: a markedly and persistently unstable self-image or sense of self. They are not really sure who they are and their assumed identity can easily change.

They are impulsive with money, sex, alcohol, driving, etc. and are in every sense of the word accident-prone. They might spend lavishly on one day and be miserly the next. At extremes, they can demonstrate recurrent suicidal or threatening behaviour. Most noticeable is their marked change of mood (e.g., intense episodic dysphoria, irritability or anxiety, usually lasting a few hours and only rarely more than a few days). They seem to be on an emotional rollercoaster with ups and downs even in the same day. They often talk about chronic feelings of inner emptiness. Unfortunately for their subordinates and managers, they have inappropriate, intense anger or difficulty controlling it (e.g., frequent displays of temper, constant anger and involvement in physical fights).

They are intense and demanding. Their emotional world is geological, full of volcanic explosions and the movement of tectonic plates. They can blow hot and cold very quickly. They are driven by emotions and find emotional significance in everything. As such, they are very moody. In their eyes, others can go from being idols to 'bad objects' in the space of days.

These people act on impulse and they can have a very self-indulgent side. They can change their lifestyle quite easily and do not have a strong sense of self. In this sense, they can be a little unsure of their identity.

At work, they can be passionately involved with others. They can really admire their bosses when praised, but this can just be a phase. They insist on being treated well and have a keen sense of entitlement. They can easily see themselves as more important than others do. As managers, they get very involved with their staff and expect total dedication. When their unrealistic expectations are not met, they can become very moody and churlish.

Their sense of who they are, what they believe and the purpose of their life is ever-changing. They do not like mixed feelings, ambiguity or solitariness. They prefer to see the world in terms of good and bad. They can also have great difficulty concentrating.

Some experts believe that the term 'personality disorganization' is best suited to this disorder because those suffering from it seem to be midway between the functional and dysfunctional.

Hogan and Hogan (2001) call these people 'excitable' as they expect to be disappointed in relationships; they anticipate being rejected, ignored, criticized or treated unfairly. They are on guard for signs that others have treated or will treat them badly. They erupt in emotional displays that may involve yelling, throwing things and slamming doors. Because they are so alert for signs of mistreatment, they find them everywhere, even when others cannot see them. They are neither predictable nor rewarding to deal with. As a result, they have a lot of trouble building and maintaining a team – the fundamental task of leadership.

These people have some capacity for empathy; because they know that life is not always fair, they can genuinely feels the pain of others. They sometimes tend to be enthusiastic about and to work very hard on new projects, but they are seriously high maintenance – they require a lot of hand-holding and reassurance, and they are very hard to please.

They do not handle stress or heavy workloads very well and they tend to explode rather easily. In addition, they are hard people to talk to and to maintain a relationship with. Consequently, they change jobs frequently and they have a large number of failed relationships. They are so easily disappointed in working relationships that their first instinct is to withdraw and leave. They are all self-centred – all information and experience is evaluated in terms of what it means for them personally – and they take the reaction of others personally. They personalize everything, but they do so privately; what others see are the emotional outbursts and the tendency to withdraw. To work with excitable managers, subordinates must be prepared to provide them with a lot of reassurance, to keep them well informed so as to minimize surprises and to give them advance notice so they know what is coming – think of trying to soothe a fretful child.

In lay language, Oldham and Morris (1991: 282–3) suggest that these types of people, which they call 'mercurial', have six characteristics:

1. *Romantic attachment*. Mercurial individuals must always be deeply involved in a romantic relationship with one person.

2. *Intensity*. They experience a passionate, focused attachment in all their relationships. Nothing that goes on between them and other people is trivial. Nothing is taken lightly.
3. *Heart*. They show what they feel. They are emotionally active and reactive. Mercurial types put their hearts into everything.
4. *Unconstraint*. They are inhibited, spontaneous, fun-loving and undaunted by risk.
5. *Activity*. Energy marks the Mercurial style. These individuals are lively, creative, busy and engaging. They show initiative and can stir others to creativity.
6. *Open mind*. They are imaginative and curious, willing to experience the experiment with other cultures, roles and value systems and to follow new paths.

3.3.6 Histrionic (colourful, dramatic)

Interestingly the definition of histrionic individuals comes from the outside: they see themselves as others say they see them. They therefore lack a consistent sense of who they are. They need constant reassurance and positive feedback from others. And because their heart rules their head, they can be impulsive, impetuous and impatient. They live not in the real world, but in a storybook world.

At work, such people can be persuasive and insightful. They enjoy the world of advertising, PR, sales and marketing, but need strong back-up for things like plans, budgets and details. They can be volatile and are known for being moody. They can be effusive with both praise and blame, but everything is an emotional drama and emotionally they can be both childlike and childish. They do not do stable relationships. They need to be the star, the centre of attention, otherwise they can feel powerless or desperately unworthy. They are not introspective. And it is important not to over-react to their over-reactions.

Hogan and Hogan (2001) call these types of people 'colourful' and state that they seem to be persuaded that others will find them interesting, engaging and worth paying attention to. They are good at drawing attention to themselves – they know how to make dramatic entrances and exits, and carry themselves with flair, self-consciously paying attention to their clothes and to way others react to them.

Histrionics are marked by their stage presence or persona, their self-conscious and distinctive aura – they perform extremely well in interviews, assessment centres and other public settings. According to Hogan and Hogan (2001: 49):

> They are great fun to watch, but they are also quite impulsive and unpredictable; everything that makes them good at sales (and selling themselves) makes them poor managers – they are noisy, distractible, over-committed and love to be the centre of attention. They are not necessarily extroverted, they are just good at calling attention to themselves. At their best, they are bright, colourful, entertaining, fun, flirtatious, and the life of the party. At their worst, they don't listen, they don't plan, they self-nominate and self-promote, and they ignore negative feedback.

Histrionics deal with stress and heavy workloads by becoming very busy, enjoying high-pressure situations when they can then be the star. Breathless with excitement, they confuse activity with productivity and evaluate themselves in terms of how many meetings they attend rather than how much they actually get done. A key feature of these people that others may not appreciate is how much they need and feed off approval, and how hard they are willing to work for it. This explains why they persist in trying to be a star after their lustre has faded. To work with them, subordinates have to be prepared to put up with missed appointments, bad organization, rapid change of direction and indecisiveness. This will never change, although they can be planned for. Yet by watching these individuals at work, you can learn how to read social clues, learn how to present your views effectively, forcefully and dramatically, and how to flatter and quite simply dazzle other people.

Oldham and Morris (1991: 126–7) note seven characteristics of this type of person, whom they term 'dramatic':

1. *Feelings.* Dramatic men and women live in an emotional world. They are sensation-orientated, emotionally demonstrative and physically affectionate. They react emotionally to events and can shift quickly from mood to mood.
2. *Colour.* They experience life vividly and expansively. They have rich imaginations, they tell entertaining stories, and they are drawn to romance and melodrama.
3. *Spontaneity.* Dramatic individuals are lively and fun. Their joie de vivre leads them to act on impulse to take advantage of the moment.
4. *Attention.* Dramatic people like to be seen and noticed. They are often the centre of attention and they rise to the occasion when all eyes are on them.
5. *Applause.* Compliments and praise are like food and water to persons with Dramatic style: they need them to go on.

6. *Appearance.* They pay a lot of attention to grooming and they enjoy clothes, style and fashion.
7. *Sexual attraction.* In appearance and behaviour, Dramatic individuals enjoy their sexuality. They are seductive, engaging, charming tempters and temptresses.

There are drama queens in all sectors, though they are more likely to be found in the more human resources-orientated world. They can also do very well in PR, marketing and training, particularly if they are talented, but they certainly remain hard work for their ever-suffering subordinates.

3.3.7 Narcissistic (arrogant, self-confident)

It may surprise some to learn that this disorder apparently only occurs in one per cent of the population. There are a lot of people with this disorder in business striving for adulation and power. There is of course a fine line between healthy self-esteem and serious self-defeating narcissism. The latter is characterized by an insatiable craving for adoration, a sense of special entitlement and the right to be insensitive to others, but at the same time being either enraged or crushed by criticism. It is the feeling that one deserves special treatment but then being extremely upset if one is treated like an ordinary person.

A manager with this disorder is marked by grandiosity (in terms of fantasy or behaviour), the need for admiration and a lack of empathy. Self-centred, selfish, egotistical: they are everywhere in business, alas.

These people have a grandiose sense of self-importance (e.g., exaggerated achievements and talents, and an expectation to be recognized as superior without the commensurate achievements). Most with this condition are preoccupied with fantasies of unlimited success, power, brilliance and money. They believe that they are 'special' and unique, and can only be understood by or should associate with other special or high-status people or institutions. They may try to 'buy' their way into exclusive circles. They constantly require excessive admiration and respect from everyone at work. Worse, they take advantage of others to achieve their own ends, which makes them terrible managers. They are unwilling to recognize or identify with the feelings and needs of others. They have desperately low emotional iIntelligence. Curiously, they are often envious of others and believe that others are envious of them. They consistently show arrogant, haughty behaviour or attitudes at work and at home. At times, this can be pretty amusing,for other to observe but is mostly simply frustrating.

Narcissists are highly self-confident and express considerable self-certainty. They are 'self-people' – self-asserting, self-possessed, self-aggrandizing, self-preoccupied, self-loving … and ultimately self-destructive. They really believe in themselves and that they were born lucky. At work, they are outgoing, have high energy levels and are competitive and very 'political'. They can make good leaders as long as they are not criticized or made to share glory. They seem to have an insatiable need to be admired, love and be needed. They are often a model of ambitious, driven, high self-esteem, self-disciplined, socially successful people. The world is their stage.

However, narcissism is a disorder of self-esteem: it's a cover-up. Narcissists self-destruct because their self-aggrandisement blinds their personal and business judgement and perception. At work, they exploit others to get ahead, yet they demand special treatment. But their reaction to any sort of criticism is extreme: shame, rage and tantrums. They aim to destroy that criticism, however well-intentioned and useful the criticism may be. They can be consumed with envy of and disdain for others and prone to depression, being manipulative, demanding and self-centred – even therapists don't like them.

Hogan and Hogan (1997) call these types of people 'arrogant': 'the lord of the high chair', a two year old sitting in its high chair demanding food and attention, and squealing in fury when its needs are not met. Narcissists expect to be liked, admired, respected, attended to, praised, complimented and indulged. Their most important and obvious characteristic is a sense of entitlement, excessive self-esteem and quite often an expectation of success that leads to real success. They expect to be successful at everything they undertake, believing that people are so interested in them that books will be written about them, and when their needs and expectations are frustrated, they explode with 'narcissistic rage'.

What is most distinctive about narcissists is their self-assurance, which often gives them charisma. Hogan and Hogan (2001) note that they are the first to speak in a group and that they hold forth with great confidence, even when they are wrong. They completely expect to succeed and take more credit for success than is warranted or fair, and they refuse to acknowledge failure, errors or mistakes. When things go right, it is because of their efforts, but when things go wrong, it is someone else's fault. This is a classic attribution error. It leads to some problems with truth telling because narcissists always rationalise and reinterpret their failures and mistakes, usually by blaming them on others.

Narcissists can be energetic, charismatic, leader-like and willing to take the initiative to get projects moving. They can be successful in the fields of management, sales and entrepreneurship. However, they are arrogant, vain, overbearing, demanding, self-deceiving and pompous. Yet they are so colourful and engaging that they often attract followers.

Narcissists handle stress and heavy workloads with ease, as well as being quite persistent under pressure and refusing to acknowledge failure. As a result of their inability to acknowledge failure or even mistakes and of the way they resist coaching and ignore negative feedback, they are unable to learn from their experiences.

Oldham and Morris (1991: 80) note nine characteristics of these types of people, whom they call 'self-confident':

1. *Self-regard*. Self-Confident individuals believe in themselves and in their abilities. They have no doubt that they are unique and special and that there is a reason for their being on this planet.
2. *The red carpet*. They expect others to treat them well at all times.
3. *Self-propulsion*. Self-Confident people are open about their ambitions and achievements. They energetically and effectively sell themselves, their goals, their projects and their ideas.
4. *Politics*. They are able to take advantage of the strengths and abilities of other people in order to achieve their goals, and they are shrewd in their dealings with others.
5. *Competition*. They are able competitors, they love getting to the top and they enjoy staying there.
6. *Dreams*. Self-Confident individuals are able to visualise themselves as the hero, the star, the best in their role or the most accomplished in their field.
7. *Self-awareness*. These individuals have a keen awareness of their thoughts and feelings and their overall inner state of being.
8. *Poise*. People with the Self-Confident personality style accept compliments, praise and admiration gracefully and with self-possession.
9. Sensitivity to criticism. The Self-Confident style confers an emotional vulnerability to the negative feelings and assessments of others, which are deeply felt, although they may be handled with this style's customary grace.

The business world often calls for and rewards arrogant, self-confident and self-important people. Such people seek out power and abuse it. They thrive in selling jobs and those where they have to engage in media work. But, as anyone who works with and for them knows, they can destabilize and destroy working groups by their deeply inconsiderate behaviour.

3.3.8 Avoidant (cautious, sensitive)

This disorder is equally common in men and women and is believed to affect 0.5–1 per cent of the population. People with this disorder appear to be social phobics, in that they are socially isolated and withdrawn. Feelings of possible rejection drive them towards situations where they are likely to be shunned, yet they seek acceptance, approval and affection.

These poor souls show social inhibition, feelings of inadequacy and hypersensitivity to negative evaluation. They are super-sensitive delicate flowers.

Such people avoid occupational activities that involve significant interpersonal contact because of their fear of criticism, disapproval or rejection. Any chance of receiving negative feedback is to be avoided. They are unwilling to get involved with people unless they are certain of being liked, which is pretty difficult at work (or indeed anywhere). They show restraint within intimate relationships because of their fear of being shamed or ridiculed. They are cold fish. They seem always preoccupied with being criticized or rejected in work situations. They are inhibited in new interpersonal situations because of their feelings of inadequacy. They see themselves as socially inept, personally unappealing or inferior to others. It can be puzzling to wonder how they ever became managers in the first place. Certainly, people with low self-esteem rarely make it to the top in business.

These rather sensitive types seek safety: in people and environments they know and trust. However, they can easily become anxious, guarded and worried. Beneath a polite and cool façade, they can feel very uneasy. They cope with their anxiety by being prepared for everything. They like life, their friends and work to be safe, secure and predictable. They do not like the new: strangers, unfamiliar people or new ways of working. They prefer what they know and they try to make work a home away from home. They can be effective, reliable and steady, and show little need for variety and challenge. They like routine and are pleased to help their seniors. But they are not political in organizations and can take refuge in their professionalism. They do well in technical fields that require routine, repetition and habit.

However, avoidants are so afraid of rejection that they live impoverished social lives. The paradox is that they avoid close relationships that could bring them exactly what they want: acceptance and approval. Because they feel isolated, unwanted and incompetent, they are sure that others will reject them and often they are rejected because of their cold, detached behaviour. They are super-sensitive to negative feedback and want unconditional love, yet they believe one cannot really be loved unless one is without imperfections. They are often very self-conscious and can feel strong self-contempt and anger towards others.

Hogan and Hogan (2001) call these people 'cautious' and stress their fear being criticized, shamed, blamed, humiliated or somehow disgraced. Because they are so alert to possible criticism, they see hazards and threats everywhere, even when others cannot see them. They respond to the possibility of being criticized by hand wringing, perseverance, freezing, becoming very cautious, and by taking no action at all. When they are threatened, they will also forbid their staff from taking any initiative. These people are unpopular managers because they are so cautious, indecisive and controlling.

Avoidant types can be prudent, careful and meticulous about evaluating risk. They rarely make rash or ill-advised moves and they can provide sound, prudential advice about intended future courses of action. However, they avoid innovation and resist change, even when it is apparent that something needs to be done. They seem particularly threatened by the new, the different and the strange, and they much prefer to react rather than to take the initiative. If their working world is stable, they can thrive, but if it is not, their behaviour may be maladaptive.

Under stress, avoidant people begin to adhere to established procedures and will rely on the tried and true rather than on any new technology or other procedures. They may try to control their staff out of fear that someone on the team will make a mistake and embarrass them, especially with their seniors. They do exactly what their seniors tell them and they enforce standard rules and procedures on their staff and others over whom they have any power. They hate to be criticized and what others will see is cautiousness, rigidity, adherence to standardized procedures and resistance to innovation and change.

To work with these people, employees need to keep them well informed about activities that concern them and where negative outcomes could reflect on them, as well as to consult them about intended future actions. When rapid action is required or when some form of innovation needs to be implemented, it is best to avoid them or put in writing the fact that action or innovation was recommended, then be prepared for nothing to happen.

The following five traits and behaviours are clues to the presence of what Oldham and Morris (1991: 174) call the 'sensitive' style:

1. *Familiarity.* Individuals with the Sensitive personality style prefer the known to the unknown. They are uncomfortable with, even inspired by, habit, repetition and routine.
2. *Family*. They stick close to the family and/or a few close friends. They do not require a wide network of friends and acquaintances, and they appreciate the comforts of home.
3. *Concern.* Sensitive individuals care deeply about what other people think of them.
4. *Circumspection.* They behave with deliberate discretion in their dealings with others. They do not make hasty judgements or jump in before they know what is appropriate.
5. *Polite reserve.* Socially they take care to maintain a courteous, self-restrained demeanour.

3.3.9 Dependent (devoted)

People with this disorder are more heavily reliant than most on other people for support or guidance. Like young children, they can be clingy, submissive and subservient in all relationships, fearing separation. They are carers and are most happy helping others to be happy. Others give meaning to their lives; they worry about others and need them. They find contentment in attachment and define themselves by others. They are not good at giving (or receiving) criticism and negative feedback. At work, they are co-operative, supportive, caring and encouraging. They do brilliantly in jobs like nursing, social work and voluntary organizations.

These people have a pervasive and excessive need to be taken care of by others. This leads to submissive and clingy behaviour and fears of separation. They often suffer analysis paralysis. They cannot make decisions on their own without continual advice and reassurance from others. Inevitably they are good at delegating, but they always seem to need help and reassurance. Most have difficulty expressing disagreement with others because of a fear of loss of support or approval. They publicly agree while privately disagreeing. This of course makes them difficult to read. They all have difficulty initiating projects or doing things on their own (because of a lack of self-confidence in their own judgement or abilities rather than a lack of motivation or energy). As such, they resist change, particularly where it leads to them being isolated or threatened. Some go to excessive lengths to obtain nurturance and support from others, often humiliating themselves in the process. All feel uncomfortable or helpless when left alone because of exaggerated fears of being unable to care for themselves at work and at home.

Dependent people do not make good managers because they are too quick to be apologetic, submissive and self-depreciating. They attach themselves to others who may all too easily take advantage of them. Kind, gentle, generous and full of humility, they do not believe in themselves. They have very low self-confidence in all aspects of life and acquire self-esteem through their attachments to others. Despite their smiling exterior, they often suffer from feelings of depression and dejection. Further, they can doom the relationships they value so much because they are too clingy and eager to please.

Hogan and Hogan (2001) note that such people are deeply concerned about being accepted, being liked and getting along, especially with authority figures. They are hyper-alert for signs of disapproval, for opportunities to ingratiate themselves and to be of service so as to demonstrate their loyalty to the organization. When they think that someone has taken offence at their actions, they redouble their efforts to be model citizens. People notice their good nature, their politeness, their cordiality and their indecisiveness. As managers, they will do anything their boss requires, which means that they are reluctant to stick up for their staff or to challenge authority, which inevitably erodes their legitimacy as leaders.

They are polite, conforming and eager to please. They rarely make enemies and they tend to rise in organizations. But they have problems making decisions, taking the initiative or taking stands on tough issues. Thus, their sections tend to drift and they can have trouble maintaining a team.

They respond to stress by freezing and becoming passive, and by hoping that someone else will take the initiative, step up, make a decision, assign responsibility and get things moving. They are too reliant on the initiative of others and can become a bottleneck for productivity and a source of delay and lost time.

Dependent people are deeply concerned with pleasing authority, which, in turn, is pleasing to authority, but they provide little leadership for those who must work for them. To work with them, employees must be prepared for indecisiveness, inaction and a lack of leadership. They must also be prepared to take the initiative when processes get stalled, but accept the fact that they will not be supported should their initiative fail or backfire. Hogan and Hogan (2001) believe that to work with these people, it is necessary to be prepared to flatter them, to agree with them, to be exploited, to allow them to take credit for your accomplishments and to allow them to blame others for their failures. Along the way, however, it is possible to profit from observing their pluck, stamina and ability to manipulate others to their ends.

Oldham and Morris (1991: 104) noted seven typical characteristics of what they call the 'devoted' style:

1. *Commitment.* Individuals with the Devoted personality style are thoroughly dedicated to the relationships in their lives. They place the highest value on sustained relationships, they respect the institution of marriage as well as unofficial avowals of commitment, and they work hard to keep their relationships together.
2. *Togetherness.* They prefer the company of one or more people to being alone.
3. *Teamwork.* People with this personality style would rather follow than lead. They are co-operative and respectful of authority and institutions. They easily rely on others and take direction well.
4. *Deference.* When making decisions, they are happy to seek out others' opinions and to follow their advice.
5. *Harmony.* Devoted individuals are careful to promote good feelings between themselves and the important people in their lives. To promote harmony, they tend to be polite, agreeable and tactful.
6. *Consideration.* They are thoughtful of others and good at pleasing them. Devoted people will endure personal discomfort to do a good turn for the key people in their lives.
7. *Self-correction.* In response to criticism, they will try hard to change their behaviour.

This personality disorder is nearly always associated with being a number two rather than a number one in any relationship.

3.3.10 Passive-aggressive (leisurely)

This personality type is very concerned about 'doing their own thing'. They demand the 'right to be me' and no one has the right to deprive them of it. They believe both at work and in private relationships that nobody has the right to own them. They like the companionship of others, but have a strong need to feel they are being treated fairly.

Such people do not regard the workplace as being of great importance. They can be good managers and workers, but they do not work overtime, take work home or worry much about it. They certainly will not do anything more than their contract specifies. They do not work to please their boss or feel better about themselves. They are often heard saying 'It's not my job' and they tend to be suspicious of workplace authority. If their boss asks them to work harder, faster or more accurately, they feel unfairly treated, even abused. They are super-sensitive to their rights, fairness and exploitation avoidance. They seem leisurely; they believe success is not everything. They tend not to rise above middle-management levels because they are not ambitious or thrusting enough. For them, the game is not worth the candle.

These people are not usually stressed. They sulk, procrastinate and forget when asked to do things they think are not fair. They are called passive-aggressive because they are rarely openly defiant, yet they are often angry. They snipe rather than confront. They are in essence oppositional rather than assertive. They often have downward job mobility.

Hogan and Hogan (2001) call these people 'leisurely'. They argue that such people march to the sound of their own drum, are confident about their skills and abilities, are cynical about the talents and intentions of others (especially their superiors) and insist on working at their own pace. They tend to get angry and slow down even more when asked to speed up. They tend to feel mistreated, unappreciated and put upon, and when they sense that they have been cheated, they retaliate, but always under conditions of high deniability. They are curiously quite skilled at hiding their annoyance and pretending to be co-operative, and their peevishness and foot-dragging are often very hard to detect.

They are often late for meetings, procrastinate, work at around 80 per cent of their capacity and are very stubborn and hard to coach. They will rarely directly confront others. Their prickly sensitivity, subtle co-operativeness, stubbornness and deep absorption make them both unpredictable and unrewarding to deal with. As a result, they have trouble building and maintaining a team.

Passive-aggressives handle stress and heavy workloads by slowing down, simply ignoring requests for greater output and finding ways to get out of work. They seem overtly co-operative and agreeable, and it takes a long time to realize how unproductive and refractory they actually can be. They are self-centred, they focus on their own agendas and they deeply believe in their own superior natural talent and their right to leisure. They regard themselves as having nothing to prove, are quite indifferent to feedback from others

and therefore become annoyed and resentful when criticized or asked for extra effort.

At work, people need to be aware that passive-aggressives are not nearly as co-operative as they seem and that they are only pretending to agree. It is also necessary to get them to commit to performance goals in public in front of witnesses so that a community of people can hold them to account. Social pressure will not change their views of the world, but it will serve to make their performance deficits less easily deniable.

Oldham and Morris (1991: 194–5) claim the following five traits and behaviours are clues to the presence of what they too call the 'leisurely style':

1. *Inalienable rights*. Leisurely men and women believe in their right to enjoy themselves on their own terms in their own time. They value and protect their comfort, their free time and their individual pursuit of happiness.
2. *Enough is enough*. They agree to play by the rules. They deliver what is expected of them and no more. They expect others to recognize and respect that limit.
3. *The right to resist*. Leisurely individuals cannot be exploited. They can comfortably resist acceding to demands that they deem unreasonable or above and beyond the call of duty.
4. *Mañana*. Leisurely men and women are relaxed about time. Unlike Type-A individuals, they are not obsessed by time urgency or the demands of the clock. To these individuals, haste makes waste and unnecessary anxiety. They are easy-going and optimistic that whatever needs to get done will get done, eventually.
5. *I'm okay*. They are not overawed by authority. They accept themselves and their approach to life. They are content with their place in the universe.

There are many senior managers with this rather unattractive profile. Their 'pathology' may have served them well even if the burden of it has been 'picked up' by their long-suffering staff.

3.3.11 Obsessive-compulsive (diligent, conscientious)

This disorder is more common in men than in women and around one per cent of the population exhibit symptoms of it. They are often known for their zealous perfectionism, their attention to detail, their rigidity and their formality. They are also often the workaholics – those who really 'live' the work ethic. They are competent, organized, thorough and loyal. Even during their holidays and leisure time, they enjoy intense, detailed, goal-orientated activity.

These people show a preoccupation with orderliness, perfectionism and mental and interpersonal control, at the expense of flexibility, openness and efficiency. They make for the most 'anal' of bureaucrats. They are preoccupied with details, rules, lists, order, organization or schedules to the extent that the major point of the business activity is lost and forgotten. All show perfectionism that interferes with task completion (e.g., they are unable to complete a project because their own overly strict standards are not met). They demand perfectionism in others, however unproductive it makes them. These managers are often workaholics, forgoing leisure activities and friendships as a result. They have a well-deserved reputation for being over-conscientious, scrupulous and inflexible about issues relating to morality, ethics or values.

Amazingly, such people are unable to discard worn-out or worthless objects even when they have no sentimental value. They hoard rubbish at home and in the workplace. They are reluctant to delegate tasks or to work with others unless these people submit to exactly their own way of doing things. They do not let go and pay the price. They are misers towards both themselves and others; money is viewed as something to be hoarded for future catastrophes. Because they never fully spend their budget, they never get it increased. In short, they show rigidity and stubbornness and are very unpleasant to work for.

Obsessive-compulsives rise through the ranks as a result of hard work. But at certain levels they start to derail because they have problems making quick decisions, setting priorities and delegating. They tend to want to check the details again and again. They function best as right-hand-men to leaders with strong conceptual skills and visions. They are very self-disciplined and put work first. They are often not very emotionally literate and can be fanatical and fundamentalist about moral, political and religious issues. Their relationships are marked by conventionality and coolness. They are faithful and responsible, but unromantic and unemotional. They can be seen as mean and over-cautious.

Obsessive-compulsive managers *must* have everything done perfectly. They get wrapped up in details and lose a sense of direction and priorities. They can be tyrannical bosses, being super-attentive to time, orderliness and cleanliness. They are driven by 'oughts' and 'shoulds', and expect others to do likewise.

They are the overbearing fault-finders of the business world. They are driven to achieve respect and approval and to control their dangerous impulses, desires and feelings (and those of others).

Hogan and Hogan (2001) call these people 'diligent' because they are concerned with doing a good job, being a good citizen and pleasing authority. They note that the 'diligent' person is hard-working, careful, planful, meticulous and has very high standards of performance for themselves and other people. They live by these rules and expect others to do so too, and they become irritable and erratic when others do not follow their rules. What is most distinctive is their conservatism, their orientation to detail and their risk aversion, but they are also thought of as reliable, dependable and predictable. They are often desirable organizational citizens who can always be relied upon to maintain standards, to do their work competently and professionally, and to treat their colleagues with respect.

Hogan and Hogan (2001) note that these people are good role models who uphold the highest standards of professionalism in performance and behaviour. They are popular with their bosses because they are so completely reliable, but not necessarily with those who report to them. However, they are fussy, particularly, nitpicking micro-managers who deprive their subordinates of any choice or control over their work. Their sin is micro-management. This alienates their staff, who soon refuse to take any initiative and simply wait to be told what to do and how to do it. Diligent, conscientious obsessive-compulsives also cause stress for themselves; their obsessive concern for quality and high performance makes it difficult for them to delegate and for them to prioritize their tasks. They also have problems with vision and the big picture. Consequently, they have a kind of ambivalent status as managers and can function in some environments at certain levels.

Diligent obsessionals tend to become stressed by heavy workloads. They respond to increased levels of work by working longer and harder (not smarter) and they fall further and further behind, which they find this intolerable. They often become a bottleneck to productivity because everything must pass through them and be checked, revised and approved by them, and they won't let anything go that isn't completed according to their standards.

In everyday language, Oldham and Morris (1991: 57), who call these people 'conscientious', describe them as having the following nine characteristics:

1. *Hard work.* The conscientious person is dedicated to work, works very hard and is capable of intense, single-minded effort.

2. *The right thing.* To be Conscientious is to be a person of conscience. These are men and women of strong moral principles and values. Opinions and beliefs on any subject are rarely held lightly. Conscientious individuals want to do the right thing.
3. *The right way.* Everything must be done 'right', and the conscientious person has a clear understanding of what that means, from the correct way to balance the cheque book, to the best strategy to achieve the boss' objectives, to how to fit every single dirty dish into the dishwasher.
4. *Perfectionism.* The conscientious person likes projects to be completed to the final detail, without even minor flaws.
5. *Love of detail.* Conscientious men and women take seriously all the steps of any project. No detail is too small for conscientious consideration.
6. *Order.* Conscientious people like the appearance of orderliness and tidiness. They are good organizers, cataloguers and list makers, and they appreciate schedules and routines.
7. *Pragmatism.* Conscientious types approach the world and other people from a practical, no-nonsense point of view. They roll up their sleeves and get to work without much emotional expenditure.
8. *Prudence.* Thrifty, careful and cautious in all areas of their lives, conscientious individuals do not give into reckless abandon or wild excess.
9. *Accumulation.* A 'pack rat', the conscientious person saves and collects things (storing them in orderly bundles), and is reluctant to discard anything that has, formerly had, or someday may have value for him or her.

The diligent, conscientious type can do very well in business. Certain jobs in fields like health and safety and quality control demand obsessive-compulsive checking. But like all the other disorders, it is an excess of this trait that leads to serious problems, both for the individual manager and their staff.

3.3.12 Self-defeating (self-sacrificing)

These people are the self-sacrificing altruists of the personality disordered world. They achieve meaning in life and satisfaction through serving others and making sacrifices for them. They may feel undeserving of attention and pleasure and unworthy of love, so they feel they have to earn it. They work long and hard for others and give their all in relationships, but they do not want thanks or attention and feel uncomfortable with positive compliments or praise. They are often seriously neglected and under-recognized, which causes them pain and confusion. They tend not to have their own needs met. They see life as tough, unfair and uncompromising, and their job is to help those less fortunate than themselves. They work well under stress but can become resentful if they are consistently ignored.

To a large extent, the self-defeating personality is ideal at work. Hard-working, respectful and adaptable, they are very concerned about the value and meaning of the work they do. They make reliable, loyal, undemanding, non-assertive workers. However, they rarely realize their potential, turning down the opportunity for promotion.

Self-defeatists rarely end up as managers, but their dedication and loyalty may mean they end up in middle-management positions. However, inevitably they have problems with delegation and discipline and take on too much. They may feel – quite rightly – that their staff are ungrateful and under-perform. Some (although not all) may demand that their subordinates to adopt the same self-sacrificial behaviour as themselves.

Because they have problems with success, such people may suffer from imposter syndrome and consciously or unconsciously self-destruct. And, of course, they are immensely vulnerable to exploitation by others. Their generosity makes them masochists, which was the term previously used for this disorder.

Oldham and Morris (1991: 308–9) specify seven characteristics of the 'self-sacrificing' person:

1. *Generosity.* Individuals with the Self-Sacrificing personality style will give you the shirts off their back if you need them. They don't wait to be asked.
2. *Service.* Their 'prime directive' is to be helpful to others. Out of deference to others, they are non-competitive and unambitious, comfortable coming second, even last.
3. *Consideration.* Self-Sacrificing people are always considerate in their dealings with others. They are ethical, honest and trustworthy.
4. *Acceptance.* They are non-judgemental, tolerant of others' foibles and never harshly reproving. They'll stick with you through thick and thin.
5. *Humility.* They are neither boastful nor proud, and they're uncomfortable being fussed over. Self-Sacrificing men and women do not like being the centre of attention; they are uneasy in the limelight.
6. *Endurance.* They are long-suffering. They prefer to shoulder their own burdens in life. They have much patience and a high tolerance for discomfort.
7. *Artlessness.* Self-Sacrificing individuals are rather naive and innocent. They are unaware of the often deep impact they make on other people's

> lives, and they tend never to suspect deviousness or underhanded motives in the people to whom they give so much of themselves.

The self-defeating person is frankly unlikely to ever make it to a senior management position.

3.3.13 Sadistic (aggressive)

The sadistic personality-disordered individual is aggressive. They are strong, forceful, courageous, pugilistic and confident. They want to be leader or 'top dog'. They have a need to dominate and organize others. Hence, they are autocratic and dictatorial and can also be immoral. They give orders, make rules and run the show.

At work, such people are ambitious and purposeful. They have the drive for power. They thrive in the win-lose, dog-eat-dog, rough-and-tumble of the business world. They are not squeamish or sentimental and can be very tough. They thrive when they have clear goals and directions. And for them, the end justifies the means, which is where problems may begin.

They can make brilliant managers, being goal-orientated, organized and disciplined, but they focus on results, not feelings. They demand total loyalty and hard work, and have little patience with errors, inefficiency, waste or failure of any type. They also do not like being bored. The most serious source of stress for them is losing power.

They have strong emotions but strong control over them. They tend to be more crafty and shrewd than physically aggressive, but they do bully, hurt and humiliate others who are subordinate to and dependent on them. They are disciplinarians who can easily inflict pain. Hence, they can be very malevolent.

Oldham and Morris (1991: 336–7) specify six criteria of the 'aggressive' person as they term them:

1. *Command.* Aggressive individuals take charge. They are comfortable with power, authority and responsibility.
2. *Hierarchy.* They operate best within a traditional power structure where everyone knows his or her place and the lines of authority are clear.
3. *Tight ship.* They are highly disciplined and impose rules of order that they expect others in their charge to follow.
4. *Expedience.* Aggressive men and women are highly goal-directed. They take a practical, pragmatic approach to accomplishing their objectives. They do what is necessary to get the job done.

5. *Guts.* They are neither squeamish nor fainthearted. They can function well and bravely in difficult and dangerous situations without being distracted by fear or horror.
6. *The rough-and-tumble.* Aggressive people like action and adventure. They are physically assertive and often participate in or enjoy playing competitive sports, especially contact sports.

In dealing with the 'aggressive person', the following points are worth remembering:

1. Beware of showing emotion; you will be up against a brick wall. Point out how your plan or approach directly benefits them.
2. If the aggressive person is your superior, look for ways to cope creatively with their possibly harsh rules and regulation.
3. Accept that the aggressive person has a temper and avoid pushing the predictable buttons that will ignite it. Look for other ways to solve your problems. To deal with this person's anger, don't fight back and don't blow off your steam in his or her face. Back off and let the anger wind down. (Oldham and Morris, 1991: 349–51)

3.4 Summary

The personality disorders are very common. Perhaps the ones that cause most problems for people at work are the anti-social, narcissistic, obsessive-complusive, schizotypal and histrionic disorders. Two important points need to be made:

- First, whilst having evidence of many of the behaviours associated with a disorder, still people may function effectively, yet under stress and pressure, the negative sides of that disorder become manifest and problematic.
- Second, paradoxically, some of these disorders may actually benefit someone at work up to a point. Thus, to be paranoid in the security industry or obsessional in quality control may be advantageous to an extent. It is where the disorder is very strong that problems arise.

The issue of classification is that, quite simply, there may be too much *overlap* among the diagnoses to really justify so many categories. Thus, although some personality disorders have quite unique and distinctive features, they appear to share common traits. The line between normal, rational, healthy behaviour and abnormal, self-defeating behaviour is often a fine one. It is where behaviours (suspiciousness in the paranoid person or exaggerating importance in the narcissistic person) are pervasive, inflexible and maladaptive, causing chronic and acute personal distress, that they probably should be diagnosed as a full-blown personality disorder. There are also suggestions and indeed evidence of *sex bias* – women are more likely to be diagnosed as borderline and histrionic and men as schizoid.

Most importantly perhaps, diagnosticians should not *confuse labels with explanations.* Such labelling also causes attribution errors by ignoring social, cultural and environmental factors that may play a part. Thus, a history of abuse, neglect and prejudice may lead to the maladaptive behaviour.

So, what of the theories of the origin of the illness?

Freudians look to early childhood for explanations. Thus, they argue that narcissists are actually trying to cover up deep feelings of anxiety. Much depends on how parents socialize their children and give them a sense of who they are, particularly in relation to how to develop a consistent self-identity separate from their parents.

Learning theorists are also happy to see the origins of disorders in childhood and cite examples of parental reward and punishment schedules. Thus, rigidly controlling parents or those who are over-attentive to particular behaviours (e.g., appearance) can be at the root of these disorders. Inconsistent, unpredictable or neglectful parents may have a lot to answer for. Early childhood emotional deprivation is often cited as a cause.

Genetic factors may also play a part, though these are more common in some areas than others. Other theorists point to physiological evidence (e.g., heart rate) of very (that is, abnormally) low anxiety in threatening situations. No fear of punishment renders threats and laws ineffectively and may, in part, account for an anti-social personality. People with anti-social personalities have been shown to exhibit little anxiety in anticipation of impending pain of all types.

Sociologists have also stressed *socio-cultural* factors. One argument is that people from large and poor families bought up in areas with high levels of crime, drug addiction and unemployment receive inconsistent and neglectful nurturing, and this can lead to disorders developing. Further, they are exposed to many devious and deviant role models. The idea, of course, is that the disorder is a result of and a reaction to the surrounding social environment.

No approach does very well in accounting for the origin of all these disorders. Psychoanalysts believe they can in part explain the borderline and narcissistic disorders, while those with a more physiological bent believe they are good at explaining the aetiology of the anti-social personality.

What about *treatment?* As noted earlier, personality-disordered people are more likely to be referred to treatment by others than to seek it themselves. What do they find? Interestingly, many therapists do not like dealing with patients who can be demanding, manipulative and fickle. Some even believe that people with certain disorders are really beyond the reach of therapy.

Some therapies attempt to teach acceptable interpersonal behaviours, while others actively confront a person's problems. Some try to work on a person's beliefs about themselves, trying to correct the distortions that suggest they are either all good or all bad. Personality-disordered patients need social and problem-solving skills, which can be taught. Incarcerated patients (such as in prisons or residential homes) may be put on a token economy schedule such that they get rewarded (in tokens) for good behaviour (only), which can be exchanged for all sorts of privileges. Interestingly, drug therapies are very seldom used for these disorders.

chapter 4

Alcohol and Other Addictions

4.1 Introduction

Most people think of addictions primarily in terms of drugs. There is a long list of substances that people can and do become addicted to: alcohol, stimulants (like cocaine), opiates, hallucinogens, marijuana, tobacco and barbiturates. There are fashions in drug abuse that are partly a function of availability. Addiction affects people's health and lives profoundly. In the workplace, productivity declines and absenteeism goes up.

Addiction originally meant physiological overdependence on a drug which altered the biochemistry of an individual such that increasing doses were required to have the desired effect. Addiction involves the exposure to something and the subsequent behaviour seeking to repeat the experience very often. Over time, the addiction becomes established. There is regular and increasing consumption with the takers knowing their habit is expensive, unhealthy and possibly illegal, but seemingly being unable to 'kick the habit'. It is a complex process that involves biological, psychological and social factors.

Some addiction researchers are interested in why some particular drugs or activities have such a propensity to be addictive. Others are fascinated by why some individuals seem more susceptible to addiction than others. Some scientists are interested in the environmental and social conditions and features that make addictions more or less likely. Others look at attempts at recovery and relapse from addiction.

However, the concept of addiction has been applied much more widely. Thus, there are gambling, sex and work addicts. There are now many '-aholic' terms like chocaholic or workaholic that are often used to try to imply an addiction like alcoholism.

With regard to drugs, the psychiatric literature distinguishes between substance dependence and abuse. Both have technical meanings. Dependence has very specific characteristics like *tolerance* (people take more and more for limited affect), *withdrawal symptoms* (on not taking the drug), *obsessions* (trying to get hold of the drug), a *deterioration* in all social, occupational and recreational activities and *continued use* in the full knowledge of all the danger that is being done by taking the drug.

Abuse means using the drug despite having to fulfil various school, home and work obligations; use in dangerous situations (e.g., driving at work); use despite illegal behaviour; and use despite persistent negative side-effects.

Different theories, models or approaches have arisen to describe all sorts of addictions. This partly reflects the complexity of the issue and the number of factors involved. Most of these approaches are supplementary rather than contradictory, but they clearly place their emphasis on different factors.

4.2 The addictive personality

The original idea was that people had some particular profile or flaw or vulnerability that made them prone to either specific or all addictions. This concept has been widely criticised, but, yet psychologists and psychiatrists have continued to explore the issue. Some psychiatrists see addiction as a consequence of mental illness like depression or anti-social personality disorder. The idea is that risk takers or the mentally ill are vulnerable to become reliant on drug taking, using it as a crutch to deal with the problems in their lives. They are more likely to experiment and ignore or downplay any potentially adverse consequences.

Therapists also point out how addicts and drug-dependent people use drugs to compensate or cope. Drugs are used to numb feelings, reduce painful emotional states or reduce internal conflict. It may help loneliness or make up for a lack of gratifying relationships with others. For young people, drugs may help with the anxiety associated with intimacy. They feel they can only say and do things when under the influence of certain drugs and therefore, in time, they become dependent on the specific drugs for effective social functioning. It does not usually help either the individual or those trying to help them to simply describe them as addictive personalities.

Addictions run in families. Thus, the children of alcoholics are four times more likely to themselves become alcoholics than the children of non-alcoholics. Twin studies have clearly indicated that substance abuse has genetic determinants. It is likely that complex genetic factors lead to an individual's particular biological response to drugs, probably specifically in relation to neurotransmitter systems. So people may be self-medicating with drugs that 'correct for' a biochemical imbalance in the brain that they have inherited.

4.3 Psychiatric criteria for substance dependence

The psychiatric criteria for substance dependence is as follows – a maladaptive pattern of substance use leading to impairment or distress, as manifested by many of the following, occurring at any time in the same 12-month period:

1. Tolerance, meaning either a need for markedly increased amounts of the substance to achieve intoxication or the desired effect and/or markedly diminished effect with continued use of the same amount of the substance.
2. Withdrawal, showing as withdrawal syndrome for the specific substance, or where the same (or a closely related) substance is taken to relieve or avoid withdrawal symptoms.
3. The substance is often taken in larger amounts or over a longer period than was intended.
4. A persistent desire or unsuccessful efforts to cut down or control substance use.
5. Much of the user's time is spent in activities necessary to obtain the substance or recover from its effects.
6. Important social, family, occupations or leisure activities are given up or reduced because of substance use.
7. Substance use is continued despite clear knowledge of having a persistent or recurrent physical or psychological problem that is likely to have been caused or exacerbated by the substance.

Over the years, different theories, models or approaches have have been put forward to describe all sorts of addictions. This partly reflects the complexity of the issue and the number of factors involved. Most of these approaches are supplementary rather than contradictory, but they clearly put their emphasis on different factors.

Opponent-Process Theory states that systems react and adapt to stimuli by opposing their initial effects. A desire followed by a craving for something, which did not exist before any experience of the drug, increases with exposure to it. A number of phenomena are associated with all addiction and dependence. The first is *affective pleasure* – a physical and emotional hedonic state that follows use. It could be relaxation, stress release or just feelings of sudden energy. Then there is *affective tolerance*, which means that one needs more and more of the substance to have the same effect. Third, there is *affective withdrawal*, which is what occurs if the drug is not taken.

So the drug causes a process which sets off an opposite reaction which grows in strength with repeated exposure. This is affective contrast. With more use, the dominant reaction is negative, so one needs the drug to achieve a neutral state and little pleasure is derived from taking it.

Positive-Reinforcement Theory is the simplest of all the models. Drugs make one feel good, even euphoric. In the 1960s, psychologists allowed monkeys to 'self-administer' morphine and they showed all the signs of addiction. Psychologists have become increasingly interested in the drug reward pathways in the brain, particularly the brain regions and neurotransmitters that may be involved in 'natural rewards', like food and sex, versus artificial stimulants, like drugs and electrical brain stimulation. We know that drugs such as cocaine and amphetamines increase synaptic dopamine in the region called the nucleus accumbus. There are other neurochemicals that play a role like endogenous opioids which effect a range of functions from taste to stress responses. Thus, lots of drugs give us real highs that we want to repeat.

Learning Theories argue that drug taking and the pleasures associated with it become associated with very specific situations, sights and sounds. Therefore, people associate drugs from alcohol to amphetamines with very specific cues or reminders. As such, if people are put in particular settings, they will experience drug cravings – for example, bars for alcoholics and the smell of smoke for nicotine addicts. Cues that deliver impending drug delivery can induce strong desires which 'have to be' fulfilled. In many senses, this is the old-fashioned behaviourism and conditioning theory.

4.4 Alcohol abuse

We know many things about alcohol abuse. Consider the following quotes from the American Psychiatric Association *Diagnostic Statistic Manual* (DSM-IV: 201–3).

1. Specific Culture, Age, and Gender Features

The cultural traditions surrounding the use of alcohol in family, religious, and social settings, especially during childhood, can affect both alcohol use and patterns and the likelihood that alcohol problems will develop.

Marked differences characterise the quantity, frequency, and patterning of alcohol consumption in the countries of the world. For example, in most Asian cultures, the overall prevalence of Alcohol-Related Disorders may be relatively low, and the male-to-female ratio high. In the United States, by contrast, whites and African-Americans have nearly identical rates of Alcohol Abuse and Dependence. Low educational level, unemployment, and lower socioeconomic status are associated with Alcohol-Related disorders, although it is often difficult to separate cause from effect.

Among adolescents, Conduct Disorder and repeated anti-social behaviour often co-occur with Alcohol Abuse or Dependence and with other Substance-Related Disorders. Alcohol Abuse and Dependence are more common in males than in females, with a male-to-female ratio as high as 5:1. However, this ratio varies substantially depending on the age group.

2. Prevalence

Alcohol Dependence and Abuse are among the most prevalent mental disorders in the general population. A community study conducted in the United States from 1980 to 1985 using DSM-III criteria found that about 8 per cent of the adult population had Alcohol Dependence and about 5 per cent had Alcohol Abuse at some time in their lives. per cent. 3. Course

The first episode of Alcohol Intoxication is likely to occur in the mid-teens, with the age at onset of Alcohol Dependence peaking in the 20s to mid-30s. The large majority of those who develop Alcohol-Related Disorders do so by their late 30s.

3. Familial Pattern

Alcohol Dependence often has a familial pattern, and at least some of the transmission can be traced to genetic factors. The risk for Alcohol Dependence is three to four times higher in close relatives of people with Alcohol Dependence. Higher risk is associated with a greater number of affected relatives, closer genetic relationships, and the severity of the alcohol-related problems in the affected relative.

The criteria for alcohol abuse are generally considered to be as follows: a maladaptive pattern on substance use leading to clinically significant impairment or distress, as manifested by one (or more) of the following, occurring within a 12-month period:

1. Recurrent alcohol use resulting in a failure to fulfil major role obligations at work, school or home (e.g., repeated absences or poor work performance related to alcohol use; alcohol-related absences, suspensions or expulsions from school; neglect of children or household).
2. Recurrent alcohol use in situations in which it is physically hazardous (e.g., driving a car or operating a machine when impaired by alcohol use);
3. Recurrent alcohol-related legal problems (e.g., arrests for alcohol-related disorderly conduct).
4. Continued alcohol use despite persistent or recurrent social or interpersonal problems caused or exacerbated by the effects of the alcohol (e.g., arguments with spouse about consequences of intoxication, physical fights).

Further, there are three criteria for alcohol withdrawal:

1. The development of an alcohol-specific syndrome due to the cessation of (or reduction in) alcohol use that has been heavy or prolonged.
2. The alcohol-specific syndrome causes clinically significant distress or impairment in social, occupational or other important areas of functioning.
3. The symptoms are not due to a general medical condition and are not better accounted for any another mental disorder.

It is assumed that for a significant number of young people, a sustained history of binge drinking may often predict a pattern of problematic drinking and alcohol abuse in later life.

Alcohol abuse is an increasingly serious issue and is of concern to many: politicians; advertisers and educationists, as well as health experts and the police. It is all the more so when people get involved in real *binge drinking* or drinking at work, which is especially unhealthy and dangerous. It is particularly problematic when it is associated with criminal, licentious or risky activities, like drink-driving or unprotected sex. Further, it may be associated with other illegal drug-taking activities. Over time, it can and does lead to serious physical and mental illness. There are societal costs created by excessive drinking, ranging from driving accidents to absenteeism from work, as well as impulsive behaviour and violent crime and delinquency. Table 4.1 below, consisting of data collected for the use of an article by David Nutt, Leslie King and Lawrence Phillips on behalf of the Independent Scientific Committee on Drugs in *The Lancet*, shows that of all the 'hardcore' drugs available ,alcohol tops the list of the most destructive.

Table 4.1 Harm caused by drugs in the UK

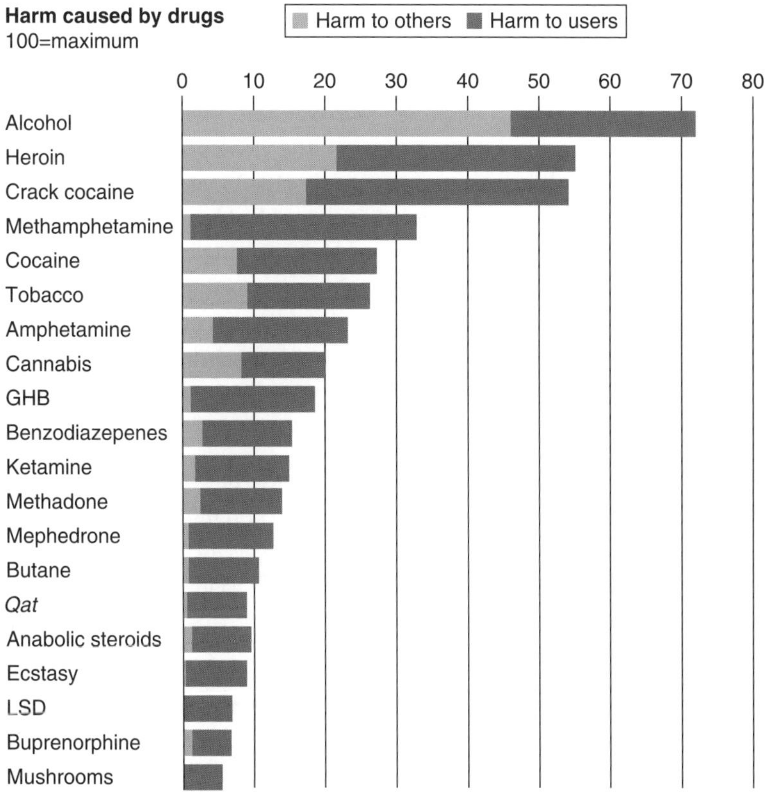

Harm caused by drugs
100=maximum

Harm to others ■ Harm to users

0 10 20 30 40 50 60 70 80

Alcohol
Heroin
Crack cocaine
Methamphetamine
Cocaine
Tobacco
Amphetamine
Cannabis
GHB
Benzodiazepenes
Ketamine
Methadone
Mephedrone
Butane
Qat
Anabolic steroids
Ecstasy
LSD
Buprenorphine
Mushrooms

Source: Nutt, King and Phillips (2010)

The causes of unhealthy drinking are both manifold and complex. Just as no simple single factor or phenomena can explain why an individual, group, community or nation seems to increase or decrease their binge drinking, equally there is no simple single cause. As a result, it is difficult to conduct research in this area. Legislators get frustrated by the equivocal and contentious nature of the research results. Further, many researchers seem to have ideological and not disinterested positions which they are not prepared to admit, but which clearly emerge in their work. However, this complexity should not prevent those interested in the area attempting a full appreciation of the issues.

The psychological effects of alcohol are well known. Alcohol makes the drinker more self-assured and more easily self-accepting. It has been called a *paradoxical stimulant* because although it is pharmacologically a depressant, it seems to act as a social stimulant, making drinkers less inhibited and more sociable. There is also evidence that doctors, politicians and diplomats themselves do (or did) drink heavily. Alcohol has symbolic and ritualistic uses. It is often used to give an enhanced sense of group cohesiveness, especially among the young.

There are many theories about the causes of alcoholism and alcohol abuse, such as biological, familial, cultural and psychological theories. Further, much work has also been undertaken on the demographic correlates of excessive drinking. We know younger people (18–34 year olds) drink more heavily than older people (those over 55 years old). Men drink more heavily than women. Younger groups are more likely to drink in bars and pubs, but this declines as people get older. Middle-class people drink less but on more occasions than working-class people. Certain trades are associated with heavy drinking and alcohol abuse: alcohol producers and retailers, heavy manual workers, business executives, travelling salesmen, journalists, entertainers, seamen and construction workers.

If one defines binge drinking as drinking twice the recommended daily allowance (more than eight units per day for men and more than six units for women), it is estimated that 29 per cent of 16–24-year-old men and 26 per cent of 16–24-year-old women fall into this bracket (Schaar Report, 2008). This trend has not changed over the past decade.

It has been pointed out that there is a contemporary British *moral panic* about young people's binge drinking and drinking in public spaces. It is believed that young people are drinking more, more often and regularly to the point of drunkenness. They start earlier, without parental knowledge or approval, and cause physical illness. For some, this is a 'problematizing' of normality.

4.5 Why do people drink?

This seemingly simple question with an obvious answer is far from straightforward. Indeed, the answer to this question dramatically illustrates the nature of the problem for those looking for easy solutions to highly complex questions. It is a long-term project to change culture and specifically the culture of drinking. From an anthropological perspective, Heath (2000: 196–8) undertook a masterful review on when, where, how, why and who drinks alcohol. His 17-point conclusion is worth summarizing here:

- Variation is an important characteristic to consider with drinking as it is with most other forms of behaviour. Patterns of behaviour will differ between populations and individuals.
- Variation within a population is as important as that between two populations. In other words, it is important to be sensitive to the rules and norms surrounding drinking for different demographic groups and social categories rather than presuming homogeneity.
- Drinking is a normal social act and the quality of social relations often tends to improve in an environment where individuals have been drinking moderately.
- Most people expect drinking to be an enjoyable activity and it usually is. Expectations about drinking are largely shaped by the shared understanding that comes from widespread experience within society.
- For that reason, the introduction of new drinks can be problematic because lack of experience in society can mean that it is only the experimental individuals who will try them out.
- Most people associate drinking with celebration and happy occasions.
- Some risk or danger is often recognized as a potential consequence of drinking, but it can usually be prevented by avoiding excess, which can vary between populations and communities.
- Drunkenness is usually viewed as risky for the individual and sometimes as dangerous for others. There are many ways of avoiding it and reducing the risks of harm, and this varies across cultures. Most cultures do not condone unfettered excessive drinking.
- Temporarily suspending the normal rules of everyday behaviour is often allowed as part of the behaviour pattern associated with drinking, but this is always subject to strict limitations.
- Alcohol, alcohol abuse and alcohol dependence are rare in most societies around the world and in history, even in the general sense of acute or chronic problem drinking.

- Societies where drinking is banned for many years and alcohol therefore holds a certain mystique and allure often tend to have young people who drink too much, too fast or for inappropriate and unrealistic reasons.
- Where drunkenness is viewed as a stupid, disgusting act or one that leads to inappropriate behaviour, it tends to be avoided. By contrast, where it is deemed 'heroic', masculine or desirable, it tends to be embraced by society.
- The quantity and frequency of drinking, both of which are often measured routinely in social surveys and by health professionals, fails accurately to represent the meanings or effects of drinking. For example, by numerically equating regular, moderate drinkers with infrequent binge drinkers, they tend to make unproblematic, normal drinking appear risky and trivialize our need to learn more about binge drinking.
- Greater attention to drinking patterns should provide a better understanding of the frequently normal role that alcohol plays in society.
- For many years, a wide variety of social and psychological benefits of moderate drinking have been recognized. In recent times, this has expanded to include physiological benefits. Such benefits, of course, cannot accurately be predicted for any given individual, so the choice must reside with the individual.
- Those who do want anything to do with alcohol and resist it should be free to leave it alone, with no pressure from society to drink.
- However, those who want to drink moderately should be confident that their behaviour is neither deviant nor indicative of addittion, but fits in well into the normal pattern of human history.

People who move from country to country and job to job become acutely aware of cultural differences in the use of and beliefs about alcohol. And, of course, drinking habits and patterns change as a result of many things, including cost, availability, role models and the availability of alternatives.

4.6 Cultural factors in alcohol use and abuse

Alcohol use and abuse is as old as man. It was consumed in Mesopotamia 5,000 years ago. The Bible in both the Old and New Testaments has parable stories and warnings about the benefits and dangers of strong drink. It seems that the message is that alcohol consumed in moderation is socially highly beneficial; indeed, wine is at the heart of both Jewish and Christian rituals.

Nearly (but not all) societies discovered alcohol and developed social conventions, mores and laws for regulating and consuming it. Climate, geography, economics, local customs and laws all influence national patterns of drinking. Immigrant groups take their patterns of drinking with them when they move, but tend over time to pick up local drinking habits.

The culture of certain socio-economic and national groups (i.e., the American Irish, the working-class Scots and the rural French) is often a powerful influence on how and how much they drink. Having been able to contrast restricted versus liberal attitudes to, as well as legislation associated with alcohol consumption, the data from Australia, the USA and Europe suggests paradoxically that liberal attitudes lead to more sensible and restrained drinking than countries and cultures that prefer rigid controls and restrictions. The question of course is cause and effect. Does liberalism lead to moderation or the other way around?

There are many socio-cultural associations with alcohol. For some, alcohol is seen as taboo, as a coping device in times of trouble, as a disinhibitor at social gatherings and as a mood changer. Alcohol consumption has been portrayed as brave, indulgent, grown-up and manly.

Drink can symbolize adulthood and independence, but it can symbolize depravity, self-indulgence and dependence. Most adults know well the 'rules' of responsible and sensible drinking:

- Drink in moderation.
- Drink for pleasure rather than to get drunk.
- Do not drink when tired or feeling ill.
- Eat when drinking.
- Drink water and soft drinks while drinking alcohol.
- Do not drink before driving, sporting activities or work.

Further, adults usually attempt to instil these behavioural rules in their children by a variety of means. In Britain about 90 per cent of the adult population drink alcohol primarily to socialize, celebrate and relax. Many quote studies that show the health benefits of moderate drinking. The alcohol industry is big in Britain: it employs around one million people and generates £7 billion in taxes per year.

Studies from around the world show the effect of culture, economics, law and policy on alcohol consumption (Grant, 1998). These show dramatic differences between countries in relation to: temporal variation in drinking; the number and characteristics of heavy drinking sessions; the social settings where drinking occurs; the activities associated with drinking; the demography of drinking groups; the types of beverages consumed; the accepted and prohibited behaviours associated with drinking; and the difference between healthy, happy drinking and that which is inappropriate, reckless and unhealthy.

Many countries have considerable religious and ethnic diversity and hence there can be very different drinking patterns within a country. Others have economic and legal infrastructure in place to try to control drinking that is considered unhealthy. Overall consumption appears to be increasing around the world and an increase in various problems is associated with it (for example, accidents and sexual activity). Curiously, even scientific societies differ in their recommendations. In Sweden, the state monopoly recommends an upper limit of alcohol, whereas in France, the French Academy of Science recommends an upper limit that is nearly 10 times higher.

There is considerable interest in European differences in drinking as well as government 'experiments' to control it. This is often portrayed as a Northern, Protestant versus Southern, Catholic difference, with guilt, restraint and taxation associated with the former. There have been many reports on the attempts of Scandinavian and Nordic countries to control binge drinking by legislative means, though it remains unclear as to whether this has been considered a success or a failure.

In contrast, 'Romanized', 'Southern Europe' or 'Mediterranean' cultures and their descendants in South America and other areas of the world do not have such great concerns about alcohol consumption. They merrily fill the drinking cup to enhance the quality of their meal and the pleasure of good company. Wine is considered part of the diet and has been since antiquity.

Such cultures frown upon drunkenness and see few problems relating to drinking, even though their per capita consumption of alcohol and liver cirrhosis rates are among the highest in the world. They have few alcohol control policies, tend to be Roman Catholic cultures, have a climate that supports viticulture and for generations had all been Roman provinces. These cultures include southern France, Spain, Portugal, Italy and Greece.

'Blended cultures' found in mid-central Western Europe and their former colonies in North America, Australasia and South Africa consume both wine and grain-based beverages, both with and without meals, and tend to frown on drunkenness. Northern-blended drinking cultures are found in the UK and its former colonies. Like Nordic cultures, they have concerns about drinking. Continental-blended cultures have more Mediterranean attitudes. In Western Europe, most blended cultures were Roman provinces in antiquity.

During the early Middle Ages, they retained the Roman urban customs of daily wine drinking and viticulture, but also incorporated the grain-based drinking preferences of the Germanic invaders and settlers into their cultures. Dominant religious beliefs include both Protestantism and Roman Catholicism. Continental-blended cultures include much of Austria and Germany, the Netherlands, Belgium, central and northern France and Switzerland.

Governments recognize and are concerned about the role of culture. In those countries with a well-established binge drinking culture, increasing access to alcohol has led to increased consumption. It remains to be seen whether the changes to the licensing laws in this country will encourage a more responsible attitude towards drinking (as the government hopes) or simply fuel a rise in binge drinking (as the medical and some other parties fear).

However, Peele and Grant (1999: 59–60) note the complexity of the cultural issue:

1. Psychoactive substance use is universal; in many non-Western societies this involves psychedelics (e.g., peyote, marijuana), opium, coca and other traditional drugs (Botswana, India, Latin America).
2. Nearly all societies have some traditional exposure to alcohol. In these societies, the supply of alcohol typically has been limited and its use highly regulated socially (Ghana, Japan, Latin America).
3. In some societies, traditional alcohol use, although planned and controlled, involves high level of consumption and intoxication (Japan, Latin America).
4. Modern societies in which alcohol is a widely available commercial product challenge, but do not eliminate, traditional drinking patterns (Ghana, India, Japan, Latin America).
5. The worst alcohol outcomes involve such disruption of traditional cultural patterns combined with overall cultural degradation and oppression (Botswana).
6. Alcohol regulation in developing nations may be sporadic and non-rationalized (Botswana, Latin America, Ghana).
7. Western styles of drinking among the economically integrated and better off in developing nations often involve more frequent but more moderate imbibing than traditional styles of drinking (Ghana, India, Japan, Latin America).
8. In this sense, the pleasure associated with drinking may need to be redefined from traditional meanings of alcohol if alcohol becomes readily available in a society.

9. Efforts to create regulated drinking in developing societies must call on both traditional and modern patterns and meanings of pleasure.

So how much do people in different cultures drink? There are interesting and important national figures on drinking and changes over time. A 2013 report (National Statistics on Alcohol) summarised its extensive 116-page report by highlighting the following points:

- 61 per cent of men and 72 per cent of women had either drunk no alcohol in the last week or had drunk within the recommended levels on the day they drank the most alcohol. This was most common among men and women aged 65 or over.
- 64 per cent of men drank no more than 21 units weekly and 63 per cent of women drank no more than 14 units weekly.
- 12 per cent of school pupils had drunk alcohol in the last week. This continues a decline from 26 per cent in 2001 and is at a similar level to 2010, when 13 per cent of pupils reported drinking in the last week.
- In 2011/12, there were 200,900 admissions where the primary diagnosis was attributable to the consumption of alcohol. This is a one per cent increase since 2010/2011, when there were 198,900 admissions of this type, and a 41 per cent increase since 2002/2003, when there were around 142,000 such admissions.
- In 2011/12, there were an estimated 1,220,300 admissions related to alcohol consumption where an alcohol-related disease, injury or condition was the primary reason for hospital admission. This is an increase of four per cent on the 2010/2011 figure (1,168,300) and more than twice as many as in 2002/2003 (510,700).

Although inconclusive, these figures suggest that binge drinking seems to be exponentially on the increase. This, coupled with the ever-increasing number of hospital admissions, makes for an uncertain future in terms of implications.

4.7 Units and recommend intakes

The strength of an alcoholic drink is indicated by the percentage of alcohol by volume (ABV). A unit corresponds to approximately 8 g (or 10 ml of pure alcohol), regardless of the amount of liquid in which it is diluted. For instance, half a pint of beer (ABV 3.5 per cent) or a small glass of wine (ABV 12–14 per cent) is the equivalent of one unit.

Guidelines issued by the Department of Health in 2013 in England (the 'lower-risk guidelines' for alcohol) state that men should not regularly drink more than 3–4 units per day and women should not regularly drink more than 2–3 units per day. 'Regularly' means drinking most days or every day. Although many people who drink do so within these guidelines, binge drinking accounts for half of all the alcohol consumed in the UK.

Drinking more than the amounts suggested by the guidelines can damage a person's health. For example, alcohol is one of the biggest behavioural risks for disease and death (along with smoking, obesity and lack of physical activity). In 2010–11, there were 1.2 million alcohol-related hospital admissions and around 15,000 deaths caused by alcohol. This is not only a burden on individuals and families, but is also a drain on hospital resources and public money: every year, alcohol-related harm costs society £21 billion.

The National Statistics report on *Adults' Behaviour and Knowledge of Drinking* in 2004 also makes interesting reading. It focused on drinkers' knowledge of units which is defined as (volume of drink in mls x alcohol by volume for that drink) ÷ 10. Most people know this as half a pint of beer, a small glass of wine or a single measure of spirits. The idea of the unit is to help people monitor their drinking. Those in the business of behaviour change always encourage behaviour monitoring and the best mechanism is through units.

The report found younger, higher-income, professional drinkers were best informed about units. It summarized its findings thus:

- Eighty-three per cent of all respondents said that they had heard of measuring alcohol consumption in units.
- Fifty-six per cent of those who had drunk beer in the last year knew that a unit is beer is half a pint, but almost one in five gave an inaccurate amount.
- Knowledge of units among both men and women had increased between 1998 and 2004: for example, the proportion of men who drank beer who knew that a unit of beer is half a pint increased from 49 per cent in 1997 to 59 per cent in 2004. Similarly, the proportion of women who drank wine who knew that a unit of wine is a glass increased from 51 per cent in 1998 to 66 per cent in 2004.
- Drinkers who knew what units were had been asked whether they kept a check on the number of units they drank: 13 per cent said that they had (similar to the 2002 figure of 11 per cent).

- There had been an increase from 54 per cent in 1997 to 61 per cent in 2004 in the proportion of the sample who had heard of daily benchmarks. There was no significant difference between men and women.
- Having heard of daily recommended levels did not necessarily mean that people knew what they were – 14 per cent thought that the recommended daily maximum for men was five units or more, and 10 per cent thought that for women, it was four units or more. There was no significant change in the knowledge of benchmark levels over the survey years.
- About one male drinker in ten (11 per cent) had discussed drinking in the last year with their GP or someone else at the surgery, or a doctor or other medical person elsewhere. Women were less likely to have had discussions (only 8 per cent had done so). There was no significant change since 2000.

In 2004, British men were consuming on average 15.2 units a week and women seven units. Around half of this was 'normal strength' beer for men, while for women it was mainly wine (37 per cent) or spirits (21 per cent). Those who drank most frequently tended to be older, professional men in higher income brackets. The Schaar Report (2008) suggests the consumption in 2008 was 18.6 units for men and 9.9 for women, but this rose to 23.5 units for men and 14.4 for women when abstainers were removed. The report found that around 40 per cent of British men and 33 per cent of women exceeded government guidelines.

In Britain it is estimated that 6.4 million people can be classified as moderate to heavy drinkers and a further 1.8 million people as very heavy drinkers. We drink less than our grandparents (nearly 25 per cent less than 1901), but more than our parents (121 per cent up on 1951). In Britain we are pretty well in the European average for consumption (Luxembourg, Ireland and Portugal being the highest and Finland and Sweden the lowest). Young people are drinking more than they used to. Interestingly, a third of British 15 year olds report having been previously drunk aged 13 or younger, but this was true of less than a tenth of French or Italian children. The greatest consumption is by 16–24 year olds, who do not drink daily, but often do so at the weekend. Aggregated over a 12-month period, the British (and the Swedes) are twice as likely to have occasions where they binge drink compared to the Italians and the French.

It has been suggested that young British women are the worst binge drinkers in the world. One recent Scottish study that looked at hazardous drinking divided it into three types: heavy (more than 14 units per week for women, 21 for men); binge (more than seven units in a day for women and ten for men) and problem drinking (based on an individual's response to a questionnaire: Emslie *et al.*, 2008). The study compared the 1990 and 2000 cohorts. Of those born in the 1930s, 17 per cent of men and two per cent of women were categorized as binge drinkers, for those born in the 1950s, the numbers rose to 35 per cent for men and nine per cent for women, while for those born in the 1970s, it had increased again to 47 per cent for men and 22 per cent for women in the 1990 cohort. Figures were similar for the 2000 cohort. Alcohol consumption had gone up. Men, particularly younger men, were more likely to be classified as heavy or binge drinkers. In the 1990 cohort, 47.2 per cent of people in the youngest group were classified as binge drinkers. The study found a significant change in young women's drinking habits, which was attributed to sociological factors.

4.8 Alcohol in the workplace

Research by the charity Alcohol Concern estimates that there are 1.6 million drinkers in the UK who are considered to be dependent drinkers and a total of 7.6 million who drink over the safe drinking guidelines. And contrary to popular belief, most of these individuals are in work, therefore presenting a real problem for employers that must be dealt with. In the USA, it is estimated that out of the total number of adults in full-time employment, nearly 15 million are heavy drinkers of alcohol.

The Health and Safety Executive (HSE) in a 2011 report highlighted two main kinds of drinking behaviour which significantly contribute to the level of work performance problems:

- *Alcohol-related absenteeism and sickness absence*: alcohol is estimated to cause 3–5 per cent of all absences from work, amounting to about 8 to 14 million lost working days in the UK each year.
- *The effects of drinking on productivity and safety*: alcohol consumption may result in reduced work performance, damaged customer relations and resentment among employees who have to make up for colleagues whose work declines because of their drinking. Safety is also a key factor, especially where there has been drinking before or during working hours or heavy drinking that causes hangovers the next day. It is widely accepted that drinking even small amounts of alcohol before or while carrying out work that is 'safety sensitive' will increase the risk of an accident.

Other problems that alcoholics can create at work include:

- poor performance on the job;
- tardiness/sleeping on the job;
- theft or damage to property;
- poor decision making;
- loss of efficiency;
- lower morale of co-workers;
- impact on relationships with co-workers/supervisors;
- higher turnover of staff;
- costs of training new employees or temporary staff who are needed to replace the alcoholic worker;
- costs of disciplinary procedures.

It is worth noting that it is not just dependent drinkers or alcoholics who generate problems in the workplace. The majority of alcohol-related work performance problems are typically associated with non-dependent drinkers who may occasionally drink quantities deemed to be over the safe drinking guidelines. Furthermore, family members living and coping with someone with problems with alcohol may also suffer significant job performance-related problems, including poor job performance, lack of focus on the task in hand, absenteeism and increased health-related problems.

In the USA, the National Council on Alcoholism and Drug Dependence reported the following facts about alcohol in the workplace:

- Workers with alcohol problems were 2.7 times more likely than workers without drinking problems to have injury-related absences.
- A hospital emergency department study showed that 35 per cent of patients with an occupational injury were at-risk drinkers.
- Breathalyzer tests detected alcohol in 16 per cent of emergency room patients injured at work.
- Analyses of workplace fatalities showed that at least 11 per cent of the victims had been drinking.
- Large federal surveys show that 24 per cent of workers report drinking during the workday least once in the past year.
- One-fifth of workers and managers across a wide range of industries and company sizes report that a co-worker's on- or off-the-job drinking jeopardized their own productivity and safety.

It is clear that alcohol abuse and dependency is a serious problem that managers must consider. It is one of the most prevalent mental disorders likely to impact on people at work and there are a number of steps that can be taken to help manage this growing epidemic.

4.9 Managing people with alcohol and drug problems

In the UK, employers (and employees) are required by law to address the issue of alcohol and drugs in the workplace under the following legislation:

- the Health and Safety at Work Act 1974;
- the Management of Health and Safety at Work Regulations 1999;
- the Misuse of Drugs Act 1971.

However, these statutory obligations often do little more than ensure that employers are carrying out the minimum requirements and offer very little practical day-to-day advice for managers and colleagues dealing with an alcoholic person in the workplace.

In the UK, it is estimated that less than 60 per cent of employers have a policy that covers drug and alcohol misuse at work and this is often focused on how to deal with employees from a disciplinary perspective rather than a supportive one. Only a minority of organizations proactively communicate such policies to all employees and less than 25 per cent of organizations train staff in how to handle the issue in an effective way (CIPD, 2007).

The provision of access to occupational health services is the most commonly provided support to help prevent individuals developing drug and alcohol problems, with almost 60 per cent of organizations surveyed in a 2007 study in the UK offering this kind of support.

This can be an effective way of dealing with alcoholism and other drug issues. Many individuals and their families face a host of difficulties closely associated with addiction and these problems inevitably spill over into the workplace. If employers are able to promote and offer assistance and support treatment, some of the negative aspects can be reduced.

Research has shown that alcohol treatment pays for itself in reduced healthcare costs, improved functioning and increased productivity almost as soon as the individual has accessed the treatment. There is considerable evidence of workplace employee assistance programmes helping millions of individuals and family members affected by alcohol problems.

Alcohol treatment pays for itself in reduced healthcare costs

4.10 Summary

Most people have worked with or for someone with an addiction. Despite one's best efforts, it is difficult to hide addictions from one's work colleagues. Yet although one might suspect serious addiction, it is not always clear what to do and there are cases of people with chronic addictions never being challenged or helped in the workplace.

There are other addictions – for instance, to gambling – which we have not dealt with here. There is also a very fine line between the heavy drinker and the functioning alcoholic as well as between the recreational drug taker and the drug addict.

Many factors, such as personal illness or tragedy, lead people to become heavily dependent on drink and drugs. People can find it very difficult to come off anti-depressants and painkillers as well as sleeping pills. Many organizations attempt to control the possibility of addictions: staff have to have liver check-ups and drinking in certain buildings is forbidden. Yet problems remain, particularly in certain work environments and cultures.

chapter 5

Workaholism

5.1 Introduction

Workaholism is not the same as working hard. A workaholic is a person who is addicted to work. Whilst there is no generally accepted medical definition of such a condition, we have included this chapter to highlight a fairly serious condition that managers and employers must be on the look-out for.

WORKAHOLISM: A SLIPPERY SLOPE

It's Saturday night and Ben is at home ... working ... again. He is 36 and this would normally be the time to relax with a few cold beers and unwind after a long week, but not anymore. Ever since he received a big promotion nine months ago, he has decided that work has to come first. Besides, he tells himself, working at home isn't that bad every now and again, right?

The problem is that it isn't just every now and again and he has recently noticed that some of his close friends have stopped calling him to invite him to take part in social activities. He hasn't seen his family in many months and his once highly trained runner's physique has begun to look suspiciously like middle-age spread as he no longer has time to exercise and maintain a healthy diet.

'Workaholic' can often sound like a buzzword for overachievers, but in today's competitive workplace, workaholism is a very common problem that is characterized by an addiction to work. Just like any addiction, it is a serious cause for concern for the workaholic, their immediate family and their friends. Their boss might think that a workaholic's long hours and superhuman work ethic are great for business, but often this is not the case.

Ben has been called a 'workaholic' on many occasions, most recently by his ex-girlfriend as she packed up her things and stormed out of his apartment. He tells himself that he is doing the right thing for his career and secretly he feels it is quite an honourable thing to devote so much of himself to his job, but what he doesn't realize is that in the long run his behaviour will hurt his career more than it will help it.

5.2 The early literature

Oates (1971) claimed to have invented the term 'workaholic', meaning the addiction to work and the compulsion or the uncontrollable need to work incessantly. But unlike other forms of addiction, which are held in contempt, workaholism is frequently lauded, praised, expected and even demanded. According to Oates, signs of this 'syndrome' included boasting about the number of hours worked, comparisons between an individual and others in terms of the amount of work achieved, an inability to refuse requests for work and general competitiveness:

> The workaholic's way of life is considered in America to be one and the same time (a) a religious virtue, (b) a form of patriotism, (c) the way to win friends and influence people, (d) the way to be healthy and wise. Therefore the workaholic, plagued though he is, is unlikely to change. Why? Because he is sort of a paragon of virtue … he is the one chosen as 'the most likely to succeed'. (Oates, 1971: 12)

Oates presented a very Christian perspective of the problem. He was a professor of the psychology of religion and examined the notion of 'Sunday neurosis' or the difficulty for a workaholic of coping with a 'work-free weekend'. He offered six pieces of advice to the workaholic:

- Admit that you are a workaholic and are powerless to do anything about it without help beyond yourself.

- Make an honest inventory of all the busy-work you do which is not essential or part of your job and stop doing this work.
- Make a plan to spend part of each weekend in meditation.
- Remember something that you enjoyed doing when you were a teenager and do it again.
- If you read at all, find something you do not have to read as part of your job.
- Meet some new people you have not met before and renew contact with some old acquaintances with whom you have lost touch.

Other advice includes re-evaluating the whole economy, pattern, productivity and purpose of holidays. The dangers of workaholism are seen to be not only the physical and mental illness of the workaholic themselves, but also of their spouse, who might become hyperactive or alcoholic, and their children.

As is customary with popularist expositions of a psychological variable, a taxonomy was provided by Oates (1971), who listed five types of workaholic:

1. *Dyed-in-the-wool* – a person with five major characteristics: high standards of professionalism; a tendency to perfectionism; vigorous intolerance of incompetence; overcommitment to institutions and organizations; and highly talented and thus in demand by employers.
2. *Converted* – a person who has given up the above but may behave like a workaholic on occasions for the rewards of money or prestige.
3. *Situational* – workaholism not for psychological or prestige reasons, but for necessity within an organization.
4. *Pseudo-workaholic* – someone who may look on occasion to be a workaholic but who has none of the commitment and dedication of a true dyed-in-the-wool character.
5. *Escapist* – someone who remains in the office simply to avoid going home or taking part in social relationships.

Finally, Oates considered the religion of the workaholic. He argued that they are worried by the future with its meaninglessness and hopelessness. Workaholics tend to be unforgiving and lacking in a sense of irony and humour, as well as a sense of wonder and awe. Once these characteristics are renounced, a workaholic experiences a much better quality of life.

Machlowitz (1980) has defined workaholics as people whose desire to work long and hard is intrinsic and whose work habits almost always exceed the prescriptions of the job they do and the expectations of the people with whom or for whom they work. According to him, all true workaholics are intense, energetic, competitive and driven, but also have *strong self-doubt*.

They prefer hard work to leisure and can – and do – work anytime and anywhere. They tend to work for the majority of their time and blur the distinctions between business and pleasure. All workaholics have these traits, but they may be subdivided into four distinct types:

- The *dedicated* workaholic is quintessentially the single-minded, one-dimensional person frequently described by laypeople and journalists. They shun leisure and are often humourless and brusque.
- The *integrated* workaholic does integrate outside features into their work. Thus, although work is 'everything', it sometimes includes extracurricular interests.
- The *diffuse* workaholic has numerous interests, connections and pursuits which are far more varied than those of the integrated workaholic. Furthermore, such people may change jobs fairly frequently in pursuit of their ends.
- The *intense* workaholic approaches leisure and hobbies (frequently competitive sport) with the same passion, pace and intensity as they show at work. They become as preoccupied by outside interests as they do with their work.

To some extent, it is thought that workaholism is an *obsessive-compulsive neurosis* characterized by sharp, narrowed, focused attention, endless activity, ritualistic behaviours and a 'strong desire to be in control'. It is perhaps linked to perfectionism, pathological ambition and even the OCD personality disorder.

However, the aetiology of this 'syndrome' is seen to lie in childhood, where workaholism is fairly easily recognized. Machlowitz (1980) argues that some children are driven from within, but others are pushed by their parents, for example, by reinforcement. In other words, parents threaten to withdraw love if ever-increasing expectations are not fulfilled:

> Seeing parental love as contingent on achievement instead of unconditional surely spurs progress, but it may also be the source of self-doubts … success is self-perpetuating, but the promise of failure is even more propelling and compelling. (Machlowitz, 1980: 41–2)

Further, parents may encourage workaholism by providing a model for their children. But because they are so busy, they may be poor parents in that they are inattentive or simply exhausted when at home. To find workaholics at play may simply be an oxymoron.

To find workaholics at play may simply be an oxymoron

Machlowitz offered a number of reasons why workaholics shun vacations and time off. They have never had a good experience of holidays for the following reasons: because they have expected too much or chose the wrong type of break; as their jobs are their passion, they do not feel that they need to get away from it all; traditional forms of recreation seem like a waste of time and incomprehensible to them; the preparation for and anxiety that precedes taking a holiday are more trouble than they are worth; and, finally, they are afraid that they would lose complete control of their jobs if they left for a holiday.

However, many workaholics do report being remarkably satisfied and content with their lives. Machlowitz found little difference between workaholic men and women's sources of joy and frustration. These were fourfold: whether in their home life, they felt free of the responsibility for supervising or performing household duties; whether their job offered them autonomy, control and variety; whether their job needed their 'particular' skills and working styles; and whether they felt healthy and fit for work. Though they appear to never feel successful, many non-frustrated workaholics do report happiness. Finally, Machlowitz offered some advice for workaholics in order to maximize the pleasures and minimize the pressures of this particular lifestyle:

- Find the job that fits – one that exercises your skills and abilities.
- Find the place that fits – one that provides the most convivial environment.
- Find the pace that fits – one that makes it possible to work at the most desirable speed.
- Create challenges in your work to deal with pressures effectively.
- Diversify each day because of potential short attention spans.
- Make sure that every day is different to improve levels of stimulation.
- Use your time; don't let it use you – establish your own circadian rhythm and plan your day around it.
- Don't deliberate excessively on decisions that don't warrant the attention.
- Let others do things for you – learn how to delegate.
- Work alone or only hire other workaholics to prevent intolerance and impatience with others.
- Become a mentor, teacher, guide and counsellor to others.
- Make sure you make time for what matters to you, such as your family or leisure pursuits.
- Get professional help if you have a job, home or health crisis as a result of your lifestyle.

The early thinking on the topic was of a more popular nature. It caught the Zeitgeist where the work-life balance was thought to be a good thing. Studies tended to emphasize all the downsides of workaholism, like problems with self-concept, rigid thinking, withdrawal symptoms, the progressive nature of the condition and denial of the problem (Porter, 1996). Many reviewers listed all the negative behavioural, emotional, interpersonal, physical, interpersonal and physical problems associated with workaholism (Gini, 1998), though some workaholism related to successful work outcomes (Burke, 2001). The workaholic was seen as a person trying to improve their personal feelings of low self-worth and insecurity. Gini (1998) suggested workaholism as a failed attempt to overcome the emptiness or unhappiness in people's lives: a cure for metaphysical angst! Some researchers even attempted to document the prevalence of workaholism. Burke (2000) made estimates of five per cent of the overall (American) population to 10–20 per cent of people in very specific careers like medicine, law and general management.

Over the last 20 years, there have been some important studies which have attempt to clarify the definition of workaholism and also to describe both the origin of the syndrome as well as the mechanisms and processes by which it operates.

5.3 Later work

Research in the topic of workaholism and related topics like burnout and engagement over the past 30 years has attempted to describe and delineate the syndrome of high work involvement and drive to work, but low work enjoyment (Aziz and Zickar, 2006; Swider and Zimmerman, 2010). It is a study of the *joylessness of work*, but almost exclusively with white-collar as opposed to blue-collar workers. Workaholism is often thought of as working both excessively and compulsively (Van den Broeck *et al.*, 2011).

The current interest around this topic is actually in the very opposite of workaholism, namely work engagement characterized by vigour, energy, resilience, dedication, enthusiasm, pride, absorption and engrossment at work (Van Beek *et al.*, 2012).

There have been some impressive attempts to build a model of the antecedents, consequences and dimensions of workaholism, such as that of Ng, Sorensen and Feldman (2007). The model specifies three types of antecedants (dispositions, socio-cultural experiences and behavioural reinforcements), dimensions of workaholism (affect, cognitive and behavioural), consequences (satisfaction, mental health and career success) and overall long-term and short-term performance.

The rise of interest in the concept of work engagement has led to an attempt to differentiate related and opposite concepts like burnout and engagement. Thus, Schaufeli, Taris and van Rhenen (2008) showed that burnout and engagement were opposites, but that workaholics and the work engaged shared some factors like excess working time as well as job satisfaction and organizational commitment.

Workaholism has been studied as the main predictor of problems at work, but also as a moderator and mediator variable (Alarcon, 2011; Taris, van Beek and Schaufeli, 2010). Some have looked at the issue of workaholism and marital estrangement and have considered whether worksholism is a cause or consequence of marital difficulties and breakdown (Yaniv, 2011). Thus, spending too much time at work may be seen as a cause of relationship break-ups, but equally work may be seen as a refuge from an unhappy marriage, which is often the case for the escapist workaholic.

Much of the research has been concerned with definitions and distinctions, using different methodology like distinguishing between the work enthusiast, the workaholic, the enthusiastic workaholic, the unengaged worker, the relaxed worker and the disenchanted worker (Spence and Robbins, 1992). Van Beek, Taris and Schaufeli (2011) in fact conceived of the engaged workaholic who did not experience burnout and had many components similar to those of genuinely engaged workers like autonomous motivation. Others too have tried to differentiate between passion for work as opposed to addiction at work (Burke and Fiksenbaum, 2009). Harpaz and Snir (2003) reference the idea of work centrality: the idea that people allocate considerable amounts of time to work-related activities and thoughts because work is more important than leisure, community, family and religion. They believe it stems from the Protestant Work Ethic viewpoint that work redeems the believer because it is a virtue, while play is a sin. Some reviewers want to move on from the concept of workaholism to things like 'heavy work investment' (Harpaz and Snir, 2003).

Many have argued that the essential criterion of a workaholic is a combination of excessive working and compulsive working. It is funless, joylessness at work which leads to mental and physical ill-health (Gorgievski and Bakker, 2010).

Some studies have looked at very specific issues, while others have focused on personality. Burke, Matthiesen and Pallensen (2006) found that extroversion was positively correlated with work involvement and joy in work, while neuroticism was related to the feeling of being driven to work. Thus, Clark, Lelchook and Taylor (2010) found that workaholics tended to be neurotic, narcissistic and characterized by negative affectivity and high standards. Andreassen, Hetland and Pallesen (2010) found weak but explicable correlations between personality and two features of workaholism: enjoyment (positive) and drive (negative). Conscientiousness correlated with both positive and negative facets; extroversion and openness correlated with the positive facet and neuroticism with the negative facet.

Evidence would suggest, therefore, that the term 'workaholic' may be slightly misleading and that in some instances it can be a positive indicator of engagement and passion. As a result, the tide seems to have turned and most researchers have extended their focus to examine passion and joy at work

5.4 Work passion

Over a 20-year period, Vallerand and his colleagues worked on the psychology of passion. Vallerand (2008: 1) defined passion as a 'strong inclination toward an activity that people like, find important and in which they invest their time and energy'. Over time, people discover that some activities rather than others seem to satisfy their needs for competence, autonomy and relatedness. They thus become a passionate, self-defining, identity-determining activity into which people invest their time and energy. Passion has powerful affective outcomes and relates strongly to the persistence in various activities.

Vallerand distinguished between a healthy harmonious passion (HP) and unhealthy obsessive passion (OP). He suggests that HP is the autonomous internalization of an activity into a person's identity when they freely accept the activity as important to them. This is done with volition and not compunction. HP for an activity is a significant but not overpowering part of identity and is in harmony with other aspects of a person's life. On the other hand, the drivers of OP are essentially specific contingencies like self-esteem, excitement or self-acceptance. People feel compelled to engage in particular activities because of these contingencies, which then come to control them. OP clearly has an addictive quality about it because it is perhaps the only source of important psychological rewards. In this sense, workaholism is a sign of OP, not HP.

This theory suggests that HP leads to more *flexible* task engagement, which in turn leads to more engagement through the process of absorption, concentration, flow and positive effect. OP, on the other hand, leads to more *rigid and conflicted* task performance, which reduces engagement. HP controls the activity, while OP is controlled by it. The former promotes healthy adaptation, while the latter thwarts it.

This work has been applied to behaviour in the workplace. Vallerand and Houlfort (2003) developed a relatively simple model which suggests that HP but not OP predicts psychological adjustment at work. They argued that passion has long-term consequences. OP workers seem akin to workaholics, while HP workers show greater job satisfaction and performance. Passion is related to affect at work, work-family conflict, turnover, health and performance.

Vallerand *et al.* (2010) showed that HP was positively correlated with work satisfaction, which in turn was negatively correlated with burnout, while OP was strongly correlated with conflict, which in turn was correlated with burnout.

The question is *how* can organizations encourage HP rather than OP in their workplace? The answer is to 'provide employees with a healthy, flexible, and secure working environment, one where their opinion is valued, will create conditions that facilitate the development of harmonious passion … organisational support seems to foster an autonomous-supportive context that allows individuals to internalise the activity in their identity in an autonomous fashion' (Vallerand *et al.*, 2010: 193).

Others have been inspired by Vallerand's work. Thus, Burke and Fiksenbaum (2009) administered a questionnaire which measured 'feeling driven to work because of inner pressure' and 'work enjoyment', which they called *passion* and *addiction*, to different groups in Australia, Canada and Norway. They found that those who scored higher on passion than addiction were more heavily invested in their work and had greater job satisfaction, while showing less work obsessive behaviours and higher psychological well-being. Equally, Gorgievski and Bakker (2010) distinguished between *work engagement* and *workaholism.*

5.5 The manifestations and correlates of passion at work

5.5.1 Energy and vigour at work

Personal energy is equally important and has various components. The *first* is *physical energy*. Older people have less energy than younger people. Sick people have less energy than well people. Sleep-deprived people are less energetic than the well-rested.

The *second* is *psychological energy*. This has been conceived of in different ways. The Freudians conceived of a psychic energy: a force that drives us to want and do things we barely understand. Thus, we can be driven to irrational and bizarre behaviours because of these unconscious libidinous springs.

Personality factors are related to energy. Extroverts appear more (socially) energetic, but burn up easily with their impulsivity and impatience. Introverts have a much slower burning fuse and are able to sustain longer periods of attentiveness under conditions of poor arousal. Neurotics waste their energy, burning it up on the irrelevant and the imaginary. They can easily become anxious and then depressed by small things. They fritter away their additional nervous energy rather than conserve it for the long haul or the really important things. Paradoxically, then, they appear to have more energy than their stable opposites, but waste it on worry and end up exhausted.

The *third* is *intellectual energy*. The bright have more intellectual energy: more curiosity and more openness to new experiences. They use their energy more efficiently. Indeed, one definition of intelligence is about energy-efficient brain processing.

Shirom (2011) has defined this as physical strength, emotional energy and cognitive liveliness. He argues that genetic, physiological and psychological factors impact on vigour, which in turn is related to job performance and satisfaction, as well as physical and mental health. He sees vigour as a personal resource related to energy and the way it can be directed in the workplace. His argument is that vigour predicts interaction with others at work and leadership style as well as group processes and the use of organizational resources to be successful at work.

5.5.2 Flow

Over 15 years ago, a Transylvanian psychologist called Mihaly Csikszentmihalyi wrote a book called *Flow*. People felt best, he found, when *engrossed* in some challenging activity. During flow, they lost track of time, felt more capable, more sensitive and more self-confident, even though the activities were work-based challenges. The activity was its own reward. Flow banishes depression, distraction and creeping dispiritedness. So what are the preconditions of flow?

Csíkszentmihályi identified the following factors as accompanying an experience of flow:

1. *Clear goals* – expectations and rules are discernible and goals are attainable and align appropriately with one's skill set and abilitie). The challenge level and skill level should both be high.

2. *Concentrating* – a high degree of concentration on a limited field of attention (a person engaged in the activity will have the opportunity to focus and to delve deeply into it).
3. *A loss of the feeling of self-consciousness* – the merging of action and awareness.
4. *Distorted sense of time* – one's subjective experience of time is altered.
5. Direct and immediate *feedback* – successes and failures in the course of the activity are apparent so that behaviour can be adjusted as needed.
6. *Balance between ability level and challenge* – the activity is neither too easy nor too difficult.
7. A sense of personal *control* over the situation or activity.
8. The activity is *intrinsically rewarding* – there is an effortlessness of action.
9. A *lack of awareness of bodily needs* – to the extent that one can reach a point of great hunger or fatigue without realizing it.
10. Absorption into the activity, narrowing of the focus of awareness down to the activity itself, *action awareness merging*.

Vallerand (2008) sees Flow as the consequence of harmonious passion. Thus, for flow to be experienced at work, a person needs to have a clear goal in mind, reasonable expectations of completing satisfactorily the goal in mind, the ability to concentrate, regular and specific feedback on their performance and the appropriate skills to complete the task.

We all know the Flow experience both at home and work. One can observe flow in those jobs where people experience the greatest work satisfaction. Such people include artisans – potters and painters, writers and weavers, thatchers and designers. They exercise their talents, work at their own pace and are not alienated from the products of their labours; indeed, they are the products of their labour. They are what they produce and are bound up in the product. Their identity, their being is in the product of their talents.

5.6 Managing a workaholic

In today's post-recession era, it can be tempting for managers to encourage their staff to work harder and longer. However, the results can be counterproductive and if it appears that an employee's passion and effort is manifesting itself in a negative way, then there are a number of things that a manager can do to help the employee regain some balance:

- *Lead by example* – leave the office at a reasonable time and avoid sending excessive emails after hours. If you do need to catch up on emails in the evenings or at weekends, make use of the tools and tricks on your email software to delay the time at which they get sent. This sends a message to the workaholics in your team that excessive work at the weekends and evenings is not the norm.

- *Encourage extracurricular activities* – talk about the fun you had over the weekend, but also point out how non-office experiences help your creativity on the job. The best way to subtly nudge a workaholic into expanding their activities is to tie outside activities to work in some way. Similarly, organizing regular opportunities for team activities outside work may also help if the workaholic can see how engaging in this type of activity may help them at work.
- *Help them to prioritize* – keep the employee focused on a limited set of priorities with defined tasks. Workaholics are driven to overcommit and go beyond what is asked of them, so if you can get into a habit of being very specific about expectations, it will help them over time to just focus on those important tasks.
- *Don't reinforce the behaviour* – workaholism is an addiction; you don't want to enable a workaholic further by legitimizing the belief that they are overloaded. Workaholics often overload themselves. Avoid offering to pick up some of their extra work because they will inevitably find something else to fill the void. Also resist the temptation to take advantage of their addiction by giving them more to do, especially when the team is overstretched.

5.7 Summary

This chapter has been about work addiction: the idea that people spend excessive time and effort in the workplace trying to achieve some end, but essentially failing. Psychological concepts like workaholism tend to go through phases. Once the description/discovery is made, some effort is spent in clarifying it and often coming up with subtypes or factors. This often leads to measurement issues and model building. The research on workaholism is no exception. The literature is now 40 years old and is considerably more sophisticated than it was. We are now much clearer about the components and antecedents of workaholism. Perhaps the greatest change has been to see some of the positive sides of what was previously thought of as almost exclusively negative. Spending a long time at work can be seen as positive and can have many positive consequences. Managers can play a role in ensuring the impact is positive and acting appropriately when they believe the situation has become negative.

chapter 6

Sector-Specific Illnesses

6.1 Introduction

So far, we have explored the mental illnesses and personality disorders that can rear their head in the workplace. We have also examined the nature of these conditions and how they might manifest themselves in a workplace setting. But how does a manager identify the illness or illnesses that their staff may be most susceptible to? Is it possible to consider the context of any particular business and identify if there is a higher risk of one particular illness? The indications seem to suggest that the answer to this question is yes.

Kets de Vries and Miller (1984) propose that whole organizations, for example, can be neurotic – paranoid, compulsive or depressive. Sometimes these patterns of behaviour may reflect the style of the leader or leadership team and this can in turn permeate the entire organization. They argue that neurotic senior managers influence the organizational style in their image. Strategy, process, structure, selection and even advertising reflect their personal pathology. Powerful but disturbed leaders create businesses in their image in order to deal (often unsuccessfully) with their personal pathologies. Thus, the whole organization takes on the pathology of the single manager. We shall revisit these concepts in Chapter 7. What Kets de Vries does is to take selective personality disorder categories and show how powerful leaders with these psychiatric disorders actually form a company in their own image that shares similar pathologies.

Kets de Vries identifies five neurotic styles, though to be accurate some are actually psychotic (Kets de Vries and Miller, 1984):

1. The *paranoid organization*: when power is highly centralized in a leader with paranoid tendencies ('everybody is out to get me'), there will tend to be a great deal of vigilance caused by distrust of subordinates and competitors alike. This may lead to the development of many control and information systems and a conspiratorial fascination with gathering intelligence from inside and outside the firm. Paranoid thinking will also lead to a centralization of power as the top executive tries to control everything themselves (nobody can be completely trusted). The strategy is likely to emphasize 'protection' and reducing dependency on particular consultants, sources of data, markets or customers. There is likely to be a good deal of diversification, with tight control over divisions and much analytical activity. A leader who is obsessed with fantasies relating to distrust can set a very distinctive tone for the strategy, structure and culture of an organization.

   The characteristics of these organizations are: suspiciousness and mistrust of others; hypersensitivity and hyper-alertness; readiness to combat perceived threats; excessive concern with hidden motives and special meanings; intense attention span; and cold, rational and unemotional interpersonal relations. The paranoid organization is defensive and hyper-vigilant. It is pervaded by an atmosphere of distrust. However, this can have benefits – certainly, such organizations will be alert to threats and opportunities both inside and outside of it. This is perhaps only a small advantage though and at a great cost.
2. An obsessive-compulsive manager leads to the development of a *compulsive organization*. Such an organization emphasizes ritual; it plans every detail in advance and carries out its activities in a routine, pre-programmed style. Thoroughness and conformity are valued. Such organizations are hierarchical and generally have elaborate policies, rules and procedures. The strategies of compulsive firms reflect their preoccupation with detail and established rituals. Each compulsive organization has a distinctive area of competence and specializes in this area, whether or not the area is related to the market or sector in which they operate .

   For Kets de Vries and Miller (1984), these organizations are characterized by: perfectionism; preoccupation with trivial details; insistence that others submit to an established way of doing things; relationships defined in terms of dominance and submission; lack of spontaneity; inability to relax; and meticulousness, dogmatism and obstinacy.

Compulsive managers are inward looking, indecisive, cautious and fearful about making mistakes. They are deeply involved in the minutiae of facts and figures, and love promulgating rules and regulations to make their lives easier. They are often inflexible, oriented towards the past and unwilling to change. They typically have excellent internal control and audit mechanisms and well-integrated procedures, but all too often they are anachronistic bureaucracies that seem out of touch with the flexible and adaptive companies of today. The faster the world changes, the more incompetent they are … change is an enemy, not an opportunity.

3. The impulsive, creative, intuitive manager will also stamp their organization in characteristic ways. The *dramatic organization* that results is hyperactive, impulsive and uninhibited. In such an organization, decision makers prefer to act on hunches and impressions, and take on widely diverse projects. Top managers reserve the right to start bold ventures independently; subordinates have limited power.

   Such organizations are characterized by: self-dramatization and excessive emotional displays; incessant self-displays organized around crises; a need for activity and excitement; an alternation between the idealization and devaluation of others; exploitativeness; and an inability to concentrate or sharply focus attention.

   Dramatic managers are not risk averse. They often make rash, intuitive decisions, swinging company policy in radically different directions. They are impulsive and unpredictable. At their best, they can revitalize tired companies and provide the necessary momentum at crucial periods in a company's history (such as during mergers and acquisitions or the start-up phase), but most of the time they simply create instability, chaos and distress. A major task of any manager is to bring order and predictability to business issues, not the opposite.

4. Many people are prone to depression or may experience periods of depression caused by stress or trauma. But some managers seem always to have depressive symptoms and this can lead to *depressive organizations*. The depressive organization lacks confidence, is inactive, conservative, insular and has an entrenched bureaucracy. The only things that get done are routine activities. Such organizations are well established and often serve a single mature market.

   The characteristics of a depressive manager and the organization they create in their own image are: feelings of guilt, worthlessness, self-reproach, inadequacy and a sense of helplessness and hopefulness – of being at the mercy of events; a diminished ability to think clearly; a loss of interest and motivation; and an inability to experience pleasure.

Depressives are negative, pessimistic and inhibited. Apathetic, inactive and hopeless managers are prevalent in these organizations. The gloom pervades everything.

5. The *schizoid organization* lacks leadership. Its top executive discourages interaction. Sometimes the second level of executives makes up for the leader's lack of involvement, but often they simply fight to fill the leadership vacuum. In such organizations, strategy often reflects individual goals and internal politics rather than the external threats or opportunities that the organization needs to take into account.

   These organizations are characterized by: detachment, non-involvement and a sense of withdrawal; a sense of estrangement; a lack of excitement or enthusiasm; an indifference to praise or criticism; a lack of interest in the present or the future; and a cold and unemotional climate. These organizations are quite political and the resulting climate of distrust inhibits normal collaboration.

Kets de Vries suggests that the unconscious and neurotic needs of the key people in an organization lead them to do things to the organization that create incompetence. Observations suggest that neurotic managers choose, create and maintain dysfunctional work groups that have shared organizational myths, and these myths often distract them from their primary tasks. Their neuroticism means that they transfer their anxieties and odd imaginings onto their staff (superiors, subordinates, peers and even shareholders and customers) and this frustrates and angers staff who may be somehow bound to or curiously abandoned by their neurotic managers.

In this chapter we will examine some of the trends that can lead to mental illness occurring more in certain sectors than others and will offer some thoughts on how managers can use this awareness to improve outcomes for their employees.

6.2 Career selection

There are numerous reasons why individuals choose certain careers and certain sectors. Typically, both positive and negative personality traits play a part in vocational selection and Chatman, Wong and Joyce (2008) have noted how the process of *attraction-selection-attrition* (ASA) leads organizations and groups within them to become increasingly homogeneous. In other words, an individual may be attracted to a certain organization or sector because of a belief that their personality, abilities and values will align with the culture of the organization and that in turn this will lead to career success for them. Their tendency to exhibit certain traits may then be magnified depending on the degree to which these traits are commonplace and are even rewarded by the organization. In the previous chapter we explored workaholism and in this case it is easy to imagine how certain organizations could reinforce and reward such behaviour.

The idea that some disorders, addictions and illnesses may be beneficial in certain occupations has been noted by many writers, particularly those using clinical case studies where personality disorders in particular have been examined in detail. Whilst some disorders are rarely associated with success in any jobs (borderline, avoidant), others have been implicated as potentially beneficial (narcissistic, anti-social and obsessive-compulsive). There is also evidence to suggest that this will vary between different job types and sectors; for example, schizotypal disorder is often associated with creativity, innovation and sales potential. There has also been speculation (although few studies) on the prevalence of these various disorders in those who choose to work in different sectors, particularly in relation to differences between private and public sector workers (Brewer and Brewer, 2011; Lyons, Duxbury and Higgins, 2006).

Over the years, work psychologists have compared the motives, traits and values of people in different sectors and in different job, trying of course to control for age, education and the like. Further, by and large, some of the stereotypes have been confirmed. Thus, people in the private sector are often more materialistic and are driven more by extrinsic factors. Overall, they are less committed to their organization and are happier to take risks. They tend to express more job satisfaction and cope better with ambiguity.

Those in the public sector have been shown to value work-life balance issues more highly. They seem more sensitive to having good relationships in the office and see the work ethic as both outmoded and unhealthy.

Furnham, Hyde and Trickey (2013) showed that comparative groups from the private and public sectors had very different 'dark side' profiles (see Table 6.1). People in the private sector were much more bold, mischievous and colourful, for which read arrogant, adventurous and melodramatic. They are tended to be more eccentric, imaginative and quirky, and less trusting, being ever vigilant of what was going on. Those in the public sector were more cautious and sensitive to criticism, as well as more reserved and detached, hence the difference in corporate cultures between the two sectors.

Table 6.1 Means of the public and private sectors showing dark side trait and higher-order factors against population norms

DSM IV Descriptor	Hogan Descriptor	Public		Private	
		Mean	SD	Mean	SD
Borderline	Excitable	3.19	2.79	3.23	2.57
Paranoid	Sceptical	4.49	2.65	4.75	2.39
Avoidant	Cautious	3.58	2.80	3.30	2.47
Schizoid	Reserved	4.41	2.34	4.19	2.06
Passive-aggressive	Leisurely	4.99	2.31	4.81	2.25
Narcissistic	Bold	6.63	2.66	7.53	2.62
Anti-social	Mischievous	6.15	2.46	7.06	2.43
Histrionic	Colourful	7.20	2.97	8.06	3.00
Schizotypal	Imaginative	5.20	2.31	5.52	2.29
Obsessive-compulsive	Diligent	8.96	2.49	8.84	2.60
Dependent	Dutiful	7.33	2.11	7.23	2.14
Moving away		1.28	1.21	0.97	1.17
Moving against		0.98	1.08	0.89	1.03
Moving towards		0.45	0.62	0.42	0.61

6.3 Work-induced mental illness

Career selection can play an important role in mental illness, but what if the job itself is the cause of the illness? A common assumption is that mental health issues are caused by factors outside of the workplace and whilst many mental health problems are unrelated to issues at work, there may well be associations with workplace conditions, such as long work hours, work overload, lack of autonomy, lack of participation in decision making, poor social support and lack of role clarity.

The CIPD's autumn 2011 Employee Outlook Focus on mental health at work survey found that 65 per cent of people reporting poor mental health said that this was due to a combination of both work *and* non-work factors. Only 20 per cent of those surveyed said their poor mental health was attributable only to non-work issues, while 15 per cent said that in fact their poor mental health was the result of work alone.

In a 2009 report on common mental health problems at work, the Sainsbury Centre for Mental Health reported that work situations characterized by high pressure and low support have been shown to correlate with worsening depressive symptoms (Paterniti *et al.*, 2002). With most mental illnesses and personality disorders, the situation is not a black and white one – most conditions exist on a continuum, like a dial that can be turned up and down rather than like an on/off switch. With illnesses such as depression, work can play a significant role in exacerbating previously manageable symptoms.

There is also a suggestion of a gender difference, with evidence that women who work for managers who do not lead in an inclusive or considerate way are more susceptible to depression and anxiety, whilst men present a higher risk of experiencing the illness if they feel they have been excluded from decision making (Kivimaki *et al.*, 2003a; Kivimaki *et al.*, 2003b; Ylipaavalniemi *et al.*, 2005). This is important information for managers to be aware of; the actions that can have a detrimental impact on their female employees will not be the same behaviours they need to be aware of in relation to their male employees.

Various other adverse psychosocial work characteristics have been shown to predict mental illness in a range of situations. In a recent meta-analyses, job strain, low job control, poor social support, high psychological demands, an imbalance between effort and reward (perceived or otherwise) and high job insecurity have all been associated with an approximately 20 to 80 per cent excess risk of depression and mental ill health in general (Bonde, 2008; Netterstrøm *et al.*, 2008; Stansfeld and Candy, 2006).

The causes of mental illness are complex, multiple and varied, but as we have explored earlier in this book, there is often an environmental trigger, and findings such as this would suggest that the work environment could well be that trigger and can have a significant impact on the degree to which an individual experiences mental illness. There also appears to be a bidirectional relationship between personality and work, so that people are drawn to particular occupations, but the occupations then have an effect on them.

We will now explore the various aspects of work that can induce mental illness.

6.4 High-risk jobs

Certain jobs have been found to be more closely linked to mental illness and it is hypothesized in these instances that the job itself can cause or exacerbate a pre-existing condition.

Certain jobs have been found to be more closely linked to mental illness

6.4.1 Occupations at risk of depression

In a number of studies, some occupational groups were found to have significantly elevated rates of depression than others and this includes lawyers, teachers, counsellors and secretaries. There is still a lack of research that enables us to accurately confirm whether the role itself acts as a temporary stressor to cause a period of depression or if the job stress triggers an underlying illness to come to the surface.

An Australian longitudinal study examined the occurrence of depression in teachers and found that there were no significant differences in the rates of DSM-IV major depression between those who stayed in teaching and those who left the profession, but rates of depression were relatively high in the group overall (Wilhelm *et al.*, 2004). This would suggest that removing oneself from the job may not be the most effective means of tackling the illness.

A study carried out by Health.com reported that workers in the following ten careers are most likely to report having an episode of major depression:

1. Nursing home/childcare workers – long hours and constantly being required to devote yourself to other people.
2. Food service staff – low pay, long, exhausting hours and little thanks from anyone.
3. Social workers – the ongoing pressure of dealing with people in extreme need and the frustrations of working with a highly bureaucratic system.
4. Healthcare workers – long, irregular hours and the stress of having to deal with sickness and death on a daily basis.
5. Artists, entertainers and writers – irregular pay, uncertain hours and isolation. Creative people may also have higher rates of mood disorders.
6. Teachers – dealing with multiple pressures, children, parents and other teachers, plus fairly low pay and long hours.
7. Administrative support staff – high demand but low control, taking orders from everyone.
8. Maintenance and ground workers – unusual hours, shift patterns and often called upon to deal with other people's mess.
9. Financial advisors and accountants – the pressure of managing and looking after other people's hard-earned cash can be a huge burden
10. Salespeople – uncertainty of income, pressure to meet sales targets and long hours.

6.4.2 Occupations at risk of suicide

The newspapers are often populated by stories of workers throwing themselves in front of a train on their way to work rather than having to face another day of living hell in a job they hate. In the City of London there is a restaurant that has become notorious as a popular location for city bankers to attempt suicide. But just how prevalent is this trend? And are there certain occupations where you are more likely to be driven to the brink of suicide?

The academic literature on suicide has identified consistent relationships between occupation and suicide. The following occupations have been identified as being high risk in this respect: farmers, doctors and nurses, dentists, veterinarians, pharmacists, police, the military, people working at sea and artists. Easy access to a means of committing suicide (drugs, guns or dangerous environments such as drowning) has become widely regarded as a major determinant of high suicide rates in most of these occupations (Hawton *et al.*, 1998; 2000; Mahon *et al.*, 2005; Marzuk *et al.*, 2002; Meltzer *et al.*, 2008; Platt *et al.*, 2010). But this does not necessarily tell us the whole story and there can often be a complex interplay of factors, such as stress caused by work or family pressures, the presence of a mental illness, age, etc. Therefore, it is important to consider things such as previous history of psychiatric problems when considering the rate of work-related suicide.

Stack (2001) also points out that increased risk of suicide in occupations that are neither client-dependent (i.e., health workers) nor have easy access to the means of suicide may also be explained by psychiatric morbidity; in other words, people with suicidal personality traits may seek out occupations that have high suicide rates.

Some new analysis has examined whether there has been a change in the past 30 years in terms of those occupations most likely to lead to suicide. The world of work has changed quite dramatically since the 1980s and so to examine the impact this may have had on the nature and prevalence of suicide in the workplace, a study was carried out to compare the UK suicide rates for dozens of occupations between 1979 and 1983 with those of similar data recorded between 2001 and 2005 (Roberts *et al.*, 2013).

In the late 1970s, vets, pharmacists, dentists, doctors and farmers were all among the top 15 occupations with the highest suicide rates, and this is consistent with the theory that those with the easiest access to a means of suicide would be more likely to take their own life. However, in the early part of the twenty-first century, none of these professions were in the top

30 occupations in terms of suicide rates. In modern society the occupations with the highest rates of suicide are largely manual, including coal miners, builders, window cleaners, plasterers and refuse collectors.

Out of a total of 55 high-risk occupations, 14 of these showed a reduction in suicide rates in the period 2001–5 compared with the period 1979–83, and these were almost exclusively highly educated professional roles. In contrast, five of the 55 high-risk professions showed an increased rate of suicide in the later data, and these were exclusively manual professions: coal miners, labourers, plasterers, fork-lift truck drivers and carpenters.

6.4.3 Occupations at risk of alcohol and substance abuse

Some studies have correlated occupational stress as a risk factor for alcohol dependence. Evidence to support this remains inconclusive, although there is a clear link between alcohol and substance abuse and occupation, which we will now explore. Let's revisit some evidence from the 1970s. A study by Plant (1977) reported on male liver cirrhosis mortality rates for England and Wales and found that company directors had the highest rates (22 times the average), followed by publicans and innkeepers (suggesting a link between the availability of alcohol and abuse), followed by workers in the entertainment industry (actors, entertainers and musicians). Military personnel also reported high rates (3.5–4.0 times the average), as did doctors (3.5 times the average). Finally, workers in the legal profession (judges, advocates, barristers and solicitors) had rates that were twice the average.

A more recent study by the National Office for Statistics in 2007 explored the trend further and examined the prevalence of alcohol-related deaths in a range of occupations. The study looked at 13,011 deaths among men aged 20–64 and 3,655 deaths among women aged 20–64. It showed that male bar staff were 2.23 times more likely to die from alcohol than average, while the figure for their female colleagues was 2.03 times more likely. Male seafarers, including those in the Royal Navy, were the second-highest risk group (2.16 times more likely), while for women, it was bar managers (1.93 times more likely).

A later study in 1992 (Mandell *et al.*, 1992) reported that construction workers, carpenters, waiters/waitresses, transportation workers and those in moving occupations were more likely to have drug abuse disorders (alcohol and stimulants).

A key consideration in assessing the link between occupation and alcohol and drug abuse is the degree to which the organizational culture accepts and perhaps even encourages this kind of behaviour. This is not always limited to the obvious choices, such as bar staff and those working in the entertainment industry. Do you work in a role that involves boozy client lunches and after-hours entertaining? Does your team tend to gravitate to the local pub at the end of the day to indulge in a few pints? Whilst often this can be a normal part of corporate life, in some instances it can be the start of a slippery slope.

Ames and Janes (1992) suggested four broad categories of problem drinking/drug abuse among the working population: 'normative regulation of drinking', which includes elements of work that 'form and maintain alcohol beliefs, values and behaviors' (e.g., pressure to join in drinking rituals during or after work, easy availability of alcohol); the 'quality and organization of work', which includes factors implicit in the demand-control model as well as factors affecting the culture of drinking behaviour (e.g., sources of stress, boredom and how these are dealt with); factors external to the workplace, such as family (e.g., history of alcohol problems in the family); and drinking subcultures, where there are groups that arise within an organization (due to such factors as age or job identity) where drinking is considered the norm.

6.4.4 Occupations exposed to trauma linked to mental health

Exposure to death, personal injury and violence can often be a normal feature of the job for occupations such as the military, the police and security personnel. For others, such as emergency service workers and undertakers, the exposure to violence relates to that inflicted on other people. These experiences have been associated with the onset of various types of mental illness, including PTSD and somatization disorder. Engel (2002) has described a syndrome of multiple idiopathic physical symptoms for individuals working in these environments following exposure to highly traumatic events.

There are also increasing levels of violence in other occupational settings previously considered to be safe environments (for example, for high school teachers and hospital staff, especially where there is exposure to intoxicated patients). Several studies have pointed to the relationship between the use of emotion-suppressing defences (Wastell, 2002) and later mental health problems (stress, alexithymia).

Wastell (2002) concludes that there are workplace factors involving exposure to danger and crisis that lead to PTSD, substance abuse (including stimulants) and depersonalization. Workplace risk factors for depression include situations where the individual has a lack a of autonomy in their role and those involving 'caring' for others as part of the work role.

6.5 Job characteristics

Hackman and Oldham (1980) proposed the original job characteristics model. They argued that the motivating potential of any job is not simply an additive function of the five job dimensions, but rather a multiplication function.

$$\text{Motivating Potential Score (MPS)} \quad \frac{[\text{skill variety + task identity + task significance}]}{\text{3 factors}} \times \text{autonomy} \times \text{feedback}$$

The theory suggests that there are three critical psychological states that are relevant to the world of work:

- *Experienced meaningfulness*: job holders must feel that the work has personal meaning and is worthwhile according to their system of values.
- *Experienced responsibility*: job holders must feel that they are responsible for work processes and outcomes.
- *Knowledge of results*: job holders need to be given information on a regular basis about whether or not their job performance is leading to appropriate and satisfactory results.

Psychological states are affected by the nature of the job and five core job dimensions. Three of these affect the meaningfulness of the job:

- *skill variety* – whether the job requires the use of a range of job skills and offers a variety of tasks to perform;
- *task identity* – whether the job holder is able to complete a 'whole' and identifiable piece of work;
- *task significance* – whether the job is perceived to have an impact upon others and their lives in the organization and/or in general.

Each of these is necessary for the work to be experienced as meaningful. The fourth and fifth dimensions are related to experienced responsibility and knowledge of results respectively:

- *autonomy* – the degree of freedom, independence and discretion that job holders may exercise in their work so as to be personally responsible for job process and outcome;
- *feedback* – the extent to which the work process itself offers direct and frequent feedback about the effectiveness of performance.

When these core job dimensions are positively present, they impact on the critical psychological states and lead to positive outcomes, such as increased motivation, higher-quality performance and work satisfaction, and lower absenteeism and labour turnover. The extent to which the relationships hold depends upon the strength of the individual's growth needs.

A job with a high MPS score should have more motivating potential than a job with a lower score. From inspecting the formula, it is the case that autonomy and feedback are the most important factors in the MPS because, if either is zero, the MPS is zero. However, skill, variety, task identity and/or task significance can be zero or low and the MPS could still be reasonably high if autonomy or feedback is high.

The relevance of this when considering mental illness in the workplace is that there are a number of job characteristics that can increase the likelihood of an individual experiencing a mental health problem. These include job control, low levels of autonomy and decision-making authority.

A British longitudinal study of over 11,000 civil servants (Stansfeld *et al.*, 1997; Stansfeld *et al.*, 1999) found that psychological problems could be predicted by poor work social support and low decision-making authority, high job demands and effort-reward imbalances. In other words, individuals were more likely to experience mental health problems if they worked in an environment where they had little support and little freedom to carry out their role as they saw fit, where high demands placed on them and where there was an imbalance between the work they carried out and the rewards they received in return.

In a further study, Wall *et al.* (1997) investigated minor psychiatric illness amongst British National Health Service (NHS) employees and compared these rates to those from the British Household Panel Survey (BHPS) (Freed Taylor *et al.*, 1995) consisting of data from 5,000 employed adults from a representative sample of British households over the same period (1993–4). Here, high job demands (conflicting tasks, role conflict, high work pace and work overload) predicted future psychiatric problems, with conflicting demands having a greater impact than work pace.

A perceived lack of control over work has been linked to depression (Wilhelm and Parker, 1989), but cross-sectional studies make it impossible to distinguish between cause and effect. One longitudinal study of 468 factory and blue-collar workers studied over three years in Japan (Wilhelm, Dewhurst-Savellis and Parker, 2000) indicated that a perceived lack of control over work, unsuitable jobs and poor workplace relations were predictors of depression identified using the Zung scale.

The results of the meta-analyses show a small but significant positive trend of increased psychological and physical symptoms with increasing hours of work. These results seem to offer support to the majority of the studies qualitatively reviewed above in suggesting that working long hours can be detrimental to the health of employees.

6.6 Summary

We can all think of a number of stereotypes – the psychopathic CEO of an FTSE 100 company, the narcissistic advertising executive and the histrionic theatre actress – but do these caricatures actually point towards a serious trend? The answer is to a large extent yes and research would suggest that sector- and organization-specific illnesses do exist. In this chapter we have examined some of the trends that can lead to entire organizations and sectors becoming 'ill'. Furthermore, there is increasing evidence to suggest that the nature of some jobs can lead the incumbent to develop mental health issues. Sometimes this can be attributed to fairly obvious reasons, such as the nature of the work itself being illness-inducing (e.g., healthcare workers). In other occupations the reasons are less obvious and can come down to factors such as whether the individual has autonomy and control over their work. Two important questions that managers must ask themselves are as follows: is my organization a toxic one which attracts and breeds certain behaviours? And does my style of management create a set of conditions that could cause people to develop problems?

chapter 7

Illness at the Top: The Paradox of Managerial Success

7.1 Introduction

This chapter is about the observation that frequently the very and often abnormal characteristics that help a person achieve career success are the same things that derail them in the end. This could be an example of the potential benefits of mild mental illness.

Paradoxically, mental illness and particularly personality disorders may serve some people well and there are a remarkable number of examples of high achievers in the corporate environment who have been able to use their personality disorder as an asset in securing senior positions. A number of recent developments in the research on personality disorders have pointed to the strong likelihood that personality disorders are prevalent amongst some managers in organizations and could ironically be proving to be an asset in acquiring these management roles.

To get to the top of any organization requires considerably ability and effort. Top jobs are nearly always very stressful and top people are usually very resilient and robust with good coping strategies. Inevitably, top executives do suffer burnout, stress and depression. Most often this is first noticeable in the form of psychosomatic illnesses like stomach ulcers, irritable bowel syndrome, etc. However, what is most common is that some of the strengths that CEOs have turn to weaknesses. In other words, the very characteristics that were in part responsible for them 'getting to the top' are those that derail them.

Some of the strengths that CEOs have turn to weaknesses

There is an extensive, compulsive and fascinating literature on the psychopaths amongst us. Films have made people think that psychopaths are all deranged axe-murderers and serial killers, but they are also convicts and mercenaries.

Empirical evidence and case studies of psychopathy in the corporate world are, to date, still very limited and are largely confined to self-report measures of constructs related to psychopathy, such as narcissism, Machiavellianism and self-promotion. This is largely because of the difficulties faced by clinical and forensic psychologists in accessing research subjects from a corporate setting, and whilst there are numerous studies demonstrating the importance of personality as a predictor of career success (Hogan, 2004 and 2005; Judge *et al.*, 2002), there have been fewer studies that have examined the impact of personality disorder on career outcomes. Those that have point towards a clear link between personality disorder and career derailment in some instances, but in many cases there is evidence that psychopaths can utilise their charm, manipulation, intelligence, recklessness and appetite for risk to great effect (Benning *et al.*, 2005).

As with all psychiatric illnesses, there have been discussions and debates about definitions and terms. Babiak and Hare (2006: 19) clarified the distinction between three overlapping terms:

> *Psychopathy* is a personality disorder described by the personality traits and behaviours. Psychopaths are without conscience and incapable of empathy, *guilt, or loyalty to anyone but themselves. Sociopathy is not a formal* psychiatric condition. It refers to patterns of attitudes and behaviours that are considered anti-social and criminal by society at large, but are seen as normal or necessary by the subculture or social environment in which they developed. Sociopaths may have a well-developed conscience and a normal capacity for empathy, guilt and loyalty, but their sense of right and wrong is based on the norms and expectations of their subculture or group. Many criminals might be described as sociopaths.
>
> Anti-social personality disorder (APD) is a broad diagnostic category found in the American Psychiatric Association's *Diagnostic and Statistic Manual of Mental Disorders,* 4th edition (DSM-IV). Anti-social and criminal behaviours play a major role in its definition and, in this sense, APD is similar to sociopathy. Some of those with APD are psychopaths but many are not. The difference between psychopathy and anti-social personality disorder is that the former includes personality traits such as lack of

empathy, grandiosity and shallow emotion that are not necessary for a diagnosis of APD. APD is three or four times more common than psychopathy in the general population and in prisons. The prevalence of those we would describe as sociopathic is unknown but likely is considerably higher than that of APD.

The defining characteristics of psychopathy tend to fall into two dimensions. The *first* is socio-emotional, where the psychopath is superficial and lacking in empathy, guilt or remorse. They are also deceitful and manipulative while being prone to egocentricity and grandiosity. The *second* is their social deviance associated with their susceptibility to boredom, impulsivity and lack of self-control. In childhood they show evidence of behavioural problems and in adulthood anti-social behaviour. This has led to the development of a checklist.

In a chapter on white-collar psychopaths, Hare (1999) noted how many of these people were 'trust-mongers' who, through charm and gall, obtained then very callously betrayed the trust of others. He notes how they make excellent imposters and how they frequently target the vulnerable. They focus on and exploit people's gullibility, naivety and Rousseauian view of the goodness of man.

Hare calls such people *subcriminal psychopaths* who can thrive as academics, cult-leaders, doctors, police officers and writers. They violate rules, conventions and ethical standards, always just crossing legal boundaries. He also gives a rich case study description of what he calls a 'corporate psychopath'. He notes that there is certainly no shortage of opportunities for psychopaths who think big: 'They are fast talking, charming, self-assured, at ease in social situations, cool under pressure, unfazed by the possibility of being found out, and totally ruthless' (1999: 121).

Babiak and Hare (2006) believe most of us will interact with a psychopath every day, but their skills and abilities make them difficult to spot. Often they tend to be charming, emotionally literate and socially skilled. In addition, they are often highly articulate and they are brilliant chameleon-like characters who can adapt to many situations:

> This is not to say that most people can't be charming, effective, socially facile communicators and still be honest – of course they can. Many people use impression management and manipulation techniques to influence

> others to like and trust them or to get what they want from people – very often subconsciously, but sometimes as the result of training, practice and planning. However, wanting people to like and respect you (and doing what it takes to achieve this) is not necessarily dishonest or insincere – the need for approval and validation from others is normal. Social manipulation begins to be insincere if you really don't care about the feelings of others or you try to take unfair advantage of others. The difference between the psychopathic approach and the non-psychopathic approach lies in motivation to take unfair and callous advantage of people. Psychopaths simply do not care if what they say and do hurts people as long as they get what they want and they are very good at hiding this fact. Given his or her powerful manipulation skills, it is little wonder why seeing a 'psychopathic' personality beneath someone's charming, engaging surface is so difficult.
>
> Not all psychopaths are smooth operators, though. Some do not have enough social or communicative skill or education to interact successfully with others, relying instead on threats, coercion, intimidation and violence to dominate others and to get what they want. Typically such individuals are manifestly aggressive and rather nasty and unlikely to charm victims into submission, relying on the bullying approach instead. (Babiak and Hare, 2006: 19)

Oldham and Morris (1991) call these people 'adventurous' and we have detailed their characteristics further in Chapter 3. They describe the psychopath in popular terminology which makes it easier for non-specialists to spot.

Such people have, essentially, a manipulative approach to life. Their sole aim is to get what they want with effort, emotion or fear and whether they deserve it or not, hence the importance of various groups that may be called 'the organizational police', auditors, human resources, quality controllers whose job it is to ensure compliance with standards. These people often play an important role in stopping a psychopath in their tracks.

There is a small but growing literature on the successful – that is, non-institutionalized – psychopath (Ishikawa *et al.*, 2001; Widom, 1978; Widom and Newman, 1985). They are described as carefree, aggressive, charming and impulsively irresponsible. They have the essential personality characteristics of the psychopath, but seem to refrain from serious anti-social behaviour. Researchers have identified many politicians and business leaders as non-criminal psychopaths. They are duplicitous, but not illegally so. They show many patterns of misconduct, but seem not to get caught. They seem brilliant at tactical impression management and are drawn to unstable, chaotic, rapidly changing situations where they can operate more easily. Successful, non-incarcerated psychopaths seem to have compensatory factors that buffer them against criminal behaviour like higher social class and intelligence. In this sense the successful psychopath has a wider set of coping mechanisms than less privileged and able psychopaths, who soon get caught.

The term 'psychopath' or 'sociopath' was used to describe anti-social personality types whose behaviour is amoral or asocial, impulsive and lacking in remorse and shame. Once called 'moral insanity', it is found more commonly among lower socio-economic groups, no doubt because of the 'downward drift' of these types.

Self-report measures of the psychopathic personality give a clear indication of the sort of behaviours that are relevant (Benning *et al*., 2003): impulsive non-conformity (reckless, rebellious, unconventional); blame externalisation (blames others, rationalizes own transgressions); Machiavellian egocentricity (interpersonally aggressive and self-centred); carefree non-planfulness (excessive present orientation with lack of forethought or planning); stress immunity (experiencing minimal anxiety); fearlessness (willing to take risks, having little concern with potentially harmful consequences) and general cold-heartedness (unsentimental, unreactive to others' distress, lacking in imagination). These seem to factor into *two* dimensions: one related to high negative emotionality and the other low behavioural constraint. Further research by Benning *et al*. (2005) led these authors to think about two distinct facets of the psychopath: *fearless dominance* (glib, grandiose, deceitful, low stress) and *impulsive anti-sociality* (aggressive, anti-social, low control). This suggests that within the psychopath population, one may be able to distinguish between these two groups.

In his famous book *The Mask of Sanity*, Cleckley (1941) set out ten criteria: superficial charm and intelligence; absence of anxiety in stressful situations; insincerity and lack of truthfulness; lack of remorse and shame; inability to experience love or genuine emotion; unreliability and irresponsibility; impulsivity and disregard for socially acceptable behaviour; clear-headedness with an absence of delusions or irrational thinking; inability to profit from experience; and lack of insight. The book is indeed a classic in psychology and psychiatry because of its insight. Cleckley described the slick but callous businessperson, the smooth-talking and manipulative lawyer, and the arrogant and deceptive politicians as psychopaths.

It is an interesting question to try to understand in what sorts of jobs psychopathic traits might be, at least for a time, advantageous. This may refer both to the type of job and also a particular situation, such as when an organization is changing rapidly, is in decline or is under investigation. Such people like outwitting the system – opportunistically exploiting who and what they can. They usually hate routine and administration, which are seen as drudgery. No wonder people who work for them feel so demoralized.

Such individuals make bad bosses and bad partners because they are egocentric and only continue in a relationship as long as it is good for them, rarely having long-lasting, meaningful relationships. They have two human ingredients missing which are pretty crucial to a fully functioning person: *conscience* and *compassion*. They score very low on agreeableness and conscientiousness. Hence, they can be cruel, destructive, malicious and criminal. They are unscrupulous and are exploitatively self-interested, with little capacity for remorse. They act before they think and are famous for their extreme impulsivity.

Dotlick and Cairo (2003) note that the mischievous psychopath knows that the rules are really 'only suggestions'. They are rebels without a cause, rule breakers who believe that laws and other restrictions are tedious and unnecessary. They clearly have destructive impulses and a preference for making impulsive decisions without considering the consequences. They can (and do) speak their mind and use their charms and creativity, but for no clear business goal.

Such people display five signs and symptoms: staff question the mischievous leader's commitments and projects they have initiated, but subsequently neglected; they frequently never take the time or effort to win people over; everything rates as a challenge to them; they are easily bored; and they have to spend a lot of effort covering up their mistakes.

How should the psychopath be dealt with? This is easier said than done; however, Dotlick and Cairo (2003) offer four pieces of advice for what is, no doubt, a successful psychopath: *first*, encourage them to take ownership for their action and interrogate their rule-breaking, consequence-ignoring behaviours; *second*, encourage them to think clearly about which rules they really will follow as opposed to break; *third*, they may benefit from being on the receiving end of the sort of mischief they dish out; *finally*, they might benefit from engaging in some coaching from a qualified coach.

Miller calls psychopathic bosses 'predators'. He claims they think: 'It's a dog-eat-dog world. Look out for number one. Rules are for losers. I'm smarter than all these suckers ... My needs come first. I can get over anyone' (2008: 58). He notes that psychopathic bosses are prototype cut-throat entrepreneurs. The interpersonal inquisitiveness is more about getting to know how to manipulate people than to befriend them. They take pleasure in outsmarting 'suckers', which reinforces their personal sense of cleverness and powerfulness.

They can easily become experts, cheats, embezzlers or harassers. Curiously, they often risk a lot for a little because of their love of thrills and excitement.

Miller (2008) notes two types of psychopathic bosses: first, the bright, devious, cunning, conning, natural manipulator – this is the plotting, smooth operator; and, second, the less bright psychopathic boss who is more likely to use bullying and intimidation to get what they want.

The psychopathic boss is not loyal or grateful, but will humour staff who fulfil their needs and purposes. They will disregard people once they have served their purpose. They steal credit, but hand out blame.

Babiak (1995) found five characteristics in the many studies of industrial psychopathy and various case studies. He reported case studies of individuals and began to describe how they succeed despite their predisposition:

> Comparison of the behaviour of the three subjects observed to date revealed some similarities: each a) began by building a *network of one-to-one relationships* with powerful and useful individuals, b) *avoided virtually all group meetings* where maintaining multiple facades may have been too difficult, and c) *created conflicts* which kept co-workers from sharing information about him. Once their power bases were established, d) *co-workers who were no longer useful* were abandoned and e) *detractors were neutralised* by systematically raising doubts about their competence and loyalty. In addition, unstable cultural factors, inadequate measurement systems, and general lack of trust typical of organizations undergoing rapid, chaotic change may have provided an acceptable cover for psychopathic behaviour. (1995: 184–5, emphasis added)

It is difficult to estimate the number of successful 'industrial' psychopaths. It is also sometimes difficult to explain why they 'get away with it' for so long. However, it is no mystery when asking those who work or have worked with a successful psychopath how much misery or dysfunctionality they can bring to the workplace.

Babiak and Hare (2006) believe that psychopaths are indeed attracted to today's business climate. They devised a questionnaire to help people at work spot them. According to them, there are ten markers of the problem. The successful, industrial psychopath is characterized by the following traits:

1. Comes across as smooth, polished and charming.
2. Turns most conversations around to a discussion of themselves.
3. Discredits and puts down others in order to build up own image and reputation.

4. Lies to co-workers, customers or business associates with a straight face.
5. Considers people they have outsmarted or manipulated as dumb or stupid.
6. Opportunistic; hates to lose and plays ruthlessly to win.
7. Comes across as cold and calculating.
8. Acts in an unethical or dishonest manner.
9. Has created a power network in the organization and uses it for personal gain.
10. Shows no regret for making decisions that negatively affect the company, shareholders or employees.

Psychopaths can easily look like ideal leaders: smooth, polished and charming. They can quite easily weave their dark side behaviours into day-to-day working. In the past it may be politics, policing, law, the media and religion that attracted psychopaths, but increasingly it is the fast-paced, exciting and glamorous world of business.

7.2 Creativity and madness

Simonton (2012) recently reviewed the rather sad literature on the creative artist. The evidence, called historiometric, supports the common-sense and cinematic view of the 'mad genius artist'. In the jargon, artistic creative achievers show 'conspicuous and systematic differences in the rate and intensity of psychopathological symptoms'.

Over the years, there have been in-depth studies of great (and not so great) artists, poets, dramatists and the like. Despite various exceptions, the data show that it is not healthy to be a poet: they are particularly prone to alcoholism, depression and suicide, having typically short and unhappy lives. One study, entitled *The Price of Greatness*, established that, among literary types, dramatists are prone to alcoholism and mania, non-fiction writers to excessive anxiety and poets to depression.

Do you have to pay a price for creativity at work? Is there evidence that the 'cost' of creativity is mental disorder?

7.2.1 Bipolar disorder: managing the ups and downs

What do the following have in common?

Artists

Francesco Bassano
Francesco Borromini
David Bomberg
John Sell Cotman

Richard Dadd
Thomas Eakins
Paul Gauguin
Théodore Géricault
Ernst Ludwig Kirchner
Sir Edwin Landseer
Edward Lear
Michelangelo Buonarroti
Edvard Munch
Georgia O'Keeffe
Jackson Pollock
George Romney
Dante Gabriel Rossetti
Mark Rothko
Maurice Utrillo
Hugo van der Goes
Vincent van Gogh
George Frederic Watts
Sir David Wilkie

Musicians

Ludwig van Beethoven
Hector Berlioz
Irving Berlin
Anton Bruckner
John Dowland
Sir Edward Elgar
Georg Frideric Handel
Gustav Holst
Charles Ives
Otto Klemperer
Gustav Mahler
Modest Mussorgsky
Charlie Mingus
Charlie Parker
Cole Porter
Sergey Rachmaninov
Gioacchino Rossini
Robert Schumann
Alexander Scriabin
Peter Tchaikovsky
Peter Warlock
Hugo Wolf
Bernd Alois Zimmerman

Mathematicians, philosophers and scientists

Georg Cantor
Auguste Comte
Sir Isaac Newton
Frederic Nietzsche
Comte de Saint Simon
Hugo Wolf

The above lists feature some eminent figures with probable manic depression or cyclothymia, or bipolar disorder as it is now called.

Ludwig analysed information on 1,004 subjects whose published biographies were reviewed in the *New York Times Book Review* between 1960 and 1990 (Ludwig, 1992: 330). Overall the average risk was 73 per cent for the arts and 42 per cent for all other professions. Ludwig's study suggests a link between psychopathology and creativity if creativity were to be understood solely in terms of the arts; however, it does not provide specific evidence for bipolar disorder and 'domain-general' creativity. In the study the results are not interpreted as providing evidence for an intrinsic link between mental illness

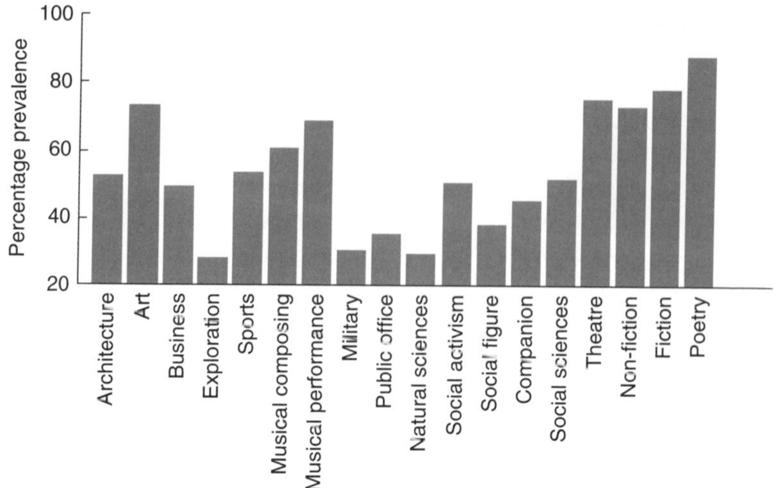

FIGURE 7.1 Lifetime prevalence of mental disorders in 1,004 eminent subjects classified by profession

Source: Ludwig, A.M. (1995) *The Price of Greatness*, Guildford Publications, Inc.

and creativity. Rather, it is hypothesized that creative people who have a mental illness may choose artistic professions because their mood changes and temperamental personalities are better tolerated than in science or business (Ludwig, 1992: 349–52).

Jamison (1993) inspected autobiographical, biographical and, where available, medical records of 36 major British poets born between 1705 and 1805. These individuals were 30 times more likely to have suffered from bipolar disorder, 10–20 times more likely to be cyclothymic, more than 20 times more likely to have been admitted to a mental asylum and at least five times more likely to have committed suicide compared to the general population (Jamison, 1993: 61–72). Jamison interprets this as persuasive evidence for a relationship between mood disorders and artistic creativity. The question of cause or effect still looms large.

Given that such highly emotional and turbulent qualities were valued in artistic creativity during this period, bipolar disorder or cyclothymia may have afforded some advantage to these poets in the production of appreciated art because of the inherent nature of their illness (Sass, 2001: 67). This may certainly explain the striking over-representation of bipolar disorder in Jamison's sample of poets. Sass asks:

> how different the results might have been if there had been more focus on neo-classical writers such as Pope, Addison or Dryden … or on the key modernist or postmodernist figures? (Sass, 2001: 68)

Jamison's cultural bias is also shown in *Touched with Fire*, where she uses a sample of 13 writers, composers and artists born between 1709 (Samuel Johnson) and 1899 (Ernest Hemingway) to draw attention to figures in whom bipolar disorder and creativity are demonstrated and to illustrate the propensity of the illness to run in families (Jamison, 1993: 192–237).

More general problems may arise with biographical studies. They may link eminence and psychopathology rather than true creativity and bipolar disorder. The reliability of biographical material such as memoirs or letters is strongly affected by their perspective and historical context, which influence emphases and interpretations. Bipolar disorder may well be more frequently ascribed to artists because society accepts their 'eccentricity' or mental illness. This is intensified by the general stigma attached to mental illness, encouraging those who do not have the excuse of being an artist to hide it. Finally, the motivation of the biographer should be considered; they may be tempted to draw more exciting conclusions from their evidence than may exist.

Furthermore, personality traits such as eccentricity and a propensity to excess and experimentation may automatically be seen as a reflection of an underlying mental illness in those characterized as creative, based on the embedded belief in a link between 'madness' and creativity (Eysenck, 1995: 116). Misdiagnosis may also occur if periods of mania are perceived as artistic inspiration (Jamison, 1993: 58).

Anecdotes about individuals and biographical studies can at best be taken as suggestive of a person-specific relationship between bipolar disorder and creativity. It is always possible to find biographical material that appears to support a specific hypothesis and the same information might well be used to link alcoholism and creativity, for example. 'Real-time' psychiatric and psychometric enquiries apply more robust scientific criteria and lead to more reliable conclusions. To eliminate the reservations that accompany biographical studies, it is necessary to examine the possible relationship between bipolar disorder and creativity using direct diagnosis and observation.

7.2.2 Schizotypal disorder: the quirky genius

Schizotypal individuals are creative. This disorder, which is more common in men than women, has been estimated to affect about 1–3 per cent of the population.

In a sense, these individuals are mild schizophrenics, but do not show the gross disorganization in thinking and feeling or such severe symptoms as someone with schizophrenia. However, they all appear to be pretty idiosyncratic and are often creatively talented and curious. They frequently hold very strange beliefs, for example, enjoying the occult. They have odd habits, eccentric lifestyles and a rich inner life.

Schizotypal people often seek emotional experiences: rapture and nirvana. Here the schizotypal manager is marked by acute discomfort with and reduced capacity for close relationships. Such people display many eccentricities of behaviour. They may look odd and have a reputation for being 'peculiar'. They often have very odd ideas about business: how to succeed, who to hire and what controls what. They can have very odd beliefs or magical thinking that influences behaviour and is inconsistent with business norms (e.g., superstitiousness or a belief in clairvoyance or telepathy).

Many organizations do not tolerate the odd behaviours of these idiosyncratic types, as they may dress oddly and work odd hours. They are not very loyal to their companies and do not enjoy the corporate world. They do not 'connect' with their staff, customers and bosses. Their quirky quasi-religious beliefs that estrange them yet further from the normal world of the other people. As such, they are often loners.

Dotlick and Cairo (2003) label the schizotypal leader as an eccentric who enjoys being different for its own sake. There a world of difference between being creative, off-beat and quirky as opposed to weird, impractical and unrealistic. The trouble with eccentric leaders is that they are full of ideas and initiatives that go nowhere. Moreover, stakeholders are confounded by their non-conformist style. They seem unable or unwilling to prioritize, collaborate and co-operate, being stubborn individualists who therefore suffer from the problem that others do not take them seriously. Like all others, they need insight and self-awareness about the consequences of their actions. They need to see and close the gap between their intentions and their impact. As such, they need dedicate staff who can and will execute their ideas. They also need to know the price they will pay for being different.

These people are curiously interesting and may be fun to be around, but they are distractible and unpredictable, and as managers they often leave people confused regarding their directions or intentions. They tend to miscommunicate in idiosyncratic and unusual ways. At their best, these people are imaginative, creative, interesting and amazingly insightful about the motives of others, but at their worst, they can be self-absorbed, single-minded, insensitive to the reactions of others and indifferent to the social and political consequences of their narrow focus on their own agendas.

Under stress and heavy workloads, such people can become upset, lose focus, lapse into eccentric behaviour and not communicate clearly. They can be moody and tend to get too excited by success and too despondent over failure. They want attention, approval and applause, which explains the lengths that they are willing to go to in order to attract it.

To work with the imaginative person, colleagues need primarily to be a good audience, to appreciate their humour, creativity and spontaneity, and to understand that they do not handle reversals very well. They will not mind suggestions and recommendations regarding important decisions, and in fact may even appreciate them. Colleagues should study their problem-solving style, listen to their insights about other people and model their ability to 'think outside the box'.

The imaginative, idiosyncratic person is unlikely to reach a very high position in an organization, although they may be promoted in the fields of advertising or academia. The absent-minded, nutty professor and the creative advertising genius may share many schizotypical behaviours. If talented, they may do well, but rarely as managers of others.

7.2.3 Histrionic disorder: the drama queen

In certain fields, such as advertising, media, fashion and the theatre, particular characteristics get people noticed and these are often the characteristics displayed by individuals with histrionic disorder. They are sometimes called outrageously disinhibited, emotional drama queens. Often they are skilled at attracting the attention of inspiring people like themselves. Kets de Vries and Miller (1985) noted how whole organizations could become drama-obsessed.

The dramatic organization is hyperactive, impulsive and uninhibited. In such an organization, decision makers prefer to act on hunches and impressions, and take on widely diverse projects. Top managers reserve the right to start bold ventures independently; subordinates have limited power.

Most histrionic people are uncomfortable in situations in which they are not the centre of attention and try always to be so. They delight in making a drama out of a crisis. Their interaction with others is often characterized by inappropriate, sexually seductive or provocative behaviour. Needless to say, this causes more of a reaction in women than men. Such people display rapidly shifting and shallow expression of emotions. They are difficult to read. Most use physical appearance (clothes) to draw attention to themselves, which may include body piercings or tattoos. They certainly get a reputation in the office for their 'unique apparel'. Many have a style of speech that is excessively impressionistic and lacking in detail. They show a tendency to self-dramatize, theatricality and an exaggerated expression of emotion (usually negative). Even the dullest topic is imbued with drama. They are easily influenced by others or circumstances and therefore are both unpredictable and persuadable. They may consider relationships to be more intimate than they actually are. Being rather dramatic, they are more likely to notice humdrum working relationships more intensely than others.

At work, such people can be persuasive and insightful. They enjoy the fields of advertising, PR, sales and marketing, but need strong back-up in relation to things like plans, budgets and details. They can be volatile and are often being known for being moody. They can be effusive with both praise and blame, but everything is an emotional drama and emotionally they can be both childlike and childish. They tend not to have stable relationships. They need to be the star, the centre of attention or else they can feel powerless or desperately unworthy. They are not introspective and it is important not to over-react to their over-reactions.

Dotlick and Cairo (2003) call the histrionic leader 'melodramatic' because they are always trying to be the centre of attention. These 'over-the-top', showman types distract too much attention from what should be the focus of the business. They dominate meetings, use attention-seeking to try and create unquestioning compliance, and employ their theatrical style to make themselves rather than the business the centre of attention; they are more flamboyant than strategic, are always 'on' and are never reflective.

According to Dotlick and Cairo (2003), such people exhibit four classic signs and symptoms:

1. Lack of focus; confused priorities; wasted energy.
2. A failure to develop people because they are too self-focused.
3. A tendency to attract other show-offs, so executive teams mimic this unhealthy style.
4. A tendency to elevate the expectations of others and develop a following, although they cannot and do not follow through on commitments.

Dotlick and Cairo recommend some 'corrective' actions for such people, like seeing some feedback of themselves in action, identifying and therefore avoiding the situations that increase the level of drama in a situation, and making time to reflect and listen to others.

Miller (2008) calls such people 'emoters'. Their attention-seeking, intuitive and highly impressionistic style can lead to impulsivity and fickle decision making. They are enthusiastic and fun-oriented, being optimistic and energetic but often very impractical. They tend to be personally poorly organized, which is not a recommendation for those who run organizations.

Because histrionic bosses do not deliver, they can cause many problems. Further, they can have difficulty separating work and pleasure – the task and the social. They need to be better prepared and find those with complementary skills to work alongside them. They have to learn to know when it is appropriate to have fun and to when it is not. In addition, they need not to take things personally.

Histrionics deal with stress and heavy workloads by becoming very busy, enjoying high-pressure situations where they can then be the star. Breathless with excitement, they confuse activity with productivity and evaluate themselves in terms of how many meetings they attend rather than how much they actually get done. A key feature of these people that others may not appreciate is how much they need and feed off approval, and how hard they are willing to work for it. This explains why they persist in trying to be a star after their lustre has faded. To work with them, colleagues have to be prepared to put up with missed appointments, bad organization, rapid changes of direction and indecisiveness. These will never change, although they can be planned for. Yet by observing them, you can learn how to read social cues, to present your views effectively, forcefully and dramatically, and to flatter and quite simply dazzle other people.

7.3 Summary

This chapter discussed a paradox: that having some indication of a mental disorder may help people in the workplace. This is based on the spectrum hypothesis, which argues that mental illness is not categorical, but dimensional. In other words, it is not a case of having or not having a mental disorder, but how severe or extreme it is.

This chapter covered a number of disorders, the most famous of which is the psychopath. We noted that the cold, rule-breaking, mischievous psychopath can thrive in the cut-throat world of business, as can the quirky, creative type. Indeed, hints of pathology can be very helpful in climbing the greasy pole of business and organizational life.

chapter 8 Spotting Illnesses

8.1 Introduction

We all bring a certain level of baggage to our workplace, whether this be stress from home (including problems in our personal relationships or with our children), financial burdens, weight problems or having to care for ageing parents. So how does one differentiate between a colleague who is going through a period of increased acute stress and something more serious? How do we tell if John from Accounts has a difficult personality style that clashes with our own or if he is exhibiting the signs and symptoms of a mental illness or personality disorder?

Despite the evidence of increasing rates of mental illness and a more widespread understanding of mental health issues in society as a whole, many managers still feel that mental health is a personal issue unconnected to the workplace and that it is not their place to intervene when they suspect a colleague may be experiencing mental health problems. Further, despite the high rates of mental ill-health discussed in Chapter 1, there are indications that almost 50 per cent of employers think that the number of their employees who will ever experience a mental health problem falls somewhere between zero and 1/20 (Trust, 2006). We are clearly turning a blind eye to this silent epidemic that is impacting on businesses the world over.

It is estimated that only 15 per cent of employers report that they train line managers to recognize signs and symptoms of mental illness and how to deal with them. This often leads to a situation where symptoms can go unchecked and unmanaged, and to more serious and extreme behaviour. The signs can be difficult to spot, even when an individual opens up about their mental well-being. Confusion over terminology and general embarrassment can make it difficult to determine if there really is a serious problem. For example, how do we differentiate between clinically diagnosed depression and the casual use of the term 'depression' to describe feeling a bit down in the dumps?

Mental illness includes a broad range of symptoms and behaviours, and it is not always easy to determine whether someone is mentally ill. One key indicator is that someone may begin to act uncharacteristically – an energetic person may seem lethargic for a considerable time or a person who is usually pretty modest may make grandiose claims about their abilities. This is the key: noticing behaviour when it becomes uncharacteristic of that person.

8.2 Mental health literacy

The concept of 'health literacy' was defined by Nutbeam *et al.* (1993) as 'the ability to gain access to, understand, and use information in ways which promote and maintain good health'. For example, in physical health, this would include the knowledge of the importance of exercise or the implementation of a healthy diet. The importance of physical health literacy is widely agreed upon, but the area of mental health literacy has been relatively neglected (Jorm *et al.*, 1997a).

The term 'mental health literacy' was coined by Jorm *et al.* (1997a) and was defined thus: 'knowledge and beliefs about mental disorders which aid their recognition, management or prevention'. According to Jorm *et al.* (1997a), there are many aspects to mental health literacy: 'the ability to recognise specific disorders', 'knowing how to seek mental health information', 'knowledge and beliefs about risk factors and causes', 'knowledge and beliefs about self-help interventions', 'knowledge and beliefs about professional help available' and 'attitudes which facilitate recognition and appropriate help-seeking'. A considerable amount of research has been done in the area of mental health literacy by Jorm and others (Chen *et al.*, 2000; Jorm *et al.*, 2000) and the concept appears to be becoming more widespread.

Mental illness (and depression in particular) accounts for a large proportion of the world's health burden. According to the World Development Report 1993, depression is the seventh most frequent cause of morbidity among men and the fifth most frequent cause among women. By 2020, the WHO predicts that depression will be the second most frequent cause of disability worldwide. Studies in certain countries suggest that the lifetime likelihood of developing a mental illness is high, such as nearly 50 per cent in the USA (Kessler *et al.*, 1994). This suggests that most people are likely, at some point, to experience a mental illness or come across a person who suffers from one. However, Jorm *et al.*'s (2000) review of public mental health literacy concluded that many laypeople cannot recognize (by applying the correct label) specific mental disorders and have difficulties understanding psychiatric terms. For example, a survey by Jorm *et al.* (1997a) on the mental health literacy of the Australian population found that only 39 per cent of participants correctly labelled depression and only 27 per cent correctly labelled schizophrenia.

It is estimated that mental illness affects 27 per cent of Europeans every year; however, 74 per cent of those affected receive no treatment. The relative neglect of mental health in comparison to physical health can be seen when it is noted that just eight per cent of diabetes sufferers in Europe receive no treatment. The WHO reviewed 37 studies worldwide and showed figures for the proportion of people untreated for particular disorders, such as schizophrenia (32 per cent), bipolar disorder (50 per cent) and OCD (57 per cent).

Typically, vignette identification methodology is used in studies of public mental health literacy, where participants are provided with vignettes describing characters, which they have to label. An example is a recent study which was concerned with whether laypeople could identify a person as having psychopathy. Furnham, Daoud and Swami (2009) used three vignettes, which accurately referred to depression, schizophrenia and psychopathy respectively. They found that 97 per cent of participants could identify depression and 61 per cent schizophrenia. However, only 39 per cent could correctly identify a psychopath (anti-social personality disorder).

8.2.1 A test of your mental health literacy

Can you recognize people with a mental disorder? This is called mental health literacy and is usually assessed by the vignette technique.

They might be asked the following questions:

What, if anything, would you say is X's main problem?____________________

How distressing do you think it would be to have X's condition?
Not at all 1 2 3 4 5 6 7 *Extremely*

How sympathetic would you be towards someone with X's problem?
Not at all 1 2 3 4 5 6 7 *Extremely*

In general, how happy do you think X is?
Not at all 1 2 3 4 5 6 7 *Extremely*

In general, how successful at his/her work do you think X is?
Not at all 1 2 3 4 5 6 7 *Extremely*

In general, how satisfying do you think X's personal relationships are?
Not at all 1 2 3 4 5 6 7 *Extremely*

Have a go at the following examples, which are derived from many sources and part of our current research programme on mental health literacy. If you think the people have a problem, how would you describe it?:

1. Kerry is 24 years old. Recently, she has been having trouble getting out of bed; she randomly burst into tears at the dinner table a couple of days ago and had to be excused from the table. This didn't really matter to her because she wasn't hungry anyway. She saw her future as very bleak and believed she would never be accepted by any graduate school and that she would never again find anyone she would love.

What would you diagnose Kerry as? ______________________________

2. Leo is 16 years old and lives at home with his step-parents. Since he started in a new school last year, he has become more shy than usual and has only made one friend. He wishes to make more friends, but is afraid that he will say or do something embarrassing around others. Although his work is OK, he rarely says a word in class and becomes incredibly nervous. He trembles and blushes and even feels like vomiting when he is asked to speak in front of the class. At home, he is quite talkative with his family, but becomes quiet if anyone he doesn't know as well comes over. He never goes out to socialize and refuses to attend gatherings. He is aware that his fears are unreasonable, but he can't seem to control them. This really upsets him.

What would you diagnose Leo as? ______________________________

3. Mary is 16 years old and was doing pretty well until about a year ago. While nothing much was going wrong in her life, she had a few problems that were really beginning to get to her. She started to feel worried and a little sad, and had trouble sleeping at night. Things bothered her more than they bothered other people, and she started to get nervous and annoyed when things went wrong. Otherwise she is doing OK. She enjoys being with other people, and though she sometimes argues with her family, she has generally been getting on pretty well with them.

What would you diagnose Mary as? ______________________________

4. Terry is 50 years old and lives alone. He has for many years had virtually no conversational contact with other human beings except to say 'hello' or 'how are you'. He reads newspapers avidly and is well informed in many areas, but he has no interest in the people around him. He prefers to be by himself, finds talk a waste of time and feels awkward when people initiate a relationship with him. He works as a security guard and is known by his co-workers as 'loner' or 'cold fish'. After a while, they no longer even notice him or tease him, since he never seems to notice or care about their teasing anyway. He considers himself different from other people and regards emotionality in others as strange. He experienced the death of his parents without emotion and feels no regret whatsoever at being completely out of contact with the rest of his family.

What would you diagnose Terry as? ______________________________

5. Alan is 27 years old and he was driving with his wife to a computer store when he felt dizzy. As soon as he noticed this sensation, he experienced a rapid and intense surge of sweating, accelerated heart rate, hot flashes, trembling and a feeling of detachment from his body. Fearing he was going to crash his car, he pulled off the road. After ten minutes, the feelings passed and Alan began to feel better, but now he worries extensively that it will happen again and he is reluctant to drive long distances.

What would you diagnose Alan as? ______________________________

6. Rose is 17 years old and lives at home. She is very shy and doesn't socialize much with her work colleagues. One of the reasons for this is that she never goes out to parties or clubs for fear that they might be dirty and contaminated. If she does go out, it would only be to a place she knows well and even then she would avoid touching anything as much as possible. She always carries an anti-bacterial soap with her which she uses often. She avoids shaking hands and touching door handles and coins since many people before her have touched them. Her biggest fear is that she would be responsible in some way for harm done to vulnerable people, especially children and the elderly, and so finds it difficult to visit her sister and her newborn niece. Her fears cause her great anxiety, so she engages in cleaning and checking her behaviours to relax herself.

What would you diagnose Rose as? ______________________________

7. Laura is 26 years old. For the past two weeks, she has been feeling really down. She wakes up in the morning with a flat, heavy feeling that sticks with her all day long. She isn't enjoying things in the way she normally

would. In fact, nothing gives her pleasure. Even when good things happen, they don't seem to make her happy. She pushes on through her days, but it is really hard. The smallest tasks are difficult to accomplish. She finds it hard to concentrate on anything. She feels out of energy and out of steam. And even though she feels tired, when night comes, she can't go to sleep. She feels pretty worthless and very discouraged. Her family has noticed that she hasn't been herself for about the last month and that she has pulled away from them. She just doesn't feel like talking.

What would you diagnose Laura as? ______________________________

8. Barry is 45 years old, single and works in a post office. He enjoys this job as it involves little contact with others. He refused several promotions because he feared the social pressures. He supervises a number of employees, but still finds it hard to give instructions, even to people he has known for years. He had dated a few women he met through family introductions, but he was never confident enough to approach a woman on his own. Perhaps it was his shyness that first attracted Steph, his co-worker. Steph had asked him out, but he declined at first, claiming some excuse. When Steph asked again a week later, he agreed, thinking she must really like him if she were willing to pursue him. The relationship developed and soon they were dating every night. However, the relationship strained when he interpreted any slight hesitation in her voice as a lack of interest. He repeatedly requested reassurance that she cared for him and evaluated every word and gesture for evidence of her feelings. When Steph said she could not see him because she was tired, he assumed she was rejecting him. After several months, the relationship ended because Steph could not stand his constant nagging. As a result, he assumed that Steph had never really cared for him.

What would you diagnose Barry as? ______________________________

9. Philippa is the owner of a successful small business. When asked recently about what makes her company successful, she replied that, among other things, her leadership was the driving force. Currently, though, she is having difficulty hiring a new assistant because she feels that none of the applicants is bright enough to do the job right. She also commented that her employees went out for happy hour last Friday after work, but they did not invite her and added that they don't like that she makes more money than they do. However, she is puzzled by the fact that her friends did not seem interested in how she selected the recent car that she purchased.

What would you diagnose Philippa as? ______________________________

10. Up until a year ago, life was pretty OK for Rachel. But then, things started to change. She thought that people around her were making disapproving comments and talking behind her back. She was convinced that people were spying on her and that they could hear what she was thinking. She lost her drive to participate in her usual work and family activities and retreated to her home, eventually spending most of her day in her room. She was hearing voices even though no one else was around. These voices told her what to do and what to think. She has been living this way for six months.

What would you diagnose Rachel as? ______________________________

11. John is 30 years old. He has been feeling unusually sad and miserable for the last few weeks. Even though he is tired all the time, he has trouble sleeping nearly every night. He doesn't feel like eating and has lost weight. He can't keep his mind on his work and puts off making decisions. Even day-to-day tasks seem too much for him. This has come to the attention of his boss, who is concerned about his lowered productivity.

What would you diagnose John as? ______________________________

12. Arlene is 25 years old and lives in a large suburban house with her parents. As a child she was cheerful and outgoing, but since her adolescence she became demanding, angry and rebellious, with her mood shifting from seemingly happy and content to tearfulness and depression. She mixed with a 'fast crowd', became promiscuous, abused marijuana and ran away from home at 15 with a 17-year-old boy. Two weeks later, they both returned after her parents hired a private investigator. She re-entered school, only to drop out for good in her senior year of high school. Her relationships with men were stormy, full of passion, unbearable longing and violent arguments. After one such relationship had ended abruptly, she made her first suicide attempt, cutting her wrists, which led to her being hospitalized. She has never worked, except for a few months as a receptionist in her father's company. She has never had an idea of what she wants to do with her life apart from being with a 'romantic man'. She never had any female friends and her only source of comfort is her dog. She has often been 'eaten alive' with boredom.

What would you diagnose Arlene as? ______________________________

13. Jane is 34 years old and is a middle-class, white bank executive who has over the last couple of weeks been staying up later at night. She typically wakes up her husband to talk about the 'revolutionary' new ideas she

has about creating an international bank cartel. She is 'full of energy' and talks rapidly about her many ideas.

What would you diagnose Jane as? ______________________________

14. Tom is 19 years old and lives with his single mother. His parents have been divorced for 15 years and his mother finds disciplining him without a father figure quite difficult. He is disobedient and resentful of authority. He is also unwilling to take part in family activities and is violently argumentative when confronted by his mother about his all-night partying. He has been arrested twice for shoplifting and once for driving while intoxicated. His mother believes that he is doing fairly well at school and is the star player of his basketball team, but he has been lying to her – he never completed high school and was never on the basketball team. His lying began when he was 12 years old. He was frequently truanting from school and would spend his time loitering in pool clubs smoking cigarettes or in the outskirts of town setting fire to people's property.

What would you diagnose Tom as? ______________________________

15. Stuart is 24 years old and lives at home with his parents. He has had a few temporary jobs since finishing school, but is now unemployed. Over the last six months, he has stopped seeing his friends and has begun locking himself in his bedroom and refusing to eat with the family or to have a bath. His parents also hear him walking about in his bedroom at night while they are in bed. Even though they know he is alone, they have heard him shouting and arguing as if someone else is there. When they try to encourage him to do more things, he whispers that he won't leave home because he is being spied upon by the neighbour. They realize he is not taking drugs because he never sees anyone or goes anywhere.

What would you diagnose Stuart as? ______________________________

16. Most people agree that Adam, who is 35 years old and an investment banker, has a certain charm. He is bright, articulate and attractive. He possesses a keen sense of humour that draws people to him at social gatherings. He always positions himself in the middle of the room where he can be the centre of attention. The topics of conversation invariably focus on his 'deals', the 'rich and famous' people he has met and his outmanoeuvring of opponents. His next project is always bigger and more daring than the last. He loves an audience. His face will light up when others respond to him with praise or admiration for his business

successes, which are always inflated beyond their true measure. But when the conversation shifts to other people, he loses interest and excuses himself to make a drink or to check his voicemail. When he hosts a party, he urges guests to stay late and feels hurt if they have to leave early. He shows no sensitivity to or awareness of the needs of his friends.

What would you diagnose Adam as? ______________________________

17. Shelly is 28 years old and has had problems relating to her peers since childhood. She was an attractive and a talented gymnast, but she had few friendships. Her mother attributed the problem to her needing to be the 'focus of attention' all the time, and when she was not, she became irritable. As an adolescent, her concern with her physical appearance became excessive and she wore very provocative clothing. She was also very flirtatious with boys, encouraging their interest in her and usually having more than one boyfriend at a time. But none of her friendships with girls lasted. Other girls sometimes initiated a friendship with her and it would develop quickly and intensely, but just as quickly it would dissolve over some emotional conflict. At her first job as a receptionist, she began an affair with the vice president of the company, a married man. She was very dramatic in her conversations with other employees and shamelessly flaunted the gifts he had purchased her. When the vice president was reprimanded, he terminated the affair and she protested dramatically. She began to tell the other employees that she was pregnant and that the father was one of the company executives. She was asked to leave the company. She has been dismissed from three other jobs because of inappropriate relationships or behaviour with male supervisors.

What would you diagnose Shelly as? ______________________________

18. Sean first became upset during the funeral of a Vietnam buddy who had killed himself. When a helicopter flew overhead during the service, he panicked and thought he was back in Vietnam. This set off a series of horrific combat memories, including one in which he had stuck his gun in the face of a Viet Cong officer. 'My God!' he remembered, 'my bullet hit her above the right eye. It took her hair and ripped off her clothes. They took her head to get her earrings'. The night of the funeral, he almost killed his wife, sticking a gun in her face.

What would you diagnose Sean as? ______________________________

19. John is 17 years old and always feels energetic. He has been sleeping for as little as three hours a night for the last week. He has been working in part-time jobs and having lots of good ideas, which he feels especially confident about. He has also been spending more money than he can afford on electronics and clothes from the Internet and on Internet gambling. His family has noticed that he is much more talkative at the moment and is easily distractible.

What would you diagnose John as? ______________________________

20. Steve is 37 years old and on a typical day spends four hours washing his hands. Although he usually takes one shower a day, he spends 60–90 minutes in the shower. When he washes his hair, he keeps the soap in his hair until he has counted to 100 to ensure that his head and hair are clean enough and free of contaminants, such as germs. He also repeatedly cleans other things he comes into contact with, including dishes, clothes, furniture and doorknobs. He has difficulty in resisting his urges to rid himself of germs and contamination.

What would you diagnose Steve as? ______________________________

21. Susan is 45 years old and is often worried. She worries a great deal about her job performance, her children's well-being and her relationships with men. In addition, she worries about a variety of minor matters, such as getting to appointments on time, keeping her house clean and maintaining regular contact with family and friends. It takes her longer than necessary to accomplish tasks because she worries about making decisions. She has trouble sleeping at night and finds that she is exhausted during the day and is irritable with her family.

What would you diagnose Susan as? ______________________________

22. Jonathan is 27 years old and is a mechanic. He has few friends and prefers science-fiction novels to socializing with other people. He looks unkempt, seldom joins in conversations and hardly makes eye contact with people. At work, he seems lost in his thoughts and his co-workers have to whistle to get his attention when he is working on a car. He often looks at colleagues with a strange expression on his face. After his mother passed away, he often experienced 'feeling' his mother standing nearby. These illusions were reassuring to him and he looked forward to their occurrence. However, he realized they were not real. He never tried to reach out to touch the 'spirit', knowing it would disappear

as soon as he drew closer, but he felt that it was enough to feel her presence.

What would you diagnose Jonathan as? ______________________________

23. Laura is 45 years old and is a married lawyer. She was the youngest full partner in the firm's history and is known as the hardest-working member of the firm. She is too proud to turn down a new case and too much of a perfectionist to be satisfied with the work done by her assistants. Displeased by their writing style and sentence structure, she finds herself constantly correcting their briefs and therefore is unable to keep up with her schedule. When assignments get backed up, she cannot decide which to address first and starts making schedules for herself and her staff, but then is unable to meet them and starts working 15 hours a day. She never seems to be able to relax. Even on holidays, she develops elaborate activities schedules for every family member and gets angry and impatient if they refuse to follow her plans. Her husband is fed up with their marriage and can no longer tolerate her emotional coldness, rigid demands and long working hours.

What would you diagnose Laura as? ______________________________

24. Kevin is 35 years old and is a single accountant. He has lived at home with his mother his whole life, except for one year in college from which he returned because of homesickness. His position at work is way below his education level and capabilities. He turned down promotions because he didn't want the responsibility of supervising others and having to make independent decisions. He has worked for the same boss for ten years, gets on well with him and is regarded as a dependable worker. He has lunch everyday with one of his two best friends since childhood and feels lost if his friend is sick and misses a day. Recently, he broke up with his girlfriend, whom he wanted to marry. His mother had disapproved because the woman was from a different religion. Because 'blood is thicker than water', he had decided not to go against his mother's wishes. He is afraid of disagreeing with his mother for fear that she will not be supportive of him and he will then have to fend for himself. In the end, he thought that maybe his girlfriend wasn't right for him at all. He respects his mother's judgement and feels that his own judgement is poor.

What would you diagnose Kevin as? ______________________________

25. Bill is 24 years old and is a handsome, well-dressed employee in an advertising firm. He made a very favourable impression when applying for the job. During the interview, he was very enthusiastic about his personal accomplishments and stated that he had been instrumental in the dramatic success of a small company where he worked part time as a student. However, he began to have trouble with some of his co-workers, who found him annoying because he bragged endlessly about his success and criticized his former co-workers for their incompetence. He also speculated openly to the other male employees that several of the female employees in his department had crushes on him. He dated four women in his department in succession, but these relationships ended with him claiming that the women 'weren't interesting'. In fact, the women simply could not tolerate his self-centred attitude. He had demanded that the furniture in his office be replaced even though it was only three years old. He complained to his manager, stating that his performance exceeded that of all his co-workers and that he should be rewarded for this. At the end of his first year in the company, he was estranged from both his co-workers and his supervisors. He perceived the situation as him being victimized by them because he was so much more successful.

What would you diagnose Bill as? ______________________________

26. Celia is 19 years old and suddenly came home from work at McDonald's and screamed that she was going to die. While standing at her counter, she had experienced the worst sensations in her life. Her heart began to pound like a jackhammer, she was gripped by panic and dread, she felt the ground underneath her was about to give way and she was convinced she was having a stroke or a heart attack. She spent the next two weeks in bed and, thereafter, she refused to walk beyond the front gate.

What would you diagnose Celia as? ______________________________

27. Peter is 20 years old and spends lots of time alone. He does not react correctly when his family try to talk to him, for example, laughing at bad news. He sometimes gets his words mixed up and his family have heard him talking even when he is alone in his room. Sometimes he will go for hours without moving, even though he is not asleep. He also sometimes experiences auditory hallucinations and delusions.

What would you diagnose Peter as? ______________________________

28. Philip is 70 years old and is a retired businessman who appears to be in good health and mentally alert. He and his wife have been married for 50 years and she is the only person he had ever trusted. He has always been suspicious of others; he never confides in anyone but his wife. He is careful about revealing personal information to others, assuming that they are out to take advantage of him. He had refused sincere offers of help from his acquaintances because he suspected their motives. He has always involved himself in work and claims to have no time for play, even after his retirement. He spends most of his time monitoring his stock market investments and has changed brokers several times because he suspected that minor errors on his statements were evidence of attempts made by them to cover up fraud.

What would you diagnose Philip as? ______________________________

The following are the 'correct' answers for the above case studies:

1. Depression
2. Social phobia
3. Stress
4. Schizoid personality disorder
5. Panic disorder
6. OCD
7. Depression
8. Avoidant personality disorder
9. Narcissistic personality disorder
10. Schizophrenia
11. Depression
12. Histrionic personality disorder
13. Schizophrenia
14. Anti-social personality disorder
15. Schizophrenia
16. Narcissistic personality disorder
17. Histrionic personality disorder
18. PTSD
19. Manic depression
20. OCD
21. GAD
22. Schizotypal personality disorder
23. OCD
24. Dependent personality disorder
25. Narcissistic personality disorder

26. Agoraphobia
27. Schizophrenia
28. Schizophrenia

8.2.2 And what about you? Self-assessed mental health

Below you will find a list of the most common mental illnesses and a brief description of their clinical diagnosis. We invite you to estimate: (1) your overall mental well-being; and (2) how likely you think you suffer from each of the mental illnesses listed. If you think you suffer from a mental illness, you should indicate a high number (7, 6), but if you do think you do not suffer from a mental illness, you should indicate a low number (1, 2). A score of 1 indicates that you show no symptoms of that disorder whatsoever and are mentally healthy. There are no right or wrong answers, so you should be honest in your responses.

	Healthy						Unhealthy
1. Overall mental health.	1	2	3	4	5	6	7
2. Acrophobia: an extreme or irrational fear of heights.	1	2	3	4	5	6	7
3. Agoraphobia: a form of anxiety disorder where sufferers fear crowded situations, especially in a confined space, where anxiety may escalate into panic attacks.	1	2	3	4	5	6	7
4. Alzheimer's disease: a neurodegenerative disease characterized by progressive cognitive deterioration together with declining activities of daily living and neuropsychiatric symptoms or behavioural changes.	1	2	3	4	5	6	7
5. Amnesia: any number of conditions in which memory is disturbed.	1	2	3	4	5	6	7
6. Anorexia nervosa: a psychiatric diagnosis that describes an eating disorder characterized by low body weight and body image distortion.	1	2	3	4	5	6	7
7. Aphasia: a loss or impairment of the ability to produce and/or comprehend language.	1	2	3	4	5	6	7
8. Arachnophobia: an abnormal fear of spiders.	1	2	3	4	5	6	7
9. Attention deficit hyperactivity disorder (ADHD): a neurological syndrome that exhibit symptoms such as hyperactivity, forgetfulness, mood shifts, poor impulse control and distractibility.	1	2	3	4	5	6	7
10. Autism: a neurodevelopmental disorder which manifests itself in markedly abnormal social interaction, communication ability, patterns of interest and patterns of behaviour.	1	2	3	4	5	6	7
11. Bipolar disorder: a class of mood disorders where the person experiences states or episodes of depression and/or mania, hypomania and/or mixed states.	1	2	3	4	5	6	7

	Healthy						Unhealthy
12. Bulimia nervosa: an eating disorder in which the subject engages in recurrent binge eating followed by intentionally vomiting, excessive exercise or fasting to compensate for the intake of the food and prevent weight gain.	1	2	3	4	5	6	7
13. Claustrophobia: an anxiety disorder that involves the fear of enclosed or confined spaces.	1	2	3	4	5	6	7
14. Clinical depression: a state of sadness, melancholia or despair that has advanced to the point of being disruptive to an individual's social functioning and/or activities of daily living.	1	2	3	4	5	6	7
15. Dissociative identity disorder (split personality): the existence in an individual of two or more distinct identities or personalities, each with its own pattern of perceiving and interacting with the environment.	1	2	3	4	5	6	7
16. Epilepsy: a chronic neurological condition characterized by recurrent unprovoked seizures.	1	2	3	4	5	6	7
17. Generalized anxiety disorder: an anxiety disorder characterized by excessive and uncontrollable worry about everyday things. The frequency, intensity and duration of the worry are disproportionate to the actual source of worry.	1	2	3	4	5	6	7
18. Gender identity disorder: a condition in which a person who has been assigned one gender (usually at birth on the basis of their sex) identifies as belonging to another gender or does not conform with the gender role their society prescribes to them.	1	2	3	4	5	6	7
19. Kleptomania: an inability to resist impulses to steal.	1	2	3	4	5	6	7
20. Munchausen syndrome: a disorder where sufferers mimic real diseases, presenting a great problem to themselves and their healthcare professionals.	1	2	3	4	5	6	7
21. Obsessive-compulsive disorder: an anxiety disorder that is most commonly characterized by a subject's obsessive (repetitive, distressing, intrusive) thoughts and related compulsions (tasks or rituals) which attempt to neutralize the obsessions.	1	2	3	4	5	6	7
22. Ophidiophobia: an abnormal fear of snakes.	1	2	3	4	5	6	7
23. Panic attacks: a period of intense fear or discomfort, typically with an abrupt onset and usually lasting no more than 30 minutes.	1	2	3	4	5	6	7
24. Parkinson's disease: a movement disorder often characterized by muscle rigidity, tremor, a slowing of physical movement and, in extreme cases, a loss of physical movement.	1	2	3	4	5	6	7

	Healthy						Unhealthy
25. Post-traumatic stress disorder: a term for certain psychological consequences of exposure to, or confrontation with, stressful experiences that the person experiences as highly traumatic.	1	2	3	4	5	6	7
26. Schizophrenia: a mental disorder characterized by impairments in the perception or expression of reality and by significant social or occupational dysfunction.	1	2	3	4	5	6	7
27. Social anxiety: an experience of fear, apprehension or worry regarding social situations and being evaluated by others.	1	2	3	4	5	6	7
28. Tourette syndrome: an inherited neurological disorder with onset in childhood, characterized by the presence of multiple motor tics and at least one phonic (verbal) tic, which characteristically wax and wane.	1	2	3	4	5	6	7

8.3 Symptoms

Despite the stories we see in films and books, the scenario in which a mentally ill colleague turns violent in the workplace is extremely rare and it is estimated that less than one per cent of sufferers will exhibit such extreme behaviour. However, the signs can be acted out in different ways and some of the key signs to watch out for include the following:

- Talk of wanting to die or a desire to hurt oneself or others.
- Sharing odd delusions or conspiracy theories.
- Changes in behaviour or personality, such as an outgoing and energetic person becoming withdrawn and reclusive.
- A reduction in productivity.
- A lack of interest in work and other interests outside of work.
- An increase in absence rates and punctuality, particularly if the individual is consistently late in the morning.
- Lack of cooperation or a general inability to work with colleagues.
- Increasingly lethargic.
- Overly emotional and unable to cope with high-pressure situations.
- Increasingly erratic behaviour and working long and intense hours.
- Loss of motivation.
- An attitude of feeling resigned.
- Obsessive activity.

- Increased activity.
- Over-reacting to normal situations.
- Increased accidents or safety problems.
- Frequent complaints of fatigue or unexplained pains.
- Expressions of strange or grandiose ideas.
- Displays of anger or blaming of others.

The main issue is a change in their behaviour which seems to last a long time and causes them and those they deal with discomfort, embarrassment and social difficulty. As an employer or manager, it is not your job or your responsibility to diagnose someone in your team with a mental health problem. However, being aware of the signs that suggest someone might be experiencing a mental illness is as important as knowing whether they are suffering from a physical ailment or something else. Your awareness of the issue may be the first step in supporting them through the illness and in the subsequent chapters of this book, we will explore the things that can be done to support them.

It is important to emphasize that people behaving in odd or peculiar ways may simply be having a bad day or week, or may be working through a particularly difficult time in their lives that is a temporary state. Behaviour changes such as those listed above may reflect personal difficulties that could in fact be resolved quickly. They may be signs that the person is no longer happy in their job or is having a difficult relationship with one or more colleagues. The individual might be going through a particularly stressful time in their life for any number of reasons, including those outside of work. Divorce, bereavement, even moving house can elicit some of the same behavioural and emotional responses as many common mental illnesses.

A pattern of behaviour that continues for a longer period, however, may indicate an underlying problem and could indicate that the person is experiencing a mental health problem that goes beyond being 'stressed out' and requires professional help.

The first signs of mental health problems will differ from person to person and are not always easy to spot. In many cases of moderate depression or anxiety, which is the most common type of mental health problem, the person becoming distressed may not display symptoms or may seek to hide them because they worry about what others will say or think about them. For employers and managers, the challenge is often in spotting the more subtle signs.

8.4 Spotting subtleties

Managers need to be aware of the more subtle patterns of behaviour associated with mental disorders and how these might manifest themselves in the workplace environment. If managers and co-workers are able to identify the warning signs, they may be able to decrease the impact of mental disorders in the workplace.

There are three issues here. The *first* issue is *who* does the reporting? The people most likely to notice personal distress and bizarre or inappropriate behaviours are not managers, but those who report to a person and the person's customers. Increasingly organizations are using 360-degree feedback for training and development. They do this because different people have different exposure to and experience of other people in the organization. Often the manager is the last person to discover that an employee has a drink or drug problem or is depressed.

One implication of this is that it may be useful to add to the list of items in a 360-degree feedback form issues relating to a person's change in behaviour, mood, etc. The questions need to be subtly put, but could be very important to enable early detection.

Figure 8.1 below provides an example of the possible sources of data in this type of multi-rater feedback mechanism.

The *second* issue is what they should look for. One possible way of thinking through this is to use instruments that are used in psychiatric screening. The following list provides some useful behavioural indicators of common mental illnesses and how the symptoms may manifest themselves in the workplace. This is based on the well-known and well-used GHQ12 (General Health Questionnaire-12 item version), which describes the issues as follows:

> Have you noticed or has the person of interest talked about:
>
> - having poor concentration all the time?
> - losing lots of sleep because of worry?
> - feeling increasingly useless and unable to take part in things?
> - feeling they can't seem to make even the smallest decisions anymore?
> - feeling of being under strain the whole time?
> - the suggestion that they seem unable to overcome their day-to-day difficulties?
> - feeling that they seem to have no more enjoyment in life?

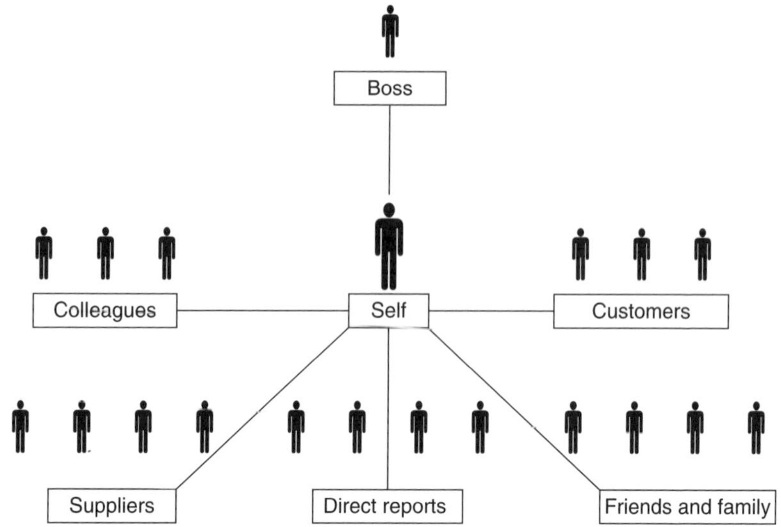

FIGURE 8.1 Multi-rater instruments

- feeling that they are unable to face up to their problems?
- feeling unhappy and depressed, and saying this a number of times?
- feeling that they seem to have lost confidence?
- feeling they are an essentially worthless person and saying this on more than one occasion?
- feeling unreasonably happy?

Another approach, based on the Langner 22 model, is to look out for people complaining of the following symptoms: that of late they have felt physically weak; that they can't seem to get going in the morning; that they are always in low spirits; that they sometimes feel hot; that they notice their heart beating hard; that they have a poor appetite; that they seem restless all the time; that they are worrying all the time about everything; that they sometimes seem short of breath; that they are nervous about lots of things; that they have experienced fainting; that they have trouble sleeping; that they have stomach troubles; that they have poor memory; that they sometimes break out into cold sweats; that they notice their hands trembling; that they report a 'fullness in the head'; that they seem to have many worries; that they say they feel apart from others; that they note that nothing seems to turn out right for them; that they have constant headaches; and that nothing is worthwhile anymore.

Many of these observations relate to anxiety (restlessness, tension, feeling scared), depression (tired, guilty, hopelessness), somatic illnesses (aches and pains, weakness, dizziness) and inadequacy (problems thinking, concentrating, irritability).

Indeed, one could look out for signs of particular problems and we outline some of the most common indicators below:

8.4.1 Signs of depression at work

People who are depressed may:

- be tearful, nervous or irritable;
- have low confidence – this should ring alarm bells if they display a lack of confidence in areas where they previously excelled;
- lose interest in their work and find it difficult to concentrate;
- feel overwhelmed and unable to deliver what is expected of them;
- lose their appetite and stop joining in on social events;
- get tired easily and leave work early.

8.4.2 Signs of anxiety

As we have discussed earlier in this book, anxiety takes many forms, from general anxiety to anxiety triggered by a particular situation (a phobia). People experiencing anxiety may:

- appear pale and tense;
- be easily startled by everyday office noises;
- have difficulty concentrating on their work;
- be irritable and short-tempered;
- try to avoid certain situations;
- suffer from panic attacks typically characterized by short breaths, feeling very hot or cold, sweating and feeling faint.

8.4.3 Signs of stress

People showing signs of stress may exhibit the following symptoms:

- a decline in physical appearance;
- chronic fatigue and tiredness;
- increase in health complaints, such as headaches, skin problems, etc.;
- being cynical and resentful of hierarchy;
- sad expressions, slumped posture, etc.;

- being irrational and quick to fly off the handle;
- reduced productivity;
- unable to concentrate or complete a task;
- a higher rate of absenteeism.

8.4.4 Signs of schizophrenia

People showing signs of schizophrenia may exhibit the following symptoms:

- deteriorating work performance;
- change in personality;
- change in personal hygiene and appearance;
- trouble concentrating for prolonged periods of time;
- withdrawal from social activities;
- appearing emotionally distant or detached;
- decreased motivation and interest in work.

Of course, there are many other forms of illness detailed in earlier chapters that are much more difficult to spot, but a good understanding of the nature of these disorders should help managers and colleagues to spot some of the early warning signs.

The *third* issue is who takes responsibility for the whole issue? Assuming peers, reports and managers notice a colleague who is showing signs of some mental problem, the question is what should they do? Who should they give this information to: their boss, HR, the in-house doctor (if one exists)? Does the organization have processes and procedures available to deal with this issue? All too frequently, if there is a policy, it is unstated, unclear or not readily available and the mentally distressed worker is not helped because nobody knows what to do or whose responsibility it really is to deal with.

8.5 Responding in a crisis

People with mental health problems sometimes experience a crisis, such as breaking down in tears, having a panic attack, feeling suicidal or losing touch with reality. Colleagues may feel a sense of crisis too, but it's important that those working with the individual also stay calm.

The following list gives some general strategies that you can use to assist you:

- Listen to your colleague without making judgements.
- Reassure them and offer practical information or support.
- Ask your colleague what would help them and involve them in the solution.
- Avoid confrontation, even if they become agitated or aggressive.
- Don't send them home if they would prefer some quiet time to themselves.
- Encourage them to seek appropriate professional help.
- If you are aware that a colleague has self-harmed, make sure they get the first aid they need.

Seeing, hearing or believing things that no one else does can be the symptom of a mental illness. It can be frightening and upsetting. Gently remind your colleague who you are and why you are there. Don't reinforce or dismiss their experiences, but acknowledge how they are making them feel.

Helping someone with a mental health problem through a crisis can be stressful and upsetting. It is important to talk it through with your HR manager, your boss or a friend without identifying your colleague.

8.6 A breakdown in coping

We all have coping strategies for when things go wrong. How people suffer from stress or not can be dependent on their coping strategies. Hence, psychologists have spent considerable effort in describing and categorizing different strategies, some of which are thought to be 'successful' and adaptive, and others less so. These strategies are stress-specific concepts; as such, they tend to be better predictors of breakdown.

How people suffer from stress or not can be dependent on their coping strategies

One distinction is between *problem*-focused coping (aimed at problem solving or doing something to alter the source of stress) and *emotion*-focused coping (aimed at reducing or managing the emotional distress that is associated with or cued by a particular situation). Others have pointed out that this distinction is too simple. Thus, Carver, Scherer and Weintraub (1989) have distinguished between both types of coping: some emotion-focused responses involve denial, others involve positive reinterpretation of events and yet others involve the seeking out of social support. Similarly, problem-focused coping can potentially involve several distinct activities, such as planning, taking direct action, seeking assistance,

screening out particular activities and sometimes stopping working for an extended period. The following list details both adaptive and non-adaptive coping strategies mentioned by Carver *et al.*:

1. Positive reinterpretation and growth.
2. Active coping.
3. Planning.
4. Seeking social support for emotional problems.
5. Seeking social support for instrumental problems.
6. Suppression of competing activities.
7. Religion.
8. Acceptance.
9. Mental disengagement.
10. Focus on/venting emotion.
11. Behavioural disengagement.
12. Denial.
13. Restraint coping.
14. Alcohol use.
15. Humour.

Most of us choose a variety of coping methods, some of which are more useful than others. However an over-reliance on certain methods (denial, drug taking) can easily indicate personal problems.

It is argued that, for various reasons, individuals tend to adopt and habitually use a few of these coping patterns, which may or may not be successful. Resilience and coping are clearly related: the resilient person has more and better coping strategies than the less resilient person.

8.7 Formal screening

One way in which employers have tried to monitor and manage mental illness has been through formal programmes to screen for certain disorders. This is particularly common in the case of alcohol and substance misuse and for conditions such as depression and stress. Effectiveness trials have demonstrated that formal depression screening and the associated care programmes can significantly improve treatment and clinical outcomes (Simon *et al.*, 2004). Given the associated costs of depression in the workplace, one would expect that employers would invest in screening programmes such as this, but widespread uptake has not occurred to date. In addition, these programmes rarely focus on the less understood disorders such as psychopathy, and as such it is clear that a more useful mechanism for spotting mental illness in the workplace is needed.

8.8 Summary

Over the course of their lives, most people have to deal with difficult issues like relationship breakdown, bereavement, physical health and other issues which can easily provoke mental illness. The term 'nervous breakdown' is used by laypeople to describe a serious episode of mental illness provoked by a variety of causes.

Those with mental health education and social awareness are more responsive to the cues of distress than others. Whilst everyone might experience a temporary, possibly dramatic change in behaviour, it is the *acuity and chronicity* of change from normal healthy functioning to dysfunctioning that is important.

Whilst it is common, if not required in law, that people in workplaces are trained in first aid, few it seems are trained in mental health awareness and noticing the early symptoms of a mental illness. Even those that are can be uncertain about how they should react – that is, what they should do in that situation.

chapter 9

Cultural Nuances and the Globalization of Mental Illness

9.1 Introduction

As organizations have continued to work in an increasingly global way, managers and HR functions have been faced with the challenge of developing systems and approaches that work across national and continental boundaries. This has created challenges when trying to develop standardized approaches to recruitment, training, diversity, etc. The approach that works in one country may not fit with the social and cultural norms of another country on the other side of the globe. With an increasing focus on international mobility, organizations must continue to focus effort on responding to global issues in a sensitive manner.

Mental illness is certainly a global issue that must be considered and workplace attitudes towards the mentally ill may be influenced by factors such as race, culture, religious belief and the condition of medical services in that country,

This highlights the need to compare the attitude towards mental illness in different countries, cultures and social groups. Indeed, there are very different cultural definitions of health:

- Health as not ill, e.g., no symptoms, no visits to doctor, therefore I am healthy.
- Health as reserve, i.e., I come from a strong family, I recovered quickly from the operation.
- Health as a description of behaviour, i.e., usually applied to other people rather than the self – for example, they are healthy because they look after themselves, exercise, etc.

- Health as physical fitness and vitality: used more often by younger respondents and often in reference to a male because the male health concept is more commonly tied to 'feeling fit', whereas females have a concept of 'feeling full of energy' and tend to describe health more in the social world in terms of being lively and having good relationships with others.
- Health as psycho-social well-being: defined in terms of a person's mental well-being.
- Health as function: the idea of health as the ability to perform one's duties, e.g., being able to do what you want when you want without being prevented in any way by ill health or physical limitations. (Blaxter, cited in Morrison and Bennett, 2009) .

It has been known for a long time that people from different cultures with exactly the same disorder and symptoms report them very differently. There are often very noticeable cultural differences when the following well-established questions are asked: 'what do you call your problem?'; 'what do you think caused your problem?'; 'why do you think it started when it did?'; 'what does your illness do to you?'; 'how severe is it?'; 'how long do you think it will last?'; 'what do you fear most about your illness?'; and 'what treatment do you think you should receive?'

Globalization and mental health are far more interrelated than one may first appreciate. Globalization is essentially the process by which businesses start to internationally integrate. That being said, while globalization mostly refers to business-related concepts, it can also occur with the immaterial, with aspects such as beliefs, religions and cultures all being transferrable. Globalization refers to processes that increase worldwide exchanges of national and cultural resources, being traceable back to 100 BC with the formation of the 'Silk Road' in Asia. In 2000, the International Monetary Fund (IMF) suggested that there are essentially four dimensions to the process of globalization: trade and transactions; capital and investment movements; the migration and movement of people; and the dissemination of knowledge.

Globalization and mental health are far more interrelated than one may first appreciate

With such a broad variety of sub-dimensions, the relationships between these are complex and are invariably difficult to understand, with some noted effects of globalization ranging from organizations to the natural environment. The concept of globalization alone should spark logical connections with mental health problems. As with disease, conditions such as depression are easily transferable. The best example to highlight this is the obscene rise in the eating disorders anorexia and bulimia in young girls. The Western stereotypical view of women and their values has through the globalization of the media become a well-known cause of such afflictions elsewhere in the world.

Through the use of examples, it can be highlighted how this problem is far more wide-ranging than was originally thought. After what may have seemed a decade of innovation, advancement and knowledge building, the West has aggressively spread its modern knowledge of mental illness around the world, the most prominent example being the DSM-V. While it is true that this has been done in the name of science, believing and proclaiming that such diagnostic manuals reveal the biological basis of illness, there is now good evidence to suggest that in the process of teaching the rest of the world, the Western 'symptom repertoire' also transferred. Indeed, a handful of disorders, such as depression, PTSD and eating disorders, appear to be spreading across cultures with the speed of contagious diseases.

While mental illness has always been around, typically by nature it has always existed in various forms. This, however, is becoming a thing of the past, with the main problem being that there is now conformity between symptoms. As with common genetic principles and that of Darwinian natural selection, failing to properly consider the variations in the long term causes problems and adaptation issues, all aspects that need to be considered for future generations.

One prominent example from the work of Dr Sing Lee may help to highlight this. During the 1980s and 1990s, Dr Lee looked at anorexics in a sample of people in Hong Kong. Rather than the typical symptoms seen today, his patients did not intentionally diet or view themselves as fat; rather, their main complaint was that of a bloated stomach. It is also important to note that the prevalence rate was very low, at around 0.01 per cent of the population. While continuing his work, an incident in 1994 changed the view of the East's perception of anorexia forever. The first death related to anorexia was reported in Hong Kong and rather than the Chinese newspapers using Eastern understanding to highlight the issue, they copied notes from the American DSM reporting that anorexia in Hong Kong was the same disorder that appeared in the USA and Europe. In the wake of this one incident, the transfer of knowledge about the nature of anorexia went only one way – from West to East – and subsequently Western ideas obscured both the understanding of the illness in Hong Kong and in turn the expression of the illness, with sufferers beginning to report symptoms much more associated with the American version of the illness.

Dr Lee, who once saw two or three anorexic patients per year, was by the end of the 1990s seeing this many new cases each month. This increase sparked another series of media reports, leading to rates of 3–10 per cent of young women in Hong Kong showing signs of an eating disorder. In contrast to Dr Lee's earlier patients, these women most often cited fat phobia as the single most important reason for their self-starvation. By 2007, about 90 per cent of the anorexics treated by Dr Lee reported fat phobia.

What has since been noted by Lee *et al.* (2007) is that: 'Culture shapes the way general psychopathology is going to be translated partially or completely into specific psychopathology. When there is a cultural atmosphere in which professionals, the media, schools, doctors and psychologists all recognize and endorse and talk about and publicize eating disorders, then people can be triggered to consciously or unconsciously pick eating-disorder pathology as a way to express that conflict.'

The problem becomes especially acute in a time of globalization, when symptom repertoires can cross borders with ease. While evidence such as this highlights the issue well, it is only recently that it is being researched widely. Even though the underlying science is sound and the intentions are good, the export of Western theory can have detrimental and unexpected consequences. While the problems of globalization are evident, there can also be positives resulting from it. For instance, the very traditional view of mental illness was that it was some sort of supernatural affliction. Those with visible symptoms were often subjected to cruel punishment and stigma. The West's research, however, suggested that it should be treated more like a 'brain disease' over which the patient has little choice or responsibility. This was promoted both culturally and scientifically with the aim that the sufferer would be protected from blame and stigma. But does the 'brain disease' belief actually reduce the stigma?

The Western push for 'mental-health literacy' or, in other words, the ability of the layperson to understand and identify mental illness, has gained ground. Studies show that much of the world has steadily adopted this medical model of mental illness. Although these changes are most extensive in the USA and Europe, similar shifts have been documented elsewhere. When asked to name the sources of mental illness, people from a variety of cultures are increasingly likely to mention 'chemical imbalance', 'brain disease' or 'genetic/inherited factors'.

The limitations of Western ideas and treatments can be witnessed in the case of schizophrenia. One interesting result from years of research is that in the cross-cultural study of mental illness, people with schizophrenia in developing countries appear to fare better over time than those living in industrialized nations. This was the startling result of three large international studies carried out by WHO over the course of 30 years, starting in the early 1970s.

McGruder (1999) carried out research which supports this trend and found that far from being stigmatizing, in an African population, these beliefs served certain useful functions, such the ill person being bound to the family and kinship group. Therefore, it seems that globalization and the impact of psychological literature has far-reaching side-effects. In places such as Africa, it seems that (at least at the time) the West's view is not a prominent one. That being said, as telecommunications and least economically developed countries (LEDCs) develop, all that will change and the similar rising patterns of prevalence as seen in Asia will be seen elsewhere too.

It is widely recognized that there are huge global inequalities in the amount of resources available to support mental health needs, with an estimate from the WHO (2005) that more than 90 per cent of the world's mental health resources are located in high-income countries.

9.2 Cultural factors in mental health

There is an extensive anthropological and psychiatric literature base on the role that cultural factors play in mental health. It has been argued and demonstrated that culture affects all aspects of mental health: how people express, experience, manage and seek help for their symptoms.

Some cultures somaticize illness and choose to express mental pain as physical pain. There are cultural differences in terms of the sensitivity to, knowledge of, empathy for and reactions to different illnesses. There are also cultural differences in the type of explanations that different cultures have for mental illnesses. Some see causes as predominantly:

1. physiological, medical or genetic;
2. psychological. including those favouring psychoanalytic explanations;
3. sociological, economic or environmental;

4. supernatural or theological;
5. fatalistic (chance, luck).

Furnham (1994) found that where people were asked to comment on the extent to which their current state of health was due to the following factors, they tended to cluster in eight directions:

1. *Emotional well-being*: my emotions (whether I feel 'on top' of my life or pressured by it); 'inner forces' of my psyche; my relationships with family and friends; my state of mind; particular events in my life at this time.
2. *Work-home interface*: my working environment; my home environment; the current circumstances at work; the circumstances of my home life.
3. *Lifestyle*: my overall lifestyle: 'taking good care of myself'; whether or not I am actively taking action to be healthy (e.g., monitoring my diet, exercise, etc.); my everyday behaviour (e.g., getting enough sleep, eating regularly).
4. *Constitution*: the constitution with which I was born; my body's natural defences.
5. *Societal factors*: the society in which I live; the culture within which I live; the care of medical professionals.
6. *Fate*: simple probability; good or bad luck.
7. *Environment*: the weather; whether or not I am being exposed at present to certain substances (e.g., pollution; additives in food).
8. *Supernatural powers*: whether there is somebody 'ill wishing' me or not (God or some other supernatural power).

To a large extent, some cultures favour one explanation over another. For instance, some *socio-centric cultures* with strong social links and bonds, where people are very interdependent and where people define themselves exclusively by their group membership, tend inevitably to favour external, social explanations. Similarly, people from an *egocentric culture* with weaker social links take a less traditional and more modern approach to illness.

Cultures also choose very different metaphors for their distress. Various studies have looked at health beliefs of ordinary people. Stainton Rogers (1991) noted that explanations for good health divided nicely into two categories (those which arise *inside* and those *outside* the individual) which were further subdivided. Four types of explanations related to internal explanations: *behaviour* (looking after yourself, adopting a healthy lifestyle, using preventive services like inoculations); *mind* (positive attitudes, not worrying, taking responsibility for yourself); *heredity* (healthy constitution); and *the body's defences* (fighting off disease).

External explanations fell into three categories: *chance*; *social policy* (public health measures, good living standards); and *medical advances* (inoculations, contraception). Asked the question 'what makes people ill?', a similar categorization occurred at least for internal factors (unhealthy behaviour, mind and heredity), but there were rather more external factors: chance; other people (upsetting one or exposing one to germs); disease organisms (infection); products of social forces (inequality, pollution, advertising); and medical intervention.

Stainton Rogers found eight quite distinct (though interrelated) 'theories' for health and illness:

1. The 'body as machine' account, within which illness is regarded as naturally occurring and 'real', and modern biomedicine as the only valid source of effective treatment for any kind of serious illness.
2. The 'body under siege' account, in which the individual is seen to be under threat and attack from germs and diseases, interpersonal conflicts and the 'stress' of modern life acting upon the body through the 'mind'.
3. The 'inequality of access' account, which is concerned about the unfair allocation of modern medicine and the lack of availability to those who need them most.
4. The 'cultural critique' of medicine account, based upon a 'dominance' sociological worldview of exploitation and oppression.
5. The 'health promotion' account, which stresses the wisdom of adopting a 'healthy lifestyle' in order for good health to be achieved and maintained, and illness to be prevented.
6. The 'robust individualism' account, which is more concerned with the individual's right to a 'satisfying life' and their freedom to choose how to live their lives than with the aetiology of illness.
7. The 'God's power' account, within which health is a product of 'right living', spiritual well-being and God's care.
8. The 'willpower' account, which sees the individual as prominently in control and stresses the moral responsibility of the individual to use their 'will' to maintain good health.

Again, certain cultures favour some of these over others.

9.3 Seeking help

There are also cultural issues in *pathways to treatment*. People try to make sense of their health and illness, and of their signs and symptoms of ill health. According to Helman (1990), they typically ask the following questions:

1. What has happened? This includes organizing the symptoms and signs into a recognizable pattern and giving it a name or identity.
2. Why has it happened? This explains the aetiology of the condition.
3. Why has it happened to me? This tries to relate the illness to aspects of the patient, such as behaviour, diet, body build, personality or heredity.
4. Why now? This concerns the timing of the illness and its mode of onset (sudden or slow).
5. What would happen to me if nothing were done about it? This considers its likely course, outcome, prognosis and dangers.
6. What are its likely effects on other people (family, friends, employers and work colleagues) if nothing were done about it? This includes loss of income or employment and strain on family relationships.
7. What should I do about it – or to whom should I turn for further help? Strategies for treating the condition include self-medication, consultation with friends or family, or going to see a doctor.

We know that cultures differ considerably in terms of their belief in, choice of, and willingness to, adhere to certain medical interventions compared to others. For instance, some strongly favour Western biological, orthodox medicine, while others are more in favour of a complementary and alternative approach. These different approaches see health and illness quite differently and suggest rather different approaches:

- *Health*: whereas conventional medicine sees health as an absence of disease, alternative medicine frequently mentions a balance of opposing forces (both external and internal).
- *Disease*: whereas conventional medical professionals see disease as a specific, locally defined deviation in organ or tissue structure, alternative and traditional practitioners stress body-wide signs, such as body language indicating disruptive forces and/or restorative processes.
- *Diagnosis*: whereas conventional medicine stresses morphological classification based on location and aetiology, alternative interpretations often consider problems of functionality to be diagnostically useful.
- *Therapy*: conventional conventional medicine often claims to destroy, demolish or suppress the sickening forces, alternative therapies often aim to strengthen the vitalizing, health-promoting forces. Alternative therapists seem particularly hostile to chemical therapies and surgery.

- *The patient*: whereas in much conventional medicine, the patient is the passive recipient of external solutions, in alternative approaches, the patient is an active participant in regaining health.

Aakster (1986) described three main models of medical thinking: the *pharmaceutical* model is a demonstrable deviation of function or structure that can be diagnosed by careful observation. The causes of disease are mainly germ-like and the application of therapeutic technology is all-important. The *integrational* model resulted from technicians attempting to reintegrate the body. This approach is not afraid of allowing for psychological and social causes to be specified in the aetiology of illness. The third model has been labelled *holistic* and does not distinguish between soma, psyche and social. It stresses total therapy and holds up the idea of a natural way of living

9.4 Depression: an example

The Southeast Asian community view depression as 'self-indulgent' and there is little tolerance for cognitions of the self. By comparing illness presentation between South Asians and White Americans, Karasz (2005) found that the South Asians interpreted the symptoms of depression in situational terms – as an emotional reaction as opposed to a pathogenic state – and were unable to label the illness. This suggests that depression may not be viewed as a disease state by the Asian community.

Whether depression is experienced or expressed in psychological, emotional or physical terms is likely to be a reflection of the cultural background of the individual. Members of ethnic minorities, particularly Asians, usually only choose to utilize mental healthcare services when they think that their altered state of functioning is related to their physical well-being. A British community survey found that there was an under-representation of British Asians in psychiatric statistics, particularly for affective disorders such as depression. Asians are known to be frequently present in primary care, but not with mental illness. Furthermore, primary care research in the UK reveals that although South Asians are found to make more frequent visits to their GPs than the white British population, they are less likely to have their psychological difficulties (and particularly depression) identified.

Furnham and Malik (1994) provided several possible explanations for this under-representation. *First*, it could imply that depression is a Western phenomenon and that Asians are psychologically healthier. Symptoms commonly manifested by sufferers from the West are rare or non-existent in non-Western cultures. *Second*, the somatization hypothesis may explain the under-representation of mental illness amongst British Asians. It has been suggested that Asians living in the UK are reluctant to disclose psychological problems to health professionals. *Third*, there is clinical evidence for Asians who become depressed to commonly present with somatic problems, usually complaints of widespread pain, headaches and difficulty in breathing. The experience of acculturation to a Western lifestyle also increases the prevalence of depression.

In a community survey in the UK, Nazroo (1997) found that there were lower rates of depression amongst Asian migrants, including British Bangladeshi's, compared with their British white counterparts. Nevertheless, this may simply be due to a failure to recognize depression by both the health professionals and the Asian sufferers themselves. It is possible that Asian women are unable to recognize depression as an illness because they are unable to dissociate symptoms of depression from the feeling of loneliness that may accompany their migration to Britain; hence, depression may be perceived as part of an everyday life experience.

The beliefs of British Asian migrants in the UK are influenced by the values of both their native culture and the host culture (Helman, 1990); however, there is evidence for traditional cultural beliefs being more deeply embedded and structured than those that exist in Western culture. In Western countries, the public attribute depression mainly to social-environmental factors, while biological causes are viewed as less important. This suggests that those who attribute mental illness to factors that are outside the control of the individual (i.e., biological factors) will have a less negative reaction towards the mentally ill, whereas those who attribute the illness to the individual themselves are less likely to have a positive attitude and interact with the mentally ill. There is a positive relationship between blaming the mentally ill individual and increasing the social distance from the mentally ill. However, the study also found a desire to increase social distance from those who had biologically based causal beliefs regarding mental illness.

In non-Western cultures, there is a tendency to regard a supernatural force, such as black magic and possession by evil spirits, as the underlying cause for mental illness. Traditional pre-immigration health beliefs and illness behaviours are likely to persist amongst immigrant communities in the UK. The use of religious or spiritual healers, who offer culture-specific approaches to mental illness and treatment, is an established form of treatment within some Asian communities. Asians living in the UK are known to use such traditional healers. Furthermore, cognitive factors (particularly religion and prayer) have been reported as important in managing depression by Pakistani Muslim women.

A number of studies have demonstrated the impact that cultural conceptions of mental illness have on help-seeking and the way in which the mentally ill are treated by health professionals and the public. Asian cultures place more emphasis on the lay referral system, particularly turning to a family member for help. This is consistent with the view that South Asian women predominantly focus on the family – and particularly their husbands – for support. The seeking of professional help is relatively rare in many non-Western societies and among immigrant and minority groups in the West (Sussman, Robins and Earls, 1987); moreover, ethnic minority members are less likely to utilize voluntary specialty mental health services (Ying and Miller, 1992).

Asian cultures have a tendency to conceal mental illness from the wider community as the reputation of the family is at stake. They seem to attach greater stigma to mental illness compared to their British white counterparts. It is possible that in Asian cultures, the disclosure of mental illness in the family reduces the prospects of an arranged marriage. Thus, the interests of the family supersedes individual interests. This may lead to a preference for private coping strategies.

9.5 Culture shock

Culture shock is a form of (temporary) mental illness that is the result of moving from one country, culture or region to another. Over the years, various researchers have tried to refine the definition of the term, looking at very specific psychological factors or facets that make up the experience. It has been seen as a loss of one's culture, a marker of moving from one culture to another and as a resocialization in another culture. It comes as a 'hurtful surprise' to many who travel for various reasons.

There remains no clear definition of culture shock and various attempts have been made to 'unpack' the definition (Ward, Bochner and Furnham, 2001):

1. *Strain* due to the effort required to make the necessary psychological adaptations.

2. A *sense of loss* and *feelings of deprivation* with regard to friends, status, profession and possessions.
3. Being *rejected* by/and or rejecting members of the new culture.
4. *Confusion* in terms of role, role expectations and values in the new culture.
5. *Surprise*, *anxiety* and even *disgust* and *indignation* after becoming aware of cultural differences.
6. *Feelings of impotence* due to not being able to cope with the new environment.

People recognize culture shock immediately, though they are often surprised by it. There are many related definitions, but nearly all of them convey a similar meaning. The concepts quoted are 'disorientation', 'anxious confusion', 'mental shock' or 'transition shock'. It is agreed that culture shock is the disorientating experience of suddenly finding that the perspectives, behaviours and experience of an individual, group or whole society are not shared by others. However, it is also agreed that it is a ubiquitous and normal stage in any acculturative adaptive process and is one that all 'travellers' experience. Going to 'strange places' and losing the power of easy communication can disrupt self-identity, worldviews and indeed all systems of acting, feeling and thinking.

There are long lists of the symptoms of culture shock, which include cognitive, emotional, physiological and other reactions. Some researchers have attempted to specify personal factors that seem to predict who and to what extent individuals suffer from culture shock, like openness, neuroticism, language proficiency and tolerance for contradiction. Zhou *et al*. (2008) suggested that there are essentially three contemporary theories in the area: *stress and coping* (cross-culturally, travellers need to develop coping strategies to deal with stress because life changes are inherently stressful); *culture learning* (cross-cultural travellers need to learn culturally relevant social skills to survive and thrive in their new settings); and *social identification* (cross-cultural transition may involve changes in cultural identity and intergroup relations). They propose that there are both individual-level (relating to the person or situation) and societal-level variables (relating to the society of origin and the society of settlement) that jointly determine stress and skills deficits, which in turn determine stress coping and skills acquisition.

Culture shock is conceived as a serious, acute and sometimes chronic affective reaction to a new (social) environment. However, there are other closely related 'shocking' experiences, which include the following:

- *Invasion shock*: this occurs in places where tourists or other visitors suddenly appear in large numbers in a particular setting and overwhelm the locals, who become a minority in their own living space. Because the 'invaders' retain their cultural morals (for example, dress and social interaction), they can surprise, frustrate and offend the locals. In this sense, the locals have culture shock without actually going anywhere.

- *Reverse culture shock*: this occurs when returning to one's home culture to find it different from that which was recalled. In this sense, you can never go home again because it does not exist. It is about re-adjusting, re-acculturating and re-assimilating in the home culture .
- *Re-professionalization and re-licensing shock*: this occurs when trained professionals do not have their qualifications accepted by a host country and have to be retrained and accepted.
- *Business shock*: this is the realization that so many subtle business practices vary considerably from one culture to the next.
- *Race culture shock*: this concerns being a racial minority in an institution within one's country. Class and race-specific styles of dress, speech, etc. can seriously shock people who do not expect them.

9.6 Culture-bound syndromes

> Recurrent and locality specific patterns of abnormal behaviour and troubling experience that may not be linked to a particular diagnostic category. They are indigenously considered to be 'illness' or at least afflictions … and have local names. They are localised, folk, diagnostic categories that frame coherent meaning for certain repetitive, patterned and troubling sets of experiences and observations. (DSM-IV, American Psychiatric Association)

9.7 Summary

As the burden caused by mental illness around the world continues to grow, employees and managers working in global, multinational companies should have an awareness and appreciation of the cultural factors that can impact on the identification, diagnosis and treatment of mental health problems in different countries.

chapter 10

Coping with Illness: Responding to and Managing the Situation Effectively

10.1 Introduction

The topic of mental illness in a workplace can be uncomfortable for employees and organizations that have a duty to create an atmosphere where mental health wellness is encouraged and where issues can be dealt with sensitively.

Identifying mental illness and promoting mental well-being can significantly improve not only clinical outcomes but also workplace outcomes. The financial value associated with promoting mental well-being alone suggests that many employers would experience a *positive return on investment* from outreach and enhanced treatment of employees experiencing mental health problems. In other words, investing in mental health wellness is a good business decision.

There are at least three reasons why employers and organizations tend to shy away from the whole issue. *First*, mental illness remains a taboo in society, supposedly bringing shame on individuals and their families. *Second*, many are worried about encouraging malingering and the possibility that a small but significant number of employees will abuse mental health policies by 'going off sick'. *Third*, many feel helpless, not really knowing what the best way is to spot and then help those with mental health issues.

However, there are several ways in which this may be done, including encouraging early treatment through the use of Employee Assistance Programmes (EAPs), company-sponsored services designed to provide confidential off-site mental health counselling to employees on a short-term basis free of charge. In addition, the manager may work with the company's Occupational Health Services to create a work environment that will promote recovery.

One straightforward way to spot mental health problems is to look at short measures used by psychiatrists to assess mental illness. One such is the General Health Questionnaire. Thus, one could look at the items and try to assess if people at work have complained about having any of the symptoms included in this. These include: loss of concentration; poor sleep, feeling one is a nuisance to others; not being able to make decisions; complaining about continuous strain; feeling pessimistic about overcoming difficulties; having little joy in life; not wanting to face up to daily problems; feeling gloomy and depressed; expressing low self-confidence; feeling worthless, etc.

Employers have an important role to play in preventing and treating worker mental health issues and overall organizational health problems. These activities should be approached at both the individual worker and the organizational levels. Further, interventions should run the gamut from *primary prevention* to effective disease management programmes. Primary prevention might include education and training programmes that teach employees how to spot mental health problems early on and how to respond to them effectively. Regular screening for depression and stress as part of a company-sponsored health promotion initiative is another way to identify individuals and groups who are at risk of suffering from mental health problems.

Teaching employees stress management and coping skills is yet another form of primary prevention. *Secondary prevention* programmes involve the detection of potential mental health issues and referral to the appropriate healthcare professionals for treatment. Finally, *tertiary prevention* involves reducing the severity, discomfort, long-term impairment and disability associated with mental health conditions through appropriate treatment, improved compliance with medications and psychotherapy, and prevention of relapse.

In the next chapter we will examine the proactive steps an organization can take to promote and encourage a healthy culture and environment. In this chapter we will examine the steps that may need to be taken if an individual has already begun to exhibit the signs of mental illness and how both the employee, their colleagues and their managers should respond in this situation.

10.2 Confronting myths

One important way to deal with misinformation is to confront myths. In the most recent exploration of psychological myths, Lilienfeld *et al.* (2010) published a highly popular and successful book entitled *50 Great*

Myths of Popular Psychology, which was subtitled 'Shattering Widespread Misconceptions about Human Behaviour'. The book has 11 chapters, some of which deal with mental illness. In addition, Lilienfeld *et al.* (2010) present 250 other 'mythlets' worth exploring. Against each described as fiction, the authors provided the 'fact' which was based on experimental evidence. Inevitably, some of the assertions that statements are a myth may be challenged, as indeed may be the concept of 'myth' as opposed to 'truth'.

Using the Lilienfeld *et al.* (2010) 'mythlets', Furnham (2014) set out to survey the extent to which an adult population endorsed these modern psychological myths. They asked 829 British participants to complete the questionnaire. The questionnaire used each myth as an item. As all of the items presented within the questionnaire are myths, the 'correct' answers are DF and PF:

- Definitely True (DT): there is good scientific evidence to support the statement.
- Probably True (PT): there is enough evidence pointing to the fact that it is more-or-less correct.
- Probably False (PF): there is little good scientific evidence to support the statement.
- Definitely False (DF): there is no evidence to support the statement and indeed the opposite may be true.
- Don't Know (DK): you personally have no idea whether it is true or false.

The results are set out below. *Bear in mind that the 'correct' answer is either PF or DF.* The numbers in bold represent the most popular response.

Myths about mental illness	DT	PT	PF	DF	DK
Psychiatric diagnoses are unreliable.	4.3	23.4	**40.4**	11.6	20.3
Most psychotic people in Western society would be viewed as 'shamans' in non-Western cultures.	3.4	17.3	25.0	12.5	**41.8**
Hallucinations are almost always a sign of serious mental illness.	6.1	32.3	**33.0**	13.4	15.2
Most people with agoraphobia can't leave their houses.	13.5	**31.2**	22.0	6.8	26.6
Most people who experience severe trauma, like military combat, develop PTSD.	19.8	**25.9**	24.9	11.1	8.3
The symptoms of PTSD were first observed following the Vietnam War.	10.8	**24.8**	18.0	21.9	24.5

(continued)

Myths about mental illness	DT	PT	PF	DF	DK
Most phobias are traceable directly to negative experiences with the object of the fear.	15.6	**45.7**	21.9	6.0	10.8
People with fetishes are fascinated with certain objects.	28.5	**43.5**	12.5	3.8	11.7
Psychosomatic disorders are entirely in 'people's heads'.	10.1	**29.9**	24.0	10.5	25.4
People with hypochondriasis are typically convinced they are suffering from many different illnesses.	19.9	**31.8**	13.0	4.5	30.7
Most people with anorexia have lost their appetite.	10.2	21.4	26.5	**29.6**	12.3
All people with anorexia are female.	3.3	10.4	16.9	**63.2**	6.1
Eating disorders, especially anorexia and bulimia, are associated with a history of child sexual abuse.	4.7	10.8	30.4	**31.4**	22.6
Almost all people with Tourette syndrome curse.	7.0	20.7	24.9	18.4	**29.0**
The brains of children with ADHD are over-aroused.	8.9	**31.7**	19.9	9.7	29.8
Autistic individuals have a particular talent for generating prime numbers.	6.4	24.5	24.5	15.6	**29.0**
All clinically depressed people suffer from extreme sadness.	10.6	**37.0**	25.9	11.7	14.8
Depressed people are less realistic than non-depressed people.	8.9	24.8	**34.1**	14.8	17.4
Depression has been demonstrated to be due to a 'chemical imbalance' in the brain.	17.6	**42.7**	13.8	5.1	20.8
Children cannot become seriously depressed.	7.9	11.9	30.8	**39.8**	9.5
The rates of depression in women increase dramatically during the postpartum period.	16.3	**41.3**	9.9	2.8	29.6
People with bipolar disorder, formerly called 'manic depression', all experience both depressed and manic episodes.	19.2	**35.2**	17.5	5.7	22.5
Suicide typically happens without warning.	6.9	20.4	**38.7**	22.9	11.2
Most people who commit suicide leave a suicide note.	6.2	26.2	33.3	18.3	16.0
People who talk a lot about suicide are extremely unlikely to commit it.	8.1	29.2	**29.7**	11.2	21.9
Asking people about suicide increases their risk for suicide.	7.3	16.0	**40.9**	17.2	18.6
Suicides are especially likely during the Christmas holidays.	10.6	**40.6**	23.2	6.7	19.0
Suicide is especially common during the dark days of winter.	13.4	**53.8**	15.5	4.0	13.3

(continued)

Myths about mental illness	DT	PT	PF	DF	DK
The age group at highest risk for suicide is adolescents.	12.4	**34.8**	23.0	5.5	24.3
More women than men commit suicide.	8.0	17.8	28.9	10.1	**35.2**
Families play a major role in causing or triggering schizophrenia.	6.7	24.4	25.4	8.8	**34.7**
All people with catatonic schizophrenia are inactive, lying in a foetal position.	3.3	12.8	21.6	13.4	**48.9**
People with schizophrenia virtually never recover.	9.1	25.9	27.1	9.2	**28.7**
Virtually all people who use heroin become addicted to it.	18.8	**43.1**	20.7	6.3	11.1
Most transvestites are homosexual.	6.2	23.8	**30.2**	15.7	24.1
Myths about psychology and the law					
Rehabilitation programmes have no effect on the recidivism rates of criminals.	4.4	17.2	**39.1**	13.1	26.1
Most paedophiles (child abusers) have extremely high levels of recidivism.	7.5	29.1	12.3	4.8	**46.3**
All paedophiles are untreatable.	7.6	17.8	**37.1**	14.7	22.8
The best approach to treating delinquents is to 'get tough' with them.	6.6	26.9	**32.1**	19.1	15.3
The overwhelming majority of acts of domestic violence are committed by men.	20.7	**45.6**	19.7	5.5	8.4
The rates of domestic abuse against women increase markedly on Super Bowl Sunday.	5.3	26.3	16.5	8.2	**43.8**
Being a postal worker is among the most dangerous of all occupations.	4.7	16.5	**30.9**	22.7	25.3
Most psychopaths are violent.	8.2	**34.3**	32.5	10.8	14.2
Most psychopaths are out of touch with reality.	11.9	**43.6**	22.6	7.7	14.2
Psychopaths are untreatable.	5.4	18.9	**40.1**	13.7	21.8
Serial killings are especially common among whites.	11.1	19.3	23.4	9.8	**36.4**
Police officers have especially high rates of suicide.	4.5	20.7	28.8	8.1	**37.9**
There is an addictive personality.	21.3	**43.0**	12.7	3.8	19.2
Alcoholism is uniquely associated with 'denial'.	9.9	**32.1**	24.2	9.2	24.7
Most rapes are committed by strangers.	5.8	19.1	**38.7**	24.3	12.1
Police psychics have proven useful in solving crimes.	6.6	**35.9**	24.2	12.0	21.3
Homicide is more common than suicide.	9.3	**32.5**	23.1	10.4	24.7
'Insanity' is a formal psychological and psychiatric term.	12.0	27.5	20.3	10.6	**29.6**

(continued)

Myths about psychology and the law	DT	PT	PF	DF	DK
The legal determination of insanity is based on the person's current mental state.	10.4	**39.2**	16.5	5.8	28.1
Most people who plead insanity are faking mental illness.	5.3	25.1	**34.9**	10.0	24.7
The insanity verdict is a 'rich person's' defence.	4.3	19.6	**33.0**	12.7	30.4
Myths about psychological treatment					
A psychologically caused disorder requires psychotherapy; a biologically caused disorder requires medication.	13.9	**31.1**	21.0	13.8	20.1
More experienced therapists tend to have much higher success rates than less experienced therapists.	12.1	**46.8**	16.9	3.9	20.2
Psychiatrists and psychologists are essentially identical.	4.9	12.4	25.5	**45.9**	11.3
The 'school of therapy' is the best predictor of treatment effectiveness.	3.9	17.9	18.2	6.6	**53.5**
All people who call themselves 'psychotherapists' have advanced degrees in mental health.	5.7	22.1	26.5	18.8	**26.8**
Most psychotherapy involves using a couch and exploring one's early past.	6.8	24.9	**31.6**	17.1	19.6
Most modern therapies are based on the teachings of Sigmund Freud.	4.3	22.0	**29.1**	20.3	24.3
Psychotherapy did not exist prior to Freud.	13.1	18.2	26.1	10.2	**32.4**
Psychotherapies can only help, not hurt.	5.2	19.4	**39.1**	20.5	15.8
Most psychotherapies use empirically supported therapies.	7.8	31.6	19.3	5.8	**35.5**
Drug Resistance and Education (DARE) programmes are effective.	7.2	**44.6**	11.0	3.2	34.1
People who have experienced a trauma must fully 'process' the trauma to improve.	11.7	**43.4**	17.7	5.3	21.9
Psychotherapies that don't address the 'deeper causes' of problems result in symptom substitution.	7.4	**39.0**	13.3	4.6	35.7
Few people can quit smoking on their own.	14.6	32.1	**34.3**	12.5	6.5
Nicotine is far less addictive than other drugs.	3.5	15.8	**38.0**	30.9	11.8
ADHD is caused by excess sugar in the diet.	3.5	19.0	**30.7**	19.2	27.6
Anti-depressants greatly increase the risk of suicide.	4.4	22.4	**35.3**	12.4	25.5
Anti-depressants often turn people into 'zombies'.	4.1	19.5	**33.5**	23.8	19.0
Anti-depressants are much more effective than psychotherapy for treating depression.	4.3	18.4	31.8	12.2	**32.3**

(continued)

Myths about psychological treatment	DT	PT	PF	DF	DK
Most new anti-depressants, like Prozac and Zoloft, are more effective than older anti-depressants.	6.6	36.7	15.4	4.2	**37.2**
Placebos influence only our imagination, not our brains.	12.3	23.6	**29.3**	15.1	19.8
Herbal remedies are superior to anti-depressants for improving mood.	8.8	21.8	**31.3**	11.9	26.2
The fact that a substance is 'natural' means that it is safe.	9.2	12.9	24.2	**48.0**	5.7
Acupuncture works only if one inserts the needles in specific points on the body.	22.0	**41.8**	9.8	6.9	19.5
Electroconvulsive therapy is rarely administered today.	13.7	30.5	16.2	5.5	**34.0**

It is possible to use this list to encourage an understanding of mental health at work. The popularity of the book is testament to public interest in the topic which may serve to improve understanding of mental illness.

10.3 What can and should managers do?

Managers may often find it difficult to deal with someone they think has a mental health problem, particularly if the person is not open about their illness or if they themselves do not feel equipped to talk about it.

There is also a challenge in knowing when best to approach an employee. Changes in employee performance and behaviours can be linked to any number of things, from marital problems to financial concerns. It is often the case that employees with mental health problems do not realize they are having problems functioning at work until a colleague or their manager brings it up with them. It is therefore important that the situation is dealt with sensitively.

The Mental Health Foundation gives the following tips to managers facing this situation:

- Take time to talk to the person privately and ask if something is wrong. Take your steer from them. Don't try to diagnose what you think is the matter.
- Ask what would help them at work. They may need a quiet place to work or more time to perform certain tasks.
- If they haven't been performing as well as usual, they may feel guilty or fearful about it. Be honest in assessing their performance – they may feel their performance is worse than it is.

- It can be useful to agree in advance how to handle any continuing problems. Encourage the employee to identify factors that might play a role in them becoming unwell and consider how to deal with them. You may also want to agree how best to respond to a crisis.
- Don't make assumptions about what someone with an illness can and can't do.
- Be aware that new computer systems or other changes, such as restructuring or the risk of redundancy, can be especially difficult for someone who is also coping with a mental health problem.
- In the language you use and the attention you give to the person, treat them with respect and act as a model to encourage other colleagues to do the same.
- Suggest they ask for advice from your occupational health advisor or contact any support service your organization uses, such as the EAP.
- After your first conversation, fix another meeting to check how the person is coping and whether further changes to their working arrangements are needed. Then keep the dialogue going.

It is also important that you continue to treat the person fairly and without discrimination. The Equality Act 2010 makes it illegal for an employer to treat employees or job applicants suffering from mental health conditions 'less favourably' than other employees. In addition, the stigma surrounding mental illness can often prevent employees being open about their condition, so, to create a culture where this is not seen to be a barrier, employers and managers must be seen to be treating people fairly at all times.

If the individual needs to have some time off work, the manager has a duty to keep in touch with them and help them through that transition. Many people who have mental health problems dread returning to work after they have been off sick and their colleagues may find it awkward to know what to say to them, especially if the subject has never been talked about openly. The Mental Health Foundation suggests the following ways of keeping in touch to help overcome this awkwardness later on:

- Ask the person who is off work what they would like their colleagues to be told. Try to get a balance between maintaining their confidentiality and letting people understand what is happening.
- Invite them out when staff are spending leisure time together. They may decline, but will still appreciate being asked.
- Send cards and call the person if you would normally socialize with them – just as you would if they had a physical health problem.
- Have a 'cup of tea' policy where someone can come into the office informally before returning to work.

At any one time, one in six adults will be experiencing a mental health condition. It is crucial that employers are playing a full part in supporting job retention and return to work for people with such conditions. A phased return to the office can also help manage the transition more easily and will also mean that the individual can gradually get back up to speed with their workload rather than being overwhelmed by a full-time return to work.

Evidence has shown that holding down a meaningful job is beneficial for mental health and well-being, and in many instances return to work can aid recovery (Waddell and Burton, 2006). Anyone who wishes to work should be supported to do so by their employer through making work more accessible.

In many instances, simple and cost-effective adjustments to the workplace can also make a big difference and can allow people with mental health conditions to keep in touch with the working world and live healthy and productive lives. The Equality Act 2010 requires employers to make 'reasonable adjustments' for all employees with a disability, including mental illness. This does not need to be something onerous that the 'equality police' will come chasing you for – the adjustment needed could be a change in workload or an introduction of a more flexibly working pattern for the individual.

It is important that the employee is involved in any decisions about their working life as much as possible. Everyone's experience of mental illness is different, so two people with a diagnosis of stress or depression may have a very different set of circumstances, symptoms and needs. Usually the best expert to advise the employer will be the person themselves. However, this does become complicated if the nature of their illness is one in which they may have grandiose or irrational ideas about normal behaviour.

Everyone's experience of mental illness is different

The following section will outline how to respond to a number of the most common mental illnesses in the workplace that we have examined so far.

10.4 Responding to depression

Managers and colleagues can look for the following signs which may help to determine if a co-worker is depressed:

- fatigue;
- unhappiness;

- excessive forgetfulness;
- irritability;
- propensity to cry;
- indecisiveness;
- lack of enthusiasm;
- withdrawal.

These same warning signs could point to any number of a broad range of problems. It is important to resist the temptation to diagnose what you see as depression; the term is widely used today inappropriately and you should stick instead to just recognizing that something is wrong, and taking caring and respectful action to encourage the individual to seek help or to refer them to the company employee assistance professional or occupational health service. It's time to talk with an employee when you have noticed several of the warning signs listed above. The sooner you have this conversation, the better.

Individuals who feel they are suffering from depression can take a number of steps. Depression, like most mental illnesses, does not always have a direct cause, certainly not one that can easily be identified, but it may be that certain aspects of work are having a negative impact. The first step is to identify if there are certain triggers or situations that are cause for concern, particularly stressful situations, such as long working hours. The individual should first speak to their employer about reducing these or decide if their current role is having too much of an impact on their mental health. There are other coping strategies that can help the individual to manage their condition in the context of their workplace that should be encouraged:

- Ensuring timely arrival each day, well prepared, to avoid feeling stressed and overwhelmed first thing.
- Ensuring a balanced diet and regular exercise – walking to work, or at least getting off the bus a stop earlier can help the person to get in the right frame of mind.
- Breaking the day up into small chunks of tasks to avoid feelings of being overwhelmed by the amount there is to do.
- Reaching out to a trusted colleague if the individual is having a particularly bad day; often, talking things through can help.
- Taking stress breaks during the day if the individual is feeling overwhelmed; even five minutes in a quiet place can help them to gather their thoughts before going back into the office environment.

10.5 Responding to stress

Methods for managing workplace stress can take a variety of forms, some healthy and many not. The challenge for organizations is to encourage more of the positive methods of managing stress and less of the unhealthy methods. Common healthy strategies include: sleeping more, talking things through with family and friends, exercising more frequently and attempting to remove stressors from one's life. Other common, but less healthy, ways of responding to stress include eating more, engaging in promiscuous behaviour, use of illicit drugs, consuming more caffeine, and smoking and drinking more frequently.

The problem is that many of these behaviours can cause further problems and other coping strategies should be developed, such as the following:

- *Telling a trusted colleague*: knowing that someone accepts their condition can be comforting and it may reduce any anticipatory anxiety about having an incident at work.
- *Education*: employees should be encouraged to learn to recognize the symptoms of negative stress, how this is different from positive stress and how the symptoms might occur.
- *Reduce stressors where possible*: taking such steps as reducing exposure to certain aspects of the job, e.g., attending high-pressure meetings.

The role of the employer and the manager in responding to individuals who are suffering from stress is to help them reduce the sufferer's exposure to potential stressors and support them through any recovery time needed.

10.6 Responding to schizophrenia

We have already discussed the need for employers to make reasonable adjustments for employees suffering from mental illness. In the case of schizophrenia, examples could include the following:

- Moving the employee's workspace away from distractions, such as people, office equipment or a busy hall, in order to help them concentrate.
- Shifting work schedules to begin later in the day as common medications used to treat schizophrenia cause significant drowsiness.
- Permitting an employee to make up lost time due to doctor's appointments by working in a more flexible manner.

Colleagues can also help co-workers suffering from schizophrenia in a number of ways. First, it is important for people recovering from a severe episode to integrate back into normal life gradually. This involves setting realistic goals and learning to function in the world again one step at a time. When people with a mental illness are pressured and criticized, it can worsen their symptoms, so each step towards these goals should be small and incremental. The individual will need support during this time, and colleagues and managers can offer help with work-related goals. Managers in particular can have a significant impact by providing a higher than normal level of positive feedback when appropriate; telling the individual when they are doing something right is a helpful way to help them move forward.

On a day-to-day level, it can be difficult to know how to respond to someone with schizophrenia, especially if they have a tendency to make strange or false statements. An important point to remember is that these hallucinations seem very real to the person and they will not respond well if you try and disabuse them of their beliefs. At the same time, going along with the delusions is not a helpful strategy either. An alternative approach is to acknowledge that everyone has the right to see things their own way and that you have a different view of the situation. In addition, it is important to understand that schizophrenia is a biological illness. Being respectful, supportive and kind without tolerating dangerous or inappropriate behaviour is the best way to approach people with this disorder.

10.7 Encouraging people back to work

There is a strong link between the recovery of an individual with mental illness and social inclusion. The quicker people can regain their place in the world and take part in normal day-to-day activities such as going to work, the better. However, facilitating a smooth return to work for people who have suffered from mental illness must be handled in a sensitive way. The manager should involve the employee in this process as much as possible and be guided by how that person feels about returning to work. One myth that must be challenged is that a person with mental illness who states that they are not ready to come back to work is not ready. Often individuals with mental illness may be fearful at the prospect of work due to poor self-esteem or fear of the stigma that surrounds their condition. Such individuals need to have their confidence rebuilt and their manager and HR personnel may need to encourage them in an explicit way to make those first steps back to work. Back to work transition days can assist such individuals by gradually re-introducing them back into the workplace.

It is also worth considering a number of basic factors to consider when supporting an individual to make a successful return to work. These include the following:

1. The nature of the work itself and the individual's presence in the workplace should not pose a risk to the individual or their colleagues.
2. The individual should be able to access the treatment they need at all times and work should not be a barrier to this.
3. The individual must be able to perform their role at a level where they are able to make a meaningful contribution with reasonable accommodations.
4. The job itself should not require a level of mental alertness and stamina that the individual is not capable of providing.
5. The workplace environment should be one that aids recovery or at the very least should be welcoming and free from other pressures that might prevent recovery.

An assessment of these factors should go hand in hand with a conversation with the individual themselves, as they will have a good appreciation of what they need in order to succeed in the workplace. They will be able to provide useful information that can smooth their re-integration back into work. The process of engaging with them on this matter will also send a powerful message about the organization's commitment to them and their recovery.

The discussion between employer and employee should focus on the reasonable adjustments that need to be made; details about diagnosis or treatment are not necessary. Managers should also seek to lead by example by discouraging derogatory remarks and demonstrating that they still trust, respect and value the individual to do their job.

In some instances, the stress of returning to work can cause a relapse for someone with severe mental illness. However, this is not always the case and there are steps that can be taken to avoid this happening. Part of the stress response for individuals suffering from mental illness is the knowledge that the typical adjustment period might be misread as a recurrence of mental illness symptoms. In reality, all people undergo stress when starting a new job or returning after time off (e.g., maternity leave). Individuals should be taught coping skills to anticipate any potential problems in managing the transition.

10.8 Training colleagues to respond appropriately

Colleagues and co-workers can play an important role in responding to mental illness in the workplace. When an individual tells their colleague they have a mental health problem, becomes distressed or starts behaving out of character, it can be very confusing and distressing for their colleagues. In these situations the default position is often to ignore the situation or write it off as 'Mary is having a bad day'. Receiving the right support, however, can make a huge difference to the individual's ability to manage their illness.

These skills may require training, particularly in organizations where there is not a culture of 'caring and sharing'. In Australia, Mental Health First Aid (MHFA) programmes have become a popular way of educating the workforce in how to respond.

MHFA training is a course for the public that teaches how to give initial help to a person developing a mental health problem or in a mental health crisis. The first aid is given until appropriate professional help is provided. Initial evaluation of these programmes has found improvements in mental health knowledge, reduced stigma, increased confidence in providing help and increased instances of help being provided (Jorm *et al*., 2004; Jorm, Kitchener and Mugford, 2005; Jorm *et al*., 2010; Kitchener and Jorm, 2006).

10.9 Summary

It is a good business decision to take mental health at work seriously. Not only does it convey a positive message to all stakeholders, but it can be shown to save the organization money in the long run. This means educating people at work for signs of mental illness in their colleagues as well as having a clear strategy of what to do when signs are detected and how to facilitate a smooth transition back to work.

chapter 11 Creating a Healthy Workplace Environment

11.1 Introduction

Despite an improved understanding about mental illness, many employers still fail to address the issue of mental health at work in a proactive way. For example, organizations that have implemented initiatives aimed at managing workplace stress have had considerable success, but these companies are still very much in the minority and more severe health problems such as depression are largely ignored.

Part of the problem is the disparity between managers' perception of mental health problems in their workforce and the reality of how frequently it occurs. In a survey of 550 senior managers in the private and public sector for the Shaw Trust (2006), one in ten managers reported that none of their employees was likely to ever suffer from mental illness. This indicates that stereotypes about mental illness are still prevalent in British business and managers do not characterize common workplace problems such as stress and depression as mental illness. Furthermore, the interventions that are geared towards addressing mental illness in the workplace are often reactive in nature and focus on how to cope with mental illness when it becomes a problem.

In the previous chapter we have outlined a number of steps that organizations can take in terms of how to cope with mental illness, but if this epidemic is to be properly addressed in today's workplace, a more proactive approach to creating a healthy workplace is needed.

Approaching mental illness in this way should not be seen as an obligation to those who may be at risk of illness, but rather as a smart way of looking after your greatest asset: your people. A workplace environment that approaches mental health in a positive way supports the well-being of all employees, not just those at risk, and encourages a culture of openness about sensitive matters, including mental health problems. Looking after staff in this way has many benefits, such as encouraging loyalty, job satisfaction, increased productivity and organizational commitment.

Companies are in a position to do something to respond and pre-empt causal factors and these steps can be broken down into manageable chunks, consisting of the following:

1. *Promoting a positive attitude towards mental health:*
   - Encouraging mental health education.
   - Challenging stigma.
   - Promoting happiness and well-being.
2. *Understanding and addressing organizational barriers:*
   - Assessing the culture of the organization – is it one that helps or hinders a healthy state of mind? Is work perceived to be worthwhile, full of purpose and aligned to 'the greater good'?
   - Ensuring the top team in the organization is aware of and willing to address the mental health agenda.
   - Identifying potential workplace hazards and developing systems to encourage a healthy approach to work.
3. *Monitoring the situation:*
   - Actively targeting depression, stress and other mental illnesses with key performance indicators.
   - Measuring productivity and thereby promoting mental health.
   - Building a 'mental health at work' referral system.

We will now examine each of these in turn.

11.2 Promoting a positive attitude towards mental health

11.2.1 Educating the workforce

Most managers will have had, at some point, had to deal with situations where an employee is coping with a mental health issue of some sort. Part of the responsibility of today's organization and its leaders is in educating the workforce and creating a mentally healthy workplace environment. Investing in mental health education for the workforce is good for business. As we have outlined in earlier chapters, the costs of poorly managed mental health problems in the workplace are astronomical. Increasing the awareness of mental health issues and how to deal with them can have a significant impact on productivity and absenteeism, and can in fact improve the health outcomes of the affected individual through providing a more supportive workplace environment.

However, progress in providing such education is slow, even in the more enlightened societies. In the UK the government offers training for managers to help them to identify signs of mental illness and there is evidence of a small number of other organizations offering courses to help tackle awareness. These courses will often cover topics such as the following:

- What is mental health?
- What can cause mental health problems in the workplace?
- Beyond the medical model: different ways of understanding mental health problems.
- Practical toolkits for supporting someone experiencing mental health problems in the workplace.
- Depression and anxiety – signs and symptoms.
- Psychosis – signs and symptoms.
- Self-harm and eating disorders – signs and symptoms.
- How to support someone experiencing mental health problems in the workplace – legal requirements.
- How to look after your own mental health.

Such training will often include a recovery story from someone with a real experience of coping with mental health problems in the workplace and managers will be encouraged to think about the parallels with their own organization. However, it would appear that much of the training in this area is targeted towards people who work in sectors where they are likely to be dealing with mental illness as part of their job, e.g., social workers, police officers and those working in the social housing arena. Training for the general workforce appears to be optional and is certainly not mainstream.

Other forms of education about mental illness might include things such as:

- implementing an informational intervention campaign;
- signposting to local and national mental health organizations for educational materials;

- sending information brochures to employees;
- employee newsletter articles;
- providing a specific mental health section on the company website;
- providing on-site educational opportunities;
- hosting an online awareness forum.

The main problem with educating the workforce is in overcoming the stigma of mental illness and presenting an alternative view that employees can buy into.

11.2.2 Dealing with stigma

Major barriers continue to exist that prevent those with mental disorders from seeking the help they need. One of the major barriers is the stigma and discrimination associated with mental disorders (Corrigan, 2004; Stuart, 2004; Thornicroft, 2006).

Stigmatization and negative labelling can impact on many areas of the mentally ill person's life and can exacerbate the extent of their illness. Sufferers may find themselves disadvantaged in, and unable to, access a range of social environments, including such areas as employment, family life, health care and the ability to function in normal social situations. The stigma surrounding mental illness can often mean that people do not seek professional help until a very late stage because of the fear they will be labelled by society if they receive professional treatment.

In many cases it is both the public stigma of being labelled as a person with a mental illness and the reduced perceptions of self-worth that accompany self-stigma which can lead to a situation where the person does want to seek help or maintain treatment of their disorder. Blumenthal and Endicott (1996) also reported that non-help-seekers' reasons can relate to mental health literacy. In other words, those experiencing a major depressive episode will often avoid seeking help because they believe they can handle or treat the depression themselves, their disorder was not serious and they did not recognize their symptoms as a mental disorder in the first place.

One of the most prominent areas where mentally ill people suffer because of negative attitudes is in the workplace. Labelling can have a negative impact on their income, work status and ability to cope. In 2006, unemployment in the UK was at 7.1 per cent for people without mental health problems, compared to 12.7 per cent for people with mental health problems. In 2010, this rose to 9.8 per cent and 18.2 per cent respectively, corresponding to an increase of 5.5 per cent for people with mental health problems versus a 2.7 per cent increase for people without mental health problems. The ability to hold down a job is often a crucial factor in reducing the symptoms of the sufferer and improving their ability to function socially, and yet often this opportunity is not afforded to them, either because negative stereotypes prevent them from getting a job in the first place or because attitudes from co-workers make it difficult for them to be successful in their role.

The impact of this can be observed in a survey conducted by the anti-stigma and discrimination campaign *Time to Change,* which found that of 2,082 people surveyed, 56 per cent would not employ an individual who had depression even if they were the most suitable candidate. Krupa *et al*. (2009) highlighted four assumptions underlying workplace stigma:

1. People with mental health problems lack the competence to meet the demands of work;
2. People with mental health problems are dangerous or unpredictable in the workplace;
3. Working is not healthy for people with a mental health problem; and
4. Providing employment for people with mental illness is an act of charity.

These assumptions vary in their salience and intensity, based on a range of organizational, individual and societal factors.

Brohan and Thornicraft (2010) researched this area further and found that of the 502 employers who took part and shared concerns about hiring someone with a mental health problem:

- 17 per cent reported concerns about the threat of safety to other staff or clients;
- 14 per cent were concerned that the individual would not be able to handle stress;
- 11 per cent were concerned about strange or unpredictable behaviour;
- 20 per cent reported work performance concerns, particularly impaired job performance;
- 29 per cent had concerns about work personality, particularly absenteeism;
- 7 per cent related to administrative concerns, including the level of monitoring needed;
- 2 per cent were worried about the negative attitude of other employees.

Disclosure of a mental health problem in the workplace can also lead to discriminatory behaviour from managers and colleagues, such as micro-management, lack of opportunities for advancement, over-inferring of mistakes to illness, gossip and social exclusion (Corrigan and Lundin, 2001).

The theory of the self-fulfilling prophecy suggests that when a person is stereotyped, it induces them to 'act in a manner consistent with that stereotype' (Carlson, Buskist and Martin, 2000: 528). Thus, the person with mental illness not only believes what people are thinking and saying about them, but also begins to act in a way that confirms the stereotype. Stereotypes often therefore become a reality by channelling behaviour and interaction in a way that causes the stereotype to be reinforced. In the context of mental illness in the workplace, the withdrawn, quiet individual who suffers from depression becomes more quiet and withdrawn as a consequence of the reaction they receive from colleagues.

The mere presence of other people can evoke the threat of stereotyping. In one experiment, women who took a mathematics exam along with two other women got 70 per cent of the answers right, while those doing the same exam in the presence of two men only achieved an average score of 55 per cent.

The mere presence of other people can evoke the threat of stereotyping

Fear of stigma and discrimination can also make people with mental health conditions unwilling to disclose their illness and thus prevents them from being adequately supported at work. In the Time to Change survey, it was found that 92 per cent of those sampled believed that admitting to having a mental health condition would damage their career in some way.

It is clear that negative attitudes towards mental illness need to change and that a greater and more effective level of training and education is needed. At the outset, it is worth examining some of the reasons why negative attitudes exist in the first place.

11.3 Attitude formation: where do negative attitudes come from?

Attitudes basically function as summary evaluations of people, objects, places, etc. and exist on a continuum from positive to negative. We summarize what existing knowledge we have about a person or issue and develop an attitude based on this information, even though it may not be accurate. The very nature of social interaction requires us to carry out this process and to base our judgements on the assumption that new individuals we encounter will behave as others like them have done in the past. Unless a new and different personal experience convinces us otherwise, we will form and adopt stereotypes.

This may to a large extent explain the formation of negative attitudes towards people suffering from mental illness, especially considering the history of mental illness in our society. The public may choose to adopt the old, outdated view that mentally ill people are a danger to themselves and others, and should be locked away. Even though this is an anachronistic and inaccurate opinion, if an individual has had no experience to lead them to think differently, it is highly likely that they will adopt the negative public perception that has prevailed for centuries.

The behaviour of the disadvantaged group is also a crucial factor and a single negative encounter with a mentally ill person can result in the formation of a negative opinion about all mentally ill people that will be very difficult to shift. It is also our tendency to focus solely on the behaviour of another individual when forming an opinion without adequate consideration of the situational forces and causal factors that could have influenced their behaviour.

Attitude theory tells us that unfamiliarity with the outgroup promotes and encourages hostility and negativity. Misunderstanding and lack of trust is exacerbated when we do not have contact with members of the other group and if we know very little about another group, we have a tendency to adopt the beliefs of other people, usually those of the majority. Negative attitudes towards mentally ill people may therefore exist because they have been passed down from a time when there was less understanding about the true nature and causes of mental illness, and less exposure to people experiencing mental health problems.

Often, mentally ill people and indeed other minority groups are used as scapegoats for many social problems and can be the target of frustration and aggression. It is very easy when confronted with an economic problem or a rise in criminal activity, for example, to direct our anger and emotion towards a group that is weak, helpless and often misunderstood. This makes us feel better about the problem because we have apportioned blame to others. There is no doubt that mentally ill people have suffered from this trend and this has been exacerbated by the media. Mental illness is often depicted negatively in the media and linked to violence and unpredictability.

A targeted workplace anti-stigma intervention could help reduce the stigma associated with mental disorders and improve mental health literacy and awareness within the employees of an organization. This should have a number of benefits, including an increase in employees experiencing mental health problems seeking help, a greater level of competence amongst managers in responding and dealing with mental health problems amongst

their staff, and the positive financial repercussions from a reduction in sickness absence, claims and lost productivity that would accompany such changes.

Because of the stigma of mental illness and fear of discrimination, targeted mental health interventions may be more effective if they are embedded in socially acceptable programmes such as EAPs, although this does not negate the need to deal with stigma in an appropriate way through training, education and improved general awareness. Such programmes should also be promoted and supported by senior management. Too often these types of initiatives are seen as 'another HR fad' with little relevance for the day-to-day business of work. Ensuring there is support and buy-in from the senior levels of the organization with a clear link to business benefits will increase the likelihood that employees will take it seriously.

Further research is needed to determine the impact of such programmes, but there would appear to be evidence to suggest that anti-stigma training increases mental illness literacy and knowledge (Kitchener and Jorm, 2006) and that they typically decrease stigmatizing attitudes and decreases in social distance (e.g., Gaebel *et al.*, 2008).

11.4 Promoting and understanding happiness and well-being

Have you ever walked into an office or workplace where there was an air of happiness? Where people greet each other with smiles instead of scowls and there is a general buzz of enjoyment? People who are happy at work tend to enjoy life more and have better mental health, stronger relationships and a greater sense of purpose. Of course, there are many factors which lead to happiness at work and not all of these can be influenced by managers and colleagues or even the employee themselves, but let us first examine this term 'happiness' and discuss the relevance of happiness in the wider discussion about mental illness.

The word 'happiness' means several different things (joy, satisfaction) and therefore many psychologists prefer the term 'subjective well-being', which is an umbrella term that incorporates the various types of evaluation of one's life one might make. It can include self-esteem, joy, feelings of fulfilment. The essence is that the person is making the evaluation of life. Thus, the person is the expert here: is my life going well according to the standards that I choose to use? Am I happy with my lot?

The relatively recent advent of studies on happiness, sometimes called 'subjective well-being' (SWB), has led to a science of well-being (Huppert, Baylis and Keverne, 2005).

It has also been suggested that there are three primary components of SWB: general satisfaction, the presence of pleasant affect and the absence of negative emotions, including anger, anxiety, guilt, sadness and shame. These can be considered at the global level or with regard to very specific domains like work, friendship and recreation. More importantly, SWB covers a wide-ranging scale from ecstasy to agony and from extreme happiness to great gloom and despondency. It relates to long-term states, not just momentary moods. It is not sufficient on its own, but is probably a necessary criterion for mental or psychological health.

All the early researchers in this field pointed out that psychologists had long neglected well-being, preferring to look at its opposites: anxiety, despair and depression. Just as the assumption that the absence of anxiety and depression suggests happiness, so it is true that not being happy does not necessarily mean unhappy. In the same way that much of the understanding and discussion surrounding mental illness has focused on the 'illness' side of the equation, it is time to focus more on how to promote mental well-being.

All the early writers in this area struggled with a definition. Eysenck (1990) noted both verbal and non-verbal telltale signs. Argyle (2001) commented that different researchers had identified different components of happiness, like life satisfaction, positive affect, self-acceptance, positive relations with others, autonomy and environmental mastery. It constitutes joy, satisfaction and other related positive emotions.

Myers (1992) noted the stable and unstable characteristics of happy people. Such people tend to be creative energetic, decisive, flexible and sociable. They also tend to be more forgiving, loving, trusting and responsible. They tolerate frustration better and are more willing to help those in need. In short, they feel good, so they in turn do good. Diener (2000) has defined SWB as how people cognitively and emotionally evaluate their lives. It has an evaluative (good-bad) as well as a hedonic (pleasant-unpleasant) dimension.

The Positive Psychology Centre at Penn State University has a website dedicated to answering frequently asked questions like 'isn't positive psychology just plain common sense?'. They note 13 points (abbreviated here) as an example:

- Wealth is only weakly related to happiness, both within and across nations, particularly when income is above the poverty level.

- Activities that make people happy in small doses – such as shopping, good food and making money – do not lead to fulfilment in the long term, indicating that these have quickly diminishing returns.
- Engaging in an experience that produces 'flow' is so gratifying that people are willing to do it for its own sake rather than for what they will get out of it. Flow is experienced when one's skills are sufficient for a challenging activity, in the pursuit of a clear goal, where immediate self-awareness disappears and a sense of time is distorted.
- People who express gratitude on a regular basis have better physical health, optimism, progress toward goals, well-being and help others more.
- Trying to maximize happiness can lead to unhappiness.
- People who witness others perform good deeds experience an emotion called 'elevation' and this motivates them to perform their own good deeds.
- Optimism can protect people from mental and physical illness.
- People who are optimistic or happy have better performance in work, school and sports, are less depressed, have fewer physical health problems and have better relationships with other people. Further, optimism can be measured and it can be learned.
- People who report more positive emotions in young adulthood live longer and healthier lives.
- Physicians experiencing positive emotions tend to make more accurate diagnoses.
- Healthy human development can take place under conditions of even great adversity due to a process of resilience that is common and completely ordinary.
- Individuals who write about traumatic events are physically healthier than control groups that do not. Writing about life goals is significantly less distressing than writing about trauma and is associated with enhanced well-being.
- People are unable to predict how long they will be happy or sad following an important event.

11.5 Positive psychology and happiness

Positive psychology is the study of factors and processes that lead to positive emotions, virtuous behaviours and optimal performance in individuals and groups. Although a few, mainly 'self-psychologists', were always interested in health, adjustment and peak performance, the study of happiness was thought to be unimportant, even trivial until relatively recently.

The psychology of happiness attempts to answer some very fundamental questions pursued over the years by philosophers, theologians and politicians. The first series of questions are really about the definition and measurement of happiness, the second group concern why certain groups are as happy or unhappy as they are, and the third group relate to what one has to do (or not do) to increase happiness.

Most measurements of happiness are by standardized questionnaires or interview schedules. Conversely, it could be carried out by informed observers – those people who know the individual well and see them regularly. There is also experience sampling when people have to report how happy they are many times a day, week or month when a beeper goes off and these ratings are aggregated. Yet another method is to investigate a person's memory and check for whether they feel predominantly happy or unhappy about their past. Finally, there are some as yet crude but ever-developing physical measures looking at everything from brain scanning to saliva cortisol measures. It is not very difficult to measure happiness reliably and validly.

11.6 Does happiness matter?

Some believe that if you act happy (smile, express optimism, act in an outgoing manner), it makes others react to you differently and you actually feel happy. Finding work and leisure activities that really engage your skills and passions helps a great deal, as does regular exercise, sleeping and eating well. Investing time and care in relationships is a very important feature of happiness. Affirming others, helping others and regularly expressing gratitude for life increases happiness, as does having a sense of purpose.

The advice of Myers (1992) can be applied very usefully in a workplace context when thinking of how to promote a greater degree of happiness in the workplace. Myers' suggestions for a happier life are as follows:

1. *Realize that enduring happiness doesn't come from success*
   People adapt to changing circumstances – even to wealth or a disability. Thus, wealth is life health: its utter absence breeds misery, but having it (or any circumstances we long for) doesn't guarantee happiness.
2. *Take control of your time*
   Happy people feel in control of their lives. To master your use of time, set goals and break them into daily aims. Although we often over-estimate how much we will accomplish in any given day (leaving us frustrated), we

generally under-estimate how much we can accomplish in a year, given just a little progress every day.

3. *Act happy*
   We can sometimes act ourselves into a happier frame of mind. Manipulated into a smiling expression, people feel better; when they scowl, the whole world seems to scowl back. So put on a happy face. Talk as if you feel positive self-esteem, are optimistic and are outgoing. Going through the motions can trigger the emotions.
4. *Seek work and leisure that engage your skills*
   Happy people are often in a zone called 'flow' – absorbed in tasks that challenge but don't overwhelm them. The most expensive forms of leisure (sitting on a yacht) often provide less flow experience than gardening, socializing or craft work.
5. *Join the 'movement' movement*
   An avalanche of research reveals that aerobic exercise can relieve mild depression and anxiety as it promotes health and energy. Sound minds reside in sound bodies. On your feet, couch potatoes!
6. *Give your body the sleep it wants*
   Happy people live active vigorous lives yet reserve time for renewing sleep and solitude. Many people suffer from a sleep debt, with resulting fatigue, diminished alertness and gloomy moods.
7. *Give priority to close relationships*
   Intimate friendships with those who care deeply about you can help you weather difficult times. Confiding is good for the body and soul. Resolve to nurture your closest relationships by not taking your loved ones for granted, by displaying to them the sort of kindness you display to others, by affirming them, by playing together and sharing together. To rejuvenate your affections, resolve to act lovingly in such ways.
8. *Focus beyond the self*
   Reach out to those in need. Happiness increases helpfulness (those who feel good do good), but doing good also makes one feel good.
9. *Keep a gratitude journal*
   Those who pause each day to reflect on some positive aspect of their lives (their health, friends, family, freedom, education, senses, natural surroundings and so on) experience heightened well-being.
10. *Nurture your spiritual self*
    For many people, faith provides a support community, a reason to focus beyond the self, and a sense of purpose and hope. Study after study finds that actively religious people are happier and that they cope better with crises.

11.7 Happiness myths

Many researchers have listed a number of myths about the nature and causes of happiness. These include the following, which are widely believed, but wrong:

- Happiness depends mainly on the quality and quantity of things that happen to you.
- People are less happy than they used to be.
- People with a serious physical disability are always less happy.
- Young people in the prime of life are much happier than older people.
- People who experience great happiness also experience great unhappiness.
- More intelligent people are generally happier than less intelligent people.
- Children add significantly to the happiness of married couples.
- Acquiring lots of money makes people much happier in the long run.
- Men are generally happier than women.
- Pursuing happiness paradoxically ensures that you lose it.

11.8 Achieving happiness

Positive psychology (Linley, 2008; Seligman, 2008) shifts the focus to exploring and attempting to correct or change personal weakness to a study of strengths and virtues. Its aim is to promote authentic happiness and the good life, and thereby promote positive health and mental health. A starting point for positive psychology for both popular writers and researchers has been to try to list and categorize strengths and values. This has been done, though this still attracts controversy.

Health and wellness are, it seems, systematically related to the age, sex, race, education and income states of individuals. We know the following:

1. Women report more happiness and fulfilment if their lives feel rushed rather than free and easy.
2. Women are more likely than men both to become depressed and to express joy.
3. There is very little change in life satisfaction and happiness over one's life span.
4. There are social class factors associated with mental health and happiness, but these are often confused with income, occupation and education.
5. There is a relationship between health, happiness and income, but the correlation is modest and the effect disappears after the average salary level is reached.

6. Better education – as measured by years of education – is positively associated with happiness.
7. Occupational status is also linked to happiness with dramatic differences between different social classes
8. Race differences in health and happiness in a culture are nearly always confused with education and occupation.
9. There are dramatic national differences in self-reported happiness which seems to be related to factors like national income, equality, human rights and democratic systems.
10. Physical health is a good correlate of mental health and happiness, but it is thought to both a cause and an effect of happiness.

Recent studies on personality correlates of health and happiness are also very clear. Most of the work on personality has been conceived of in terms of the 'Big Five' traits (neuroticism, extraversion, openness, agreeableness and conscientiousness). However, there are other individual difference/trait variables that are clearly related to the Big Five as well as health and happiness:

1. Extroverts are much happier than introverts partly because of their sociability, optimism and assertiveness.
2. Neurotics are far less happy and healthy than stable people because they are prone to anxiety, depression, phobias and hypochondriases.
3. Conscientious people certainly tend to be healthier than non-conscientious people partly because of their orderly and structured lifestyle and their following of health guidelines.
4. Agreeable people are marginally happier than disagreeable people because they are warm, gregarious and caring, which is reciprocated.
5. People with high self-esteem are happier, with more positive attitudes, well-being and self-confidence.
6. Those people with internal or instrumental as opposed to external fatalistic beliefs tend to be happier because they feel they can influence their lives.
7. Those with high dispositional optimism tend to be happier, healthier and have greater SWB.
8. Those with a strong sense of purpose in life, whether generated by strong values, religion or occupation, are generally more happy.

Promoting happier organizations and people can be achieved by applying this learning in a number of practical ways:

1. Encourage employees to engage in charity work and provide them with the time to do so – many global firms now actively promote charity work

and having this kind of company-wide initiative that makes a difference will make people feel connected to the greater good.

2. Advocate a strength-based approach to performance management and appraisals where individuals are encouraged to focus on their positive qualities.
3. Emphasize the values of the organization where possible to increase employees' sense of purpose
4. Job design and matching people to the right role is important – try and ensure a good fit through job redesign and effective recruitment processes.
5. Encourage leaders to act as role models by exhibiting happiness in their behaviours and day-to-day interactions.
6. Encourage teamworking and making time to build strong relationships at work.

11.9 Work engagement and passion at work

A great deal is now written about work engagement. Its opposite is called alienation: that is, being estranged from all that happens in the workplace. Work engagement matters because it directly affects the bottom line. To some extent, engagement is another word for morale. When it is high, absenteeism, theft and turnover go down and productivity and customer satisfaction go up. Good leadership creates engagement; bad management destroys it, quickly and devastatingly.

Engaged staff are marked by high levels of energy, persistence and involvement at work. They express a great deal of enthusiasm and pride in their work. They say their work is meaningful and that they have a sense of empowerment at work. Measures of work engagement typically assess:

1. energy and vigour at work;
2. dedication and enthusiasm for the work itself;
3. total absorption while at work.

There are some pretty basic but important things one needs to do to maximize engagement:

- Let every person know what is expected of them in terms of their processes and products. Be clear and check understandings, and revisit expectations as they change. All people have hopes and expectations about promotion, change and what their organization should be doing for them (and what they should be doing for the organization). These people need to be managed.

- Give people the tools for the job and keep them up to date. Train them how to use them. Make sure that processes are well thought through so that the technology that people use is appropriate for what they are required to do. In short, give technical and informational support.
- Give individuals opportunities to learn and shine at what they are good at. People like to celebrate their skills, abilities and unique gifts. Help them to find and explore them. Let them do their best all the time and encourage their development of strengths.
- Be generous but targeted in praise. Recognize effort and success and target specific individuals and how they have strived to achieve. Celebrate success notice and praise individuals when they have put in extra effort. Do this openly, naturally and regularly.
- Listen to your employees. They often have very good innovative ideas. They need to believe that their ideas count, that their voice is heard and that they can contribute to how the work is arranged.
- Help them believe in the purpose or product of the organization. People need to feel their job is important – that they are really making a contribution to society. This involves more than writing fancy mission statements; it is about giving the job a sense of meaning and purpose.
- Encourage friendship formation at work. This is more than insisting on teamwork. It is about giving people the space and time to build up a friendship network. Friends are a major source of social support. They make all the difference to the working day. And committed people commit to their friends.
- Talk to people about their progress. Give them a chance to let off steam, to dream about what might be and to have quality time with you. This is more than those detailed, often rather forced appraisals; it is about the opportunity for the boss to focus on the hopes, aspirations and plans of the individual.

11.10 Addressing organizational barriers

Often the very nature of the organizations in which we work can exacerbate mental health problems and work can sometimes be the trigger for an individual who is at risk of developing mental health problems.

11.10.1 Culture

Organizational culture is an important construct in understanding the experiences of individuals in the workplace, and particularly those who may be experiencing mental illness. Is the culture of the organization one of presenteeism and long hours? Are people rewarded based on the quantity of hours worked rather than the quality of output produced? Is there a high divorce rate amongst senior executives because they rarely have time to see their family? If this sounds familiar, the chances are that the culture of your organization is an unhealthy one where the risks of mental health problems amongst employees will be much higher.

There are various measures of corporate culture defined quite simply as 'the way we do things around here'. It is an unstated set of rules and assumptions about how to behave. It relates to that which is shared within a department or organization, such as:

- beliefs, values and attitudes;
- routines, traditions and rewards;
- meanings, narratives and sense-making.

The critical task is to determine which of the assumptions and unwritten rules that comprise an organizational culture can enhance the psychological health of the workplace and the workforce.

Some corporate cultures can be defined as win-win, co-operative and supportive, while others are win-lose, competitive and unsupportive. Some are tough, macho and aggressive, where any form of mental illness is frowned upon and seen as a sign of weakness, while others are caring, where people with problems can expect to receive help and support. Corporate culture is relatively easy to assess, but very difficult to change. It certainly relates to how mental illness is dealt with.

It is important to consider and, if necessary, address organizational culture in this context because the 'right' culture is imperative for any positive and productive social process within the workplace, and this includes the process of developing a healthy organization

It is vital to create a work culture with social support, where employee well-being is enhanced and where employees who may be suffering from psychological conditions are supported and experience a positive environment. When an organization has a positive mental health-focused culture, employee well-being, job satisfaction and organizational commitment will also be enhanced.

An unhealthy culture, on the other hand, creates increased and unnecessary stress in the workplace, which in turn lowers employee well-being. The most extreme example of this can be seen in the 'profit at all costs' culture in many financial institutions, where constant chaotic urgency is the norm and burnout and high turnover is all part of the job.

11.10.2 Ensuring top team buy-in

Gaining commitment from the executive-level leadership is a critical stage in promoting a healthier, happier workplace. Respected, senior individuals who actively and publicly demonstrate their support will go a long way towards ensuring that the rest of the organization take the matter seriously and will help reduce the stigma that can surround mental illness.

An example of this level of commitment can be seen at American Express. Gostick and Elton (2012) describe an American Express call centre that holds a monthly morale-boosting event, led by Doria Camaraza, the Senior Vice President and General Manager of the 3,000-worker office. Camaraza allegedly leads a Lady Gaga dance routine in the building atrium and singles out employees who have gone the extra mile to deliver great customer service. She also gives out recognition awards to employees each month, and the call centre offers a workout room with fitness classes, weights, trainers and a nurse, and a back-up daycare centre. Gostick and Elton report that these perks contribute to a workforce that is happy and productive.

Other more traditional methods of demonstrating a commitment to the issue include holding awareness sessions hosted by a senior member of the executive team or issuing a briefing from the CEO or an equivalent person to the general staff. The following extract comes from a briefing issued by Robert Care, Regional CEO of the large global consulting firm Arup, to the general staff in 2009.

CEO BRIEFING

I'd like to discuss some ideas about caring for our total well-being, including mental health.

We are serious about looking after our long-term health, and therefore we need to consider the whole person – physical and mental. Just as we watch what we eat and try to exercise regularly, we should also aim to keep our mental health in the best possible condition. I'm interested in exploring more active ways we can all deal with stress and some of the consequences such as depression in the workplace. Currently our Human Resources team is running lunchtime workshops for managers and team leaders. The topics covered include causes, signs and symptoms, and how to manage employees suffering from depression, anxiety or stress.

If you have already attended one of these sessions, have you discussed it with your team? What other initiatives would you find

useful to support your colleagues? Hopefully you all know that Arup provides an EAP, which is free to all staff and their families, and that the service is completely confidential.

Are there more steps we could be taking?

Taking responsibility for our health means being willing to seek help, and the EAP may be the first step. We go to professionals for all kinds of advice – general practitioners, dermatologists, dentists, podiatrists and optometrists – but we can be reluctant to seek professional help for what can be incorrectly dismissed as 'just emotional problems' or a need to 'pull yourself together'. Thankfully, attitudes are changing. Awareness of the importance of maintaining mental health has grown in recent years, particularly as a number of high-profile, high-achieving people have acknowledged their personal battles to overcome depression and other mental illness.

General practitioners are now better informed about offering help and counselling, while many health insurance funds cover these services. There are also a wide range of resources freely available for individuals, their friends and families.

Workplace stress can be a major trigger for depression, while many other factors can trigger or exacerbate it, such as the death of a loved one, divorce, moving, an illness or accident, even happy events such as planning a wedding.

It can be very difficult for co-workers to identify that someone is suffering or needs help, and we can't feel responsible for what is essentially a medical diagnosis. We can, however, be alert to overt signals and offer help where we can. Do not try to make a diagnosis yourself or force anyone to seek help, but you can express concern and support a person to seek help. Signs to watch out for include moodiness that is out of character, increased irritability and inability to take minor criticism, increased absenteeism or tardiness, and recklessness or unnecessary risk taking.

If you think a work colleague is anxious or depressed, give them information about the EAP or recommend that they see a doctor. Depression is an illness, not a character flaw. If you're feeling stressed, it's a good idea to take action before it affects you unduly. It's helpful to recognize the difference between stress and pressure. We all experience pressure on a daily basis and need it to motivate us and enable us to perform at our best. It's when we experience too much pressure without the opportunity to recover that we start to experience stress.

Try to identify the causes and what you can do to make things better. Ideally, tell your manager or another responsible senior person at an early stage. If your stress is work-related, this gives them the chance to help and prevent the situation getting worse. If it isn't work-related, they may be able to do something to reduce some of your pressure.

Recognize that you have a responsibility for your own personal stress and try to help yourself where possible. While you're working with your manager to improve the work situation, consider these steps to improve your capacity to deal with stress:

- eat regularly and well;
- exercise regularly;
- practise relaxation techniques – even a brisk walk can help;
- get a good night's sleep;
- make time for your family, friends and other interests;
- limit the use of tobacco, alcohol and other drugs.

It may be a cliché, but our health is everything. We all have much to gain by doing our best to prevent problems and then seeking assistance when it's necessary. No one has to face anything alone.

As it happens, October is beyondblue Anxiety and Depression Awareness (ADA) month, which aims to help organizations and individuals participate in activities to raise awareness of anxiety and depression, and reduce the stigma. A number of offices in the Region will display posters and have information available.

11.10.3 Identifying and removing potential work place hazards, and encouraging a balanced approach to work

Changing the culture of an organization takes many years, but there are small steps that can be taken to help remove any hazards that could be contributing to the deterioration of the mental health of the employees and promote working practices that have been proven to make a positive difference.

The pressure of an increasingly demanding working culture in today's society, particularly in the wake of the global recession, where people feel the pressure to work harder and longer just to hold on to their job, presents one of the biggest challenges to maintaining mental health at work. Often individuals suffer an imbalance between work and other aspects of life such as family and hobbies, and this can have a detrimental impact on mental health.

Wang *et al.* (2008) examined this topic and found that an imbalance between work and home was a stronger risk factor than general work stress for mental illness, and this was equally important for men and women. This could be a result of the fact that, whereas women largely still retain the primary role of caregiver, men are more involved than previous generations in their family roles (Silver and Frohlinger-Graham, 2000).

So what are the signs of an unhealthy work-life balance? In a recent survey by the UK Mental Health Foundation into the impact of an unhealthy work-life balance, the following trends emerged:

- One-third of respondents feel unhappy or very unhappy about the time they devote to work.
- More than 40 per cent of employees who responded are neglecting other aspects of their life because of work, which may increase their vulnerability to mental health problems.
- When working long hours, more than a quarter of employees who responded feel depressed (27 per cent), one-third feel anxious (34 per cent), and more than half feel irritable (58 per cent).
- The more hours you spend at work, the more hours outside of work you are likely to spend thinking or worrying about it.
- As a person's weekly hours increase, so do their feelings of unhappiness.
- Many more women report unhappiness than men (42 per cent of women compared with 29 per cent of men), which is probably a consequence of competing life roles and more pressure to 'juggle'.
- Nearly two-thirds of employees who responded experienced a negative effect on their personal life, including lack of personal development, physical and mental health problems, and poor relationships and poor home life.

Does this sound like your place of work? If so, there are practical steps to take and both organizations and individuals have a joint responsibility to ensure a healthy work-life balance is maintained.

Individuals should do the following:

- Speak up when work demands become too great.
- Take proper breaks for lunch, go outside and get fresh air and embrace the new trend of 'walking meetings' as a means of integrating some physical exercise into the daily schedule.

- Examine how you are working. Are you being as efficient as possible? Try to 'work smart, not long'. Avoid getting caught up in less productive activities, such as meetings with no agenda that tend to take up lots of time.
- Delegate as much as possible and avoid the temptation to do everything yourself.
- Draw a line between work and home. Avoid checking emails and working in the evenings, and if you do need to, dedicate an area in your home to do so where you can close the door on it when you are done.
- Seek out ways to ensure you are relaxing enough through exercise, hobbies, etc.

Organizations should do the following:

- Promote messages about work-life balance.
- Develop policies to encourage alternative ways of working (e.g., flexible or part-time working) and promote these as a smart way of doing business.
- Encourage a culture of openness about time constraints and workload where staff feel able to speak out.
- Train people in how to work smarter and ensure they are aware of the various tools at their disposal and how to use them (e.g., IT).
- Evaluate the work environment to identify elements that may be having a negative impact on work-life balance.
- Encourage leaders to set a good example by going home on time and not sending emails late at night or at the weekend.
- Provide access to activities that promote good mental health, for example, lunchtime hobby or exercise classes.

11.10.4 Monitoring the situation

Employers have the potential to significantly impact the health, well-being and productivity of their workers. By providing an environment that encourages mental wellness, employers can reduce the risk of mental illness becoming a problem for their staff. Monitoring the situation is a further key step in this. Organizations can stay on top of the issue by asking some key questions:

- Do we provide an effective employee assistance programme to support those who may be at risk of mental illness?
- Do we provide appropriate screening and early detection?
- Does our organizational culture promote a healthy and balanced approach to work? Do we provide an environment that promotes mental well-being?
- Do we encourage mental health and stress management through a comprehensive health promotions programme?

- Have we removed any barriers that may exist to prevent people receiving adequate medical, pharmacological and psychotherapeutic care?
- Are our managers trained to identify the early signs of mental illness if it should occur in their team? Does this training include identifying job performance problems that can relate to mental health?
- Do we regularly provide information about mental health issues and the support available to reduce the stigma sometimes associated with seeking help for mental health problems?
- Do our leaders walk the talk and ensure that the topic is not taboo?
- Are we collaborating with our competitors and other stakeholders to address any industry-wide issues that might exist?
- Is there a clear process in place for supporting individuals returning to work after a mental health-related absence?
- Do we regularly monitor the situation through tracking disability claims that relate to mental illness and other sources of information (e.g., HR)?

Organizations should aim to monitor the degree to which there is a culture of mental well-being in the same way that they assess other facets of culture, such as organizational commitment and engagement. The benefits will be equally rewarding.

This chapter has focused on the importance of creating an organizational environment that promotes and supports mental wellness. Of course, no organization can have an influence on the health outcomes of every individual in their employment and there will inevitably continue to be many cases where factors external to the workplace will cause an individual to experience mental ill health. However, organizations have a responsibility and an opportunity to ensure that they have removed as many potential workplace factors as possible and this is an area where many businesses continue to fail. In the same way that attitudes and approaches towards issues such as workplace health and safety and the physical well-being of employees have experienced a huge cultural shift in recent decades, the issue of mental health at work must also now be addressed in a serious way.

11.11 Conclusion

Mental illness is a complex topic and one which is subject to misunderstanding, prejudice and confusion in relation to its origins, symptoms and consequences. In this book we have attempted to debunk some of the myths surrounding the topic, with a particular focus on how mental illness can have an impact the modern workplace. We have provided an overview of the major illnesses and disorders, and how these can manifest in the work environment, and we have offered some insights as to how mental illness can be identified, prevented and managed more effectively.

Mental illness is a topic that will continue to be of significant importance to organizations and employees across the globe; it is not going away and presents a real problem if it is not addressed effectively. The warning signs are there when we consider the sheer cost of depression alone to business in recent years. The enlightened managers and organizations have taken heed of the warning signs and we can see early indicators that the necessary mechanisms are being put in place: training and awareness for staff, employee programmes to support individuals who experience mental health problems, initiatives to create more healthier workplace environments, and checks and balances to ensure that the most extreme cases of mental illness (psychopaths and the like) do not end up in the boardroom. There is more to be done, however, and whilst it is encouraging that the topic of mental health at work is, at last, moving up the agenda of many public and private sector organizations, a greater understanding and awareness amongst the general working public is essential to truly address the issue.

This chapter has concentrated on mental health literacy and the extent to which people are able to identify common mental illnesses. We know that people can be taught to be more literate with all sorts of beneficial consequences for those they interact with. The higher the level of mental health literacy a person has, the quicker they will be to identify potentially serious problems and know who to contact and for what sort of help.

References

Aakster C. (1986). Concepts in alternative medicine. *Social Science & Medicine* 22: 265–73.

Acas (2011). The Equality Act – what's new for employers?, www.acas.org.uk/media/pdf/n/8/Equality_Act_2010_guide_for_employers-accessible-version-Nov-2011.pdf (date accessed 4 February 2014).

Alarcon, G. (2011). A meta-analysis of burnout with job demands, resources and attitudes. *Journal of Vocational Behaviour* 79: 549–62.

American Psychological Association (1994). *DSM-IV-TR Diagnostic and Statistical Manual of Mental Disorders Diagnostic*, 4th edn. Washington DC: American Psychiatric Association.

——. (2000). *Diagnostic and Statistical Manual of Mental Disorders*, 4th edn. Washington DC: APA.

——. (2013). *Diagnostic and Statistical Manual of Mental Disorders*, 5th edn. Washington DC: APA.

Ames, G.M. and Janes, C. (1992). A cultural approach to conceptualizing alcohol and the workplace. *Alcohol Health and Research World* 16(2): 112–19.

Andreassen, C. Hetland, J. and Pallesen, S. (2010). The relationship between 'workaholism', basic needs satisfaction at work and personality. *European Journal of Personality* 24: 3–17.

Anxiety and Depression Association of America (2006). Highlights: workplace stress and anxiety disorders survey, www.adaa.org/workplace-stress-anxiety-disorders-survey (date accessed 4 February 2014).

Argyle, M. (2001). *The Psychology of Happiness*. London: Routledge

Aziz, S. and Zickar, M. (2006). A cluster analysis investigation of workaholism as a syndrome. *Journal of Occupational Health Psychology* 11: 52–62.

Babiak, P. (1995). When psychopaths go to work: a case study of an industrial psychopath. *Applied Psychology* 44: 171–88.

Babiak, P. and Hare, R. (2006). *Snakes in Suits*. New York: Regan Books.

Baca-Garcia, E., Perez-Rodriguez, M.M., Basurte-Villamor, I., Del Moral, A.L.F., Jimenez-Arriero, M.A., De Rivera, J.L.G. and Oquendo, M.A. (2007). Diagnostic stability of psychiatric disorders in clinical practice. *British Journal of Psychiatry* 190(3): 210–16.

Benning, S., Patrick, C., Bloniger, D., Hicks, B. and Iacono, W. (2005). Estimating facets of psychopathy from normal personality traits. *Assessment* 12: 3–18.

Bernstein, D.P., Iscan, C. and Maser, J. (2007). Opinions of personality disorder experts regarding the DSM-IV personality disorders classification system. *Journal of Personality Disorders* 21(5): 536–51.

Bjarnsasson, T. and Sigurdardotter, T. (2003). Psychological distress during unemployment and beyond. *Social Science and Medicine* 56: 973–85.

Bloom, D.E., Cafiero, E.T., Jané-Llopis, E., Abrahams-Gessel, S., Bloom, L.R., Fathima, S., Feigl, A.B., Gaziano, T., Mowafi, M., Pandya, A., Prettner, K., Rosenberg, L., Seligman, B., Stein, A.Z. and Weinstein, C. (2011). *The Global Economic Burden of Noncommunicable Diseases*. Geneva: World Economic Forum.

Blumenthal, R. and Endicott, J. (1996), Barriers to seeking treatment for major depression. *Depress Anxiety* 4: 273–8.

Bonde, J.P.E. (2008). Psychosocial factors at work and risk of depression: a systematic review of the epidemiological evidence. *Occupational and Environmental Medicine* 65(7): 438–45.

Boyle, M.H., Offord, D.R., Campbell, D., Catlin, G., Goering, P., Lin, E. and Racine, Y.A. (1996). Mental health supplement to the Ontario Health Survey: methodology. *Mental Health 41*(9): 549–58.

Bradburn, N. (1969). *The Structure of Psychological Well-Being*. Chicago: Aldine.

Brewer, G. and Brewer, G. (2011). Parsing public/private differences in work motivation and performance. *Journal of Public Administration Research* 21: 347–62.

Brohan, E. and Thornicraft, G. (2010). Stigma and discrimination of mental health problems: workplace implications. *Occupational Medicine* 60(6): 414–15.

Burke, R. (2000). Workaholism in organizations. *International Journal of Management Review* 2: 1–16.

——. (2001). Workaholism components, job satisfaction, and career progress. *Journal of Applied Social Psychology* 31: 2339–56.

Burke, R. and Fiksenbaum, L. (2009). Work motivations, work outcomes and health. *Journal of Business Ethics* 84: 257–63.

Burke, R., Matthiesen, S. and Pallesen, S. (2006). Personality correlates of workaholism. *Personality and Individual Differences* 40: 1223–33.

Carlson, N.R, Buskist, W. and Martin, G. N. (2000). *Psychology*. Harlow: Pearson.

Carver, C., Scherer, M. and Weintraub, J. (1989). Assessing coping stategies: a theoretical-based approach. *Journal of Personality and Social Psychology* 56: 267–83.

Chatman, J., Wong, E. and Joyce, C. (2008). When do people make the place? In D.B. Smith (ed.), *The People Make the Place*. New York: LEA, pp. 63–86.

Chen, H., Parker, G., Kua, J., Jorm, A. and Lou, J. (2000). Mental health literacy in Singapore. *Annals of the Academy of Medicine, Singapore* 29: 467–73.

CIPD (2007). Managing drug and alcohol misuse at work, www.cipd.co.uk/NR/rdonlyres/0731B5C2-3AAA-4A40-b80D-25521BDBA23A/0/mandrgalcmisusesr.pdf (date accessed 4 February 2014).

Clark, M., Lelchook, A. and Taylor, M. (2010). Beyond the Big Five: how narcissism, perfectionism, and dispositional affect relate to workaholism. *Personality and Individual Differences* 48: 786–91.

Cleckley, H. (1941). *The Mask of Sanity*. St Louis: Mosley.

Corrigan, P. (2004). How stigma interferes with mental health care. *American Psychologist* 59(7): 614–25.

Corrigan, P. and Lundin, R. (2001). *Don't Call Me Nuts!: Coping with the Stigma of Mental Illness*. Champaign, IL: Recovery Press.

Corrigan, P., Rafacz, J. and Rusch, N. (2011). Examining a progressive model of self-stigma and its impact on people with serious mental illness. *Psychiatry Research* 189: 339–43.

Czikszentmihalyi, M. (1990). *Flow: The Psychology of Optimal Experience*. New York: Harper & Row.

De Graaf, R., Ten Have, M., van Gool, C. and van Dorsselaer, S. (2012). Prevalence of mental disorders and trends from 1996 to 2009. Results from the Netherlands Mental Health Survey and Incidence Study-2. *Social Psychiatry and Psychiatric Epidemiology* 47(2): 203–13.

Department of Health (2012). Alcohol strategy published, 23 March, https://www.gov.uk/government/news/alcohol-strategy-published (date accessed 4 February 2014).

Deverill, C. and King, M. (2009). Common mental disorders. In S. McManus, H. Meltzer, T. Brugha, P. Bebbington and R. Jenkins (eds), *Adult Psychiatric Morbidity in England: Results of a Household Survey*. London: NHS Information Centre. Available at: www.ic.nhs.uk/pubs/psychiatricmorbidity07 (date accessed 4 February 2014).

Diener, E. (2000). Subjective wellbeing. *American Psychologist* 55: 34–41.

Dotlick, D. and Cairo, P. (2003). *Why CEOs Fail*. New York: Jossey-Bass.

Engel, C.C. (2002). Outbreaks of medically unexplained physical symptoms after military action, terrorist threat, or technological disaster. *Military Medicine* 166(12): 47–8.

Eysenck, H. (1995). *Genius: The Natural History of Creativity*. New York: Cambridge University Press.

Eysenck, M. (1990). *Happiness: Facts and Myths*. Hove: LEA.

Freed Taylor, M., Brice, J. and Buck, N. (1995). *BHPS User Manual*, vol. A, University of Essex, Colchester.

Furnham, A. (1994). A content, correlational and factor analytic study of four tolerance of ambiguity questionnaires. *Personality and Individual Differences* 16(3): 403–10.

——. (2006). Personality disorders and intelligence. *Journal of Individual Differences* 27(1): 42–6.

Furnham, A., Daoud, J. and Swami, V. (2009). How to spot a psychopath? *Social Psychiatry and Psychiatric Epidemiology* 44: 464–72.

Furnham, A., Hyde, G. and Trickey, J. (2013). Do your dark side traits fit? Dysfunctional personalities in different work sectors. *Applied Psychology* (online).

Furnham, A. and Malik, R. (1994). Cross-cultural beliefs about depression. *International Journal of Social Psychiatry* 40: 106–23.

Gaebel, W., Zäske, H., Baumann, A.E., Klosterkötter, J., Maier, W., Decker, P. and Möller, H.J. (2008). Evaluation of the German WPA 'program against stigma and discrimination because of schizophrenia—open the doors': results from representative telephone surveys before and after three years of antistigma interventions. *Schizophrenia Research* 98(1): 184–93.

Gini, A. (1998). Working ourselves to death. *Business and Society Review* 100: 45–56.

Gorgievski, M. and Bakker, A. (2010). Passion for work: work engagement vs workaholism. In S Albrecht (ed.), *Handbook of Employee Engagement*. Cheltenham: Edward Elgar.

Gostick, A. and Elton, C. (2012). *All in: How the Best Managers Create a Culture of Belief and Drive Big Results*. Doncaster: Free Press.

Grant, M. (ed.) (1998). *Alcohol and Emerging Markets*. New York: Brunner Mazel.

Greenberg, P.E., Kessler R.C., Birnbaum H.G. *et al.* (2003). The economic burden of depression in the United States: how did it change between 1990 and 2000? *Journal of Clinical Psychiatry* 64(12): 1465–75.

Hackman, J.R. and Oldham, G.R. (1980). *Work Redesign*. Boston, MA: Addison-Wesley.

Hare, P. (1999). *Without Conscience*. New York: Guilford Press.

Harpaz, I. and Snir, R. (2003). Workaholism: its definition and nature. *Human Relations* 58: 29–319.

Hawton, K. (2000). Sex and suicide: gender differences in suicidal behaviour. *British Journal of Psychiatry* 177(6): 484–5.

Hawton, K., Arensman, E., Townsend, E., Bremner, S., Feldman, E., Goldney, R. and Träskman-Bendz, L. (1998). Deliberate self harm: systematic review of efficacy of psychosocial and pharmacological treatments in preventing repetition. *British Medical Journal* 317(7156): 441–7.

Health and Social Care Informatioin Centre (2013). Statistics on alcohol – England, 2013, www.hscic.gov.uk/catalogue/PUB10932 (date accessed 4 February 2014).

Heath, D. (2000). *Drinking Occasions: Comparative Perspectives on Alcohol and Culture*. New York: Brunner/Mazel.

Helman, C. (1990). *Culture, Health and Illness*. London: Butterworth Scientific.

Hogan, R. (2004). In defence of personality measures. *Human Performance* 18: 331–41.

——. (2005). *Personality and the Fate of Organisations*. Mahwah, NJ: LEA.

——. (2007). *Comments on the Hogan Business Reasoning Inventory*. Tulsa: Hogan Assessments.

Hogan, R. and Hogan, J. (1997). *Hogan Development Survey Manual*. Tulsa: Hogan Assessment Centers.

——. (2001). Assessing leadership: a view from the dark side. *International Journal of Selection and Assessment* 9: 40–51.

Horsfall, J., Cleary, M. and Hunt, G.E. (2010). Stigma in mental health: clients and professionals. *Issues in Mental Health Nursing* 31(7): 450–5.

Huppert, F., Baylis, N. and Keverne, B. (eds) (2005). *The Science of Well-Being*. Oxford University Press.

Institute of Alcohol Studies (2013). Alcohol in the workplace factsheet, www.ias.org.uk/uploads/pdf/Factsheets/Alcohol%20in%20the%20workplace%20factsheet%20August%202013.pdf (date accessed 4 February 2014).

Ishikawa, S., Raine, A., Lenez, T., Bihrli, S. and Lacasse, L. (2001). Autonomic stress reactivity and executive functions in successful and unsuccessful criminal psychopaths from the community. *Journal of Abnormal Psychology* 110: 423–32.

Jahoda, M. (1958). *Current Concepts of Positive Mental Health*. New York: Basic Books.

Jamison, K.R. (1993). *Touched with Fire: Manic Depressive Illness and the Artistic Temperament*. New York: Free Press.

Jorm, A. (2012). Mental health literacy: empowering the community to take action for better mental health. *American Psychologist* 67: 231–44.

Jorm, A., Christensen, H. and Griffiths, K.M. (2005). The public's ability to recognise mental disorders and their beliefs about treatment: changes in Australia over 8 years. *Australia and New Zealand Journal Psychiatry* 39: 248–58.

Jorm, A., Kitchener, B. and Mugford, S. (2005). Experiences in applying skills learned in a mental health first aid training course: a qualitative study of participants' stories. *BMC Psychiatry* 5(1): 43.

Jorm, A., Kitchener, B., O'Kearney, R. and Dear, K. (2004). Mental health first aid training of the public in a rural area: a cluster randomized trial. *BMC Psychiatry* 4(1): 33.

Jorm, A., Kitchener, B., Sawyer, M., Scales, H. and Cvetkovski, S. (2010). Mental health first aid training for high school teachers: a cluster randomized trial. *BMC Psychiatry*: 10(1): 51.

Jorm, A., Korten, A., Jacomb, P., Christensen, H., Rodgers, B. and Pollitt, P. (1997a). Mental health literacy: a survey of the public's ability to recognize mental disorders and their beliefs about the effectiveness of treatment. *Medical Journal of Australia* 166: 182–6.

——. (2000). Mental health literacy. *British Journal of Psychiatry* 177(5): 396–401.

Jorm, A., Korten, A., Rodgers, B., Pollitt, P., Jacomb, P., Christensen, H. *et al.* (1997b). Belief systems of the general public concerning the appropriate treatments for mental disorders. *Social Psychiatry and Psychiatric Epidemiology* 32: 116–21.

Jorm, A., Korten, A., Rodgers, B., Pollitt, H., Christensen, H. and Henderson, A. (1997c). Helpfulness of interventions for mental disorders: beliefs of health professionals compared to the general public. *British Journal of Psychiatry* 171: 233–7.

Judge, T.A., Bono, J.E., Ilies, R. and Gerhardt, M.W. (2002). Personality and leadership: a qualitative and quantitative review. *Journal of Applied Psychology* 87(4): 765–80.

Judge, T.A., Erez, A., Bono, J.E. and Thoresen, C.J. (2003). The core self-evaluations scale: development of a measure. *Personnel Psychology* 56: 303–31.

Karasz, A. (2005). Marriage, depression and illness: sociosomatic models in a South Asian immigrant community. *Psychology and Developing Societies* 17(2): 161–80.

Kessler, R.C., Adler, L., Barkley, R., Biederman, J., Conners, C.K., Demler, O. and Zaslavsky, A.M. (2006). The prevalence and correlates of adult ADHD in the United States: results from the National Comorbidity Survey Replication. *American Journal of Psychiatry* 163(4): 716–23.

Kessler, R.C., Chiu, W.T., Demler, O. and Walters, E.E. (2005). Prevalence, severity, and comorbidity of 12-month DSM-IV disorders in the National Comorbidity Survey Replication. *Archives of General Psychiatry* 62(6): 617–27.

Kessler, R.C. and Frank, R.G. (1997). The impact of psychiatric disorders on work loss days. *Psychological Medicine* 27: 861–73.

Kessler, R.C., McGonagle, K.A. Zhao, S., Nelson, C.B., Hughes, M., Eshleman, S., Wittchen, H.U. and Kendler, K.S. (1994). Lifetime and 12-month prevalence of DSM-III-R psychiatric disorders in the United States. *Archives of General Psychiatry* 51: 8–19.

Kets de Vries, M. and Miller, D. (1984). *The Neurotic Organization*. San Francisco: Jossey-Bass.

Kirk, S.A. (2013). *Mad Science: Psychiatric Coercion, Diagnosis, and Drugs*. Piscataway, NJ: Transaction Publishers.

Kitchener, B.A. and Jorm, A.F. (2006). Mental health first aid training: review of evaluation studies. *Australian and New Zealand Journal of Psychiatry* 40: 6–8.

Kivimäki, M., Elovainio, M., Vahtera, J. and Ferrie, J.E. (2003a). Organisational justice and health of employees: prospective cohort study. *Occupational and Environmental Medicine* 60(1): 27–34.

Kivimäki, M., Virtanen, M., Vartia, M., Elovainio, M., Vahtera, J. and Keltikangas-Järvinen, L. (2003b). Workplace bullying and the risk of cardiovascular disease and depression. *Occupational and Environmental Medicine* 60(10): 779–83.

Kraepelin, E. (1987). A critical discussion of DSM-III dysthymic disorder. *American Journal of Psychiatry* 144(12): 1534–42.

Krupa, T., Kirsh, B., Cockburn, L. and Gewurtz, R. (2009). Understanding the stigma of mental illness in employment. *Work: A Journal of Prevention, Assessment and Rehabilitation* 33(4); 413–25.

Lilienfeld, S., Lynn, S.J., Ruscio, J. and Beverstein, B. (2010). *50 Great Myths of Popular Psychology*. Oxford: Wiley-Blackwell.

Linley, A. (2008). *Average to A+*. Coventry: CAPP Press.

Ludwig, A.M. (1992). Creative achievement and psychopathology: comparison among professions. In M. Runco and R. Richards (eds), *Eminent Creativity, Everyday Creativity, and Health*. New York: Praeger, pp. 33–60.

Lyons, S., Duxbury, L. and Higgins, C. (2006). A comparison of the values and commitment of private sector, public sector and parapublic sector employees. *Public Administration Review* 13: 605–18.

Machlowitz, M. (1980). *Workaholics*. New York: Mentor.

Mahon, M.J., Tobin, J.P., Cusack, D.A., Kelleher, C. and Malone, K.M. (2005). Suicide among regular-duty military personnel: a retrospective case-control study of occupation-specific risk factors for workplace suicide. *American Journal of Psychiatry* 162(9): 1688–96.

Mak, W.W., Poon, C.Y., Pun, L.Y. and Cheung, S.F. (2007). Meta-analysis of stigma and mental health. *Social Science and Medicine* 65(2): 245–61.

Mandell, W., Eaton, W.W., Anthony, J.C. and Garrison, R. (1992). Alcoholism and occupations: a review and analysis of 104 occupations. *Alcoholism: Clinical and Experimental Research* 16(4): 734–46.

Marzuk, P.M., Nock, M.K., Leon, A.C., Portera, L. and Tardiff, K. (2002). Suicide among New York city police officers, 1977–1996. *American Journal of Psychiatry* 159(12): 2069–71.

Mas, A. and Hatim, A. (2002). Stigma in mental illness: attitudes of medical students towards mental illness. *Medical Journal of Malaysia* 57(4): 433–44.

McGruder, J. (1999). Madness in Zanzibar: 'schizophrenia' in three families in the 'developing' world. Unpublished doctoral dissertation.

Meltzer, H., Griffiths, C., Brock, A., Rooney, C. and Jenkins, R. (2008). Patterns of suicide by occupation in England and Wales: 2001–2005. *British Journal of Psychiatry* 193(1): 73–6.

Merikangas, K.R., He, J.P., Burstein, M., Swanson, S.A., Avenevoli, S., Cui, L. and Swendsen, J. (2010). Lifetime prevalence of mental disorders in US adolescents: results from the National Comorbidity Survey Replication–Adolescent Supplement (NCS-A). *Journal of the American Academy of Child and Adolescent Psychiatry* 49(10): 980–9.

Michael, T., Zetsche, U. and Margraf, J. (2007). Epidemiology of anxiety disorders. *Psychiatry* 6(4): 136–42.

Middleton, H., Shaw, I., Hull, S. and Feder, G. (2005). NICE guidelines for the management of depression: are clear for severe depression, but uncertain for mild or moderate depression. *British Medical Journal* 330(7486): 267.

Miller, L. (2008). *From Difficult to Disturbed*. New York: Amacom.

Morrison, V. and Bennett, P. (2009). *An Introduction to Health Psychology*. Harlow: Pearson Education.

Mojtabai, R. (2010). Mental illness stigma and willingness to seek mental health care in the European Union. *Social Psychiatry and Psychiatric Epidemiology* 45(7): 705–12.

Muntaner, C., Eaton, W.W., Diala, C., Kessler, R.C. and Sorlie, P.D. (1998). Social class, assets, organizational control and the prevalence of common groups of psychiatric disorders. *Social Science and Medicine* 47(12): 2043–53.

Myers, D. (1992). *The Pursuit of Happiness*. New York: Avon.

National Institute of Mental Health (n.d. a). What is Generalized Anxiety Disorder?, www.nimh.nih.gov/health/topics/generalized-anxiety-disorder-gad/index.shtml (date accessed 4 February 2014).

——. (n.d. b). The numbers count: mental disorders in America, www.nimh.nih.gov/health/publications/the-numbers-count-mental-disorders-in-america/index.shtml (date accessed 4 February 2014).

National Statistics (2006). *Statistics on Alcohol: England 2006*. London: The Information Centre.

Nazroo, J. (1997). *Ethnicity and Mental Health*. London: Public Policy Unit.

Netterstrøm, B., Conrad, N., Bech, P., Fink, P., Olensen, O., Rugulies, R. and Stansfeld, S. (2008). The relation between work-related psychosocial factors and the development of depression. *Epidemiologic Review* 30: 118–32.

Nevid, J., Rathus, S. and Greene, B. (1997). *Abnormal Psychology in a Changing World.* Upper Saddle River, NJ: Prentice Hall.

Ng, T.W., Sorensen, K.L. and Feldman, D.C. (2007). Dimensions, antecedents, and consequences of workaholism: a conceptual integration and extension. *Journal of Organizational Behavior* 28: 111–36

Niedhammer, I., Goldberg, M., Leclerc, A., Bugel, I., David, S. (1998). Psychosocial factors and subsequent depressive symptoms in the Gazel cohort. *Scandinavian Journal of Work, Environment, and Health* 24: 197–205.

Nutbeam, D., Wise, M., Bauman, A., Harris, E. and Leeder, S. (1993). *Goals and Targets for Australia's Health in the Year 2000 and Beyond*. Sydney: Department of Public Health, University of Sydney.

Nutt, J., King, L. and Phillips, L. (2010). Drug harms in the UK: a multicriteria decision analysis. *The Lancet* 376(9752): 1558–65.

Oates, W. (1971). *Confessions of a Workaholic: The Facts about Work Addiction.* New York: World Publishing Company.

Oldham, J. and Morris, L. (1991). *The Personality Self-Portrait: Why You Think, Work, Love, and Act the Way You Do*. New York: Bantam Nooks.

——. (2000). *The New Personality Self-Portrait*. New York: Bantam Books.

Paterniti, S., Niedhammer, I., Lang, T. and Consoli, S.M. (2002). Psychosocial factors at work, personality traits and depressive symptoms. Longitudinal results from the GAZEL Study. *British Journal of Psychiatry* 181(2): 111–17.

Peele, S. and Grant, M. (eds) (1999). *Alcohol and Pleasure*. New York: Brunner Mazel.

Plant, M. A. (1977). Alcoholism and occupation: a review. *British Journal of Addiction to Alcohol and Other Drugs* 72(4): 309–16.

Platt, B., Hawton, K., Simkin, S. and Mellanby, R.J. (2010). Systematic review of the prevalence of suicide in veterinary surgeons. *Occupational Medicine* 60(6): 436–46.

Porter, G. (1996). Organizational impact of workaholism. *Journal of Occupational Health Psychology* 1: 70–84.

Powell, L.H., Shahabi, L. and Thoresen, C.E. (2003). Religion and spirituality: linkages to physical health. *American Psychologist* 58(1): 36–52.

Roberts, S.E., Jaremin, B. and Lloyd, K. (2013). High-risk occupations for suicide. *Psychological Medicine* 43(6): 1231–40.

Rosenheck, R., Leslie, D., Keefe, R., McEvoy, J., Swartz, M., Perkins, D. and Lieberman, J. (2006). Barriers to employment for people with schizophrenia. *American Journal of Psychiatry* 163(3): 411–17.

Sainsbury Centre for Mental Health (2007). Anti-Social Behaviour Orders and mental health: the evidence to date, www.psychminded.co.uk/news/news2007/nov07/sainsburycentre_asbo_consultation_response_nov07.pdf (date accessed 4 February 2014).

Salmans, S. (1997). *Depression: Questions You Have – Answers You Need*. Allenton, PA: People's Medical Society.

Sass, L. (2001). Self and world in schizophrenia: three classic approaches in phenomenological psychiatry. *Philosophy, Psychiatry, and Psychology* 8: 251–70.

Schaar Report (2008). Alcohol pricing and promotion effects on consumption and harm. University of Sheffield.

Schaufeli W.B., Taris, T.W. and van Rhenen, W. (2008). Workaholism, burnout, and work engagement: three of a kind or three different kinds of employee well-being? *Applied Psychology: An International Review* 57(2): 173–203.

Schneier, F.R. (2006). Social anxiety disorder. *New England Journal of Medicine* 355(10): 1029–36.

Seligman, M., Walker, E.F. and Rosenhan, D. (2001). *Abnormal Psychologist*. New York: W.W. Norton.

Seligman, M.E.P. (2008). Positive health. *Applied Psychology: An International Review* 57; 3–18.

Shirom, A. (2011). Vigor as a positive affect at work. *Review of General Psychology* 15: 50–64.

Silver, E.J. and Frohlinger-Graham, M.J. (2000). Brief report: psychological symptoms in healthy female siblings of adolescents with and without chronic conditions. *Journal of Pediatric Psychology* 25(4): 279–84.

Simon, G.E., Barber, C., Birnbaum, H.G., Frank, R.G., Greenberg, P.E., Rose, R.M., Wang, P.S. and Kessler, R.C. (2001). Depression and work productivity: the comparative costs of treatment versus nontreatment. *Journal of Occupational and Environmental Medicine* 43: 2–9.

Simon, G.E., Ludman, E.J., Tutty, S., Operskalski, B. and Von Korff, M. (2004). Telephone psychotherapy and telephone care management for primary care patients starting antidepressant treatment: a randomized controlled trial. *Journal of American Medical Association* 292(8): 935–42.

Simonton, D.K. (2012). Assessing scientific creativity: conceptual analyses of assessment complexities. Commissioned paper, the Science of Science and Innovation Policy Conference, National Academy of Sciences.

Snir, R. and Harpaz, I. (2012). Beyond workaholism: towards a general model of heavy work investment. *Human Resource Management Review* 22(3): 232–43.

Spence, J. and Robbins, A. (1992). Workaholism: definition, measurement and preliminary results. *Journal of Personality Assessment* 58: 160–78.

Stack, S. (2001). Occupation and suicide. *Social Science Quarterly* 82(2): 384–96.

Stainton Rogers, W. (1991). *Explaining Health and Illness*. London: Wheatsheaf.

Stein, M.B. and Stein, D.J. (2008). Social anxiety disorder. *The Lancet 371*(9618): 1115–25.

Stuart, H. (2004). Stigma and work. *Healthcare Papers* 5(2): 100–11.

Sussman, L.K., Robins, L.N. and Earls, F. (1987). Treatment-seeking for depression by black and white Americans. *Social Science and Medicine* 24(3): 187–96.

Swider, B. and Zimmerman, R. (2010). Born to burnout. *Journal of Vocational Behaviour* 76: 487–506.

Szasz, T. (1960). *The Myth of Mental Illness: Foundations of a Theory of Personal Conduct*. New York: Hoeber-Harper.

Taris, T., van Beek, I. and Schaufeli, W. (2010). Why do perfectionists have a higher burnout risk than others? *Romanian Journal of Applied Psychology* 12: 1–7.

Thornicroft, G. (2006). *Shunned: Discrimination against people with Mental Illness*. Oxford University Press.

Torpy, J.M., Burke, A.E. and Golub, R.M. (2011). Generalized anxiety disorder. *J AMA: The Journal of the American Medical Association* 305(5): 522.

Trust, S. (2006). Mental health: the last workplace taboo. Independent Research into What British Business Thinks.

Ustün, T.B., Ayuso-Mateos, J.L., Chatterji, S., Mathers, C. and Murray, C.J. (2004). Global burden of depressive disorders in the year 2000. *British Journal of Psychiatry* 184: 386 –92.

Vallerand, R. (2008). On the psychology of passion: in search of what makes people's lives most worth living. *Canadian Psychology* 49: 1–13.

Vallerand, R. and Houlfort, N. (2003). Passion at work: towards a new conceptualization. In Skarlicki , D., Gilliland, S. and Steiner, D (eds), *Social Issues in Management*. Greenwich, CT: Information Age, pp. 175–204.

Vallerand, R., Paquet, Y., Philippe, F. and Charest, J. (2010). On the role of passion for work in burnout. *Journal of Personality* 78: 290–311.

Van Beek, I., Hu, Q., Schaufeli, W.B., Taris, T.W. and Schreurs, B.H.J. (2012). For fun, love, or money: what drives workaholic, engaged, and burned-out employees at work? *Applied Psychology* 61(1): 30–55.

Van Beek, I., Taris, T. and Schaufeli, W. (2011). Workaholic and work engagement employees. *Journal of Occupational Health Psychology* 16: 468–82.

Van den Broeck, A., Schreurs, B., De Witte, H., Vansteenkiste, M., Germeys, F. and Schaufeli, W.B. (2011). Understanding workaholics' motivations: a self-determination perspective. *Applied Psychology: An International Review* 60: 600–21.

Waddell, G. and Burton, A.K. (2006). *Is Work Good for Your Health and Well-being?* London: HMSO.

Wall, T.D., Bolden, R.I., Borrill, C.S., Carter, A.J., Golya, D.A., Hardy, G.E. and West, M.A. (1997). Minor psychiatric disorder in NHS trust staff: occupational and gender differences. *British Journal of Psychiatry* 171(6): 519–23.

Wang, J.L., Lesage, A., Schmitz, N. and Drapeau, A. (2008). The relationship between work stress and mental disorders in men and women: findings from a population-based study. *Journal of Epidemiology and Community Health* 62: 42–7.

Wang, P.S., Beck, A., Berglund, P., Leutzinger, J.A., Pronk, N., Richling, D. and Kessler, R.C. (2003). Chronic medical conditions and work performance in the health and work performance questionnaire calibration surveys. *Journal of Occupational and Environmental Medicine* 45(12): 1303–11.

Ward, C. Bochner, S. and Furnham, A. (2001). *The Psychology of Culture Shock*. London: Routledge.

Wastell, C. A. (2002). Exposure to trauma: the long-term effects of suppressing emotional reactions. *Journal of Nervous and Mental Disease* 190(12): 839–45.

Wells, K.B., Stewart, A., Hays, R.D., Burnam, M.A., Rogers, W., Daniels, M., Berry, S., Greenfield, S. and Ware, J. (1989). The functioning and well-being of depressed patients. Results from the Medical Outcomes Study. *Journal of the American Medical Association* 262(7): 914–19.

Widom, C.S. (1978). A methodology for studying non-institutionalised psychopaths. In R.D. Hare and D. Schalling (eds), *Psychopathic Behaviour: Approaches to Research*. Chichester: Wiley, pp. 71–84.

Widom, C.S. and Newman, J.P. (1985). Characteristics of non-institutionalised psychopaths. In J. Gunn and D. Farrington (eds), *Current Research in Forensic Psychiatry and Psychology*, Vol. 2. New York: Wiley, pp. 57–80.

Wieclaw, J., Agerbo, E., Mortensen, P.B., Burr, H., Tuchsen, F. and Bonde, J.P. (2008). Psychosocial working conditions and the risk of depression and anxiety disorders in the Danish workforce. *BMC Public Health* 8(1): 280.

Wilhelm, K., Dewhurst-Savellis, J. and Parker, G. (2000). Teacher stress? An analysis of why teachers leave and why they stay. *Teachers and Teaching: Theory and Practice* 6(3): 291–304.

Wilhelm, K., Kovess, V., Rios-Seidel, C. and Finch, A. (2004). Work and mental health. *Social Psychiatry and Psychiatric Epidemiology* 39(11): 866–73.

Wilhelm, K. and Parker, G. (1989). Is sex necessarily a risk factor to depression? *Psychological Medicine* 19: 401–13.

World Development Report 1993: Investing in Health. New York: Oxford University Press.

World Development Report 1996: Fighting Disease, Fostering Development. New York: Oxford University Press, available at: http://www.who.int/whr/1996/en (date accessed 4 February 2014).

World Health Organization (2005). *Mental Health Atlas 2005*. Geneva: WHO.

Yaniv, G. (2011). Workaholism and marital estrangement. *Mathematical Social Sciences* 61: 104–8.

Ying, Y.W. and Miller, L.S. (1992). Help-seeking behavior and attitude of Chinese Americans regarding psychological problems. *American Journal of Community Psychology* 20(4): 549–56.

Ylipaavalniemi, J., Kivimäki, M., Elovainio, M., Virtanen, M., Keltikangas-Järvinen, L. and Vahtera, J. (2005). Psychosocial work characteristics and incidence of newly diagnosed depression: a prospective cohort study of three different models. *Social Science and Medicine* 61: 111–22.

Zhou, Y., Jindal-Snape, D., Topping, K. and Todman, J. (2008). Theoretical models of culture shock and adaptation in international students in higher education. *Studies in Higher Education* 33(1): 63–75.

Index

Note: italic page numbers indicate tables; bold indicate figures.

Printed and bound in Great Britain by
CPI Group (UK) Ltd, Croydon, CR0 4YY